The Reluctant Patron

The Reluctant Patron

The United States Government and the Arts, 1943–1965

GARY O. LARSON

UNIVERSITY OF PENNSYLVANIA PRESS
Philadelphia
1983

This work was published with the support of the Haney Foundation.

Library of Congress Cataloging in Publication Data

Larson, Gary O., 1949–
    The reluctant patron.

    Bibliography: p.
    Includes index.
    1. Federal aid to the arts—United States.
I. Title.
NX735.L37   1983   353.00854   82-40492
ISBN 0-8122-7876-3
ISBN 0-8122-1144-8 (pbk.)

Printed in the United States of America

To Jim Rockford

Contents

Photographs

Preface

As is true of a lot of Americans, my first encounter with government support of the arts was accidental. In my case it was 1972, and a local hero of mine, San Francisco pianist Mike Nock, was awarded a National Endowment for the Arts fellowship for $1,000. Now I had known Mike to be a struggling, deserving young jazz pianist (who had developed a small and not-very-loyal following in the Bay Area), but I was amazed that anyone connected with the *federal government* should recognize his talents. It must have been some sort of lottery, I concluded.

If the presence of federal patronage could prove so pleasantly surprising, it was also around this time that I first became aware of the *absence* of public subsidy. With visions of the Newport Jazz Festival's George Wein, I helped a friend produce jazz concerts in church basements in Berkeley, a dubious venture that made one point, at least, abundantly clear: some kinds of art—especially avant-garde jazz in musty church basements—simply cannot pay for themselves.

Other, more important lessons were to be learned about government and the arts, though. After trading the temperate climate of northern California for the more rigorous weather of Minnesota, I gradually became involved in a study of the *tradition* (if that is the right word for so fleeting an experience) of federal support of the arts in America. This investigation, too, was something of an accident, as it was the Slave Narrative Collection compiled in the thirties by the Federal Writers' Project that first attracted my attention.

The *Federal Writers' Project*. . . . That was an intriguing concept, conjuring up visions of poets and novelists turned civil servants, creating prose and poetry that one might pick up in installments at the local post office. The writers' project,

I soon discovered, was not quite so visionary as that, but the project's state guides were fascinating compendiums of local color and social history. I dug through the records of the Minnesota project at the state historical society, and even managed to track down a few project veterans. I met, too, with Clem Haupers, the painter and former head of the Minnesota branch of the Federal Art Project. Encouraged by his vivid recollections of those years ("Remember it?" he chortled when I first contacted him, "Hell, I put the project to bed!"), I soon turned my attention to the Federal Music Project and the Federal Theater Project, the other two components of the WPA's "Federal Project No. One."

It was the theater project, chronicled so delightfully in Hallie Flanagan's *Arena* and so effectively in Jane De Hart Mathew's *The Federal Theatre, 1935–1939: Plays, Relief, and Politics*, that provided the most instructive lesson for the student of federal arts support: sometimes it simply does not work. Struck down by a short-tempered Congress in 1939, the Federal Theater Project had suffered an even earlier demise in Minnesota. And even if it was a case of mistaken identity that killed the federal theater in Minnesota, the results—bad publicity and political controversy combining to thwart the federal arts effort—were the same as those of scores of episodes throughout the thirties, forties, and fifties. In the Minnesota instance an out-of-work exotic dancer, hired along with other performers to provide some Christmas entertainment at Civilian Conservation Corps camps, unwittingly killed the Minnesota theater project. Branded "Federal Fan Dancer No. 1" in a *Minneapolis Journal* headline, poor Ruby Bae helped convince state WPA officials that Minnesota could make it through the Depression without a branch office of the Federal Theater Project.

A laughable episode, to be sure, but one that was typical of the kind of controversy that public art could engender. And this was only the beginning of the federal arts fray, as I soon learned, before the House Un-American Activities Committee and the State Department got involved in the action, and long before a handful of visionaries in Washington and elsewhere decided it was time for yet another federal arts program.

A 1977 internship with the National Endowment for the Arts in Washington provided a good view of that second arts program (which had been established in 1965, and to which I returned in 1980 as a low-level bureaucrat); but I kept thinking of that earlier experiment in federal arts support, and in particular of those intervening years between the WPA and the NEA, when the foundations of the new program were laid. *The Reluctant Patron* is a study of the twenty-two-year struggle to establish a new program of federal arts patronage.

It is inexcusably self-serving to quote in this context Santayana's old saw, "Those who cannot remember the past are condemned to repeat it"; yet it is impossible to overlook some of the unfortunate parallels between the federal arts debates of the fifties and more recent developments at the federal level, as the Arts Endowment completes its second decade. For if there is no George Dondero (R-MI) on hand to condemn as "subversive" the art he cannot understand, there is William Proxmire (D-WI) to pass out "Golden Fleece" awards for the very same reason. If there is no Harold Gross (R-IA) clamoring that the federal government simply cannot *afford* to support the arts, there is David Stockman (R-OMB), who has labeled federal arts funding a "low priority." And if conservative arts groups no longer warn us of the political control of the arts, there is Francis S. M. Hodsoll, chairman of the Arts Endowment, whose major qualification for the position appears to be his connections to the White House.

It would be fatuous, certainly, to claim that we have come full circle. The arts are too much an accepted part of the "good life" in America for a repeat of the kind of congressional vandalism that frustrated the federal arts movement for over twenty years. Yet it is apparent that we can no longer point proudly to the steadily growing coffers of the Arts Endowment (as if that statistic ever really measured the state of the arts in America); nor can we assume that, budget constraints aside, all is well in the realm of government and the arts. The institutions of art themselves, most of which seem destined ever to earn their nonprofit, tax-exempt status with a vengeance, constantly court economic disaster, while it is impossible to scan the best-seller lists or the Nielsen ratings without harboring a few doubts about the nutritional content of American culture. Nor, given the vagaries of American political life, can we assume that the ship of state will continue to sail the same course of federal activism that it has followed since the New Deal. The Reagan administration's plans for the "swapping" and "turnback" of programs at the federal level, to say nothing of its abiding faith in voluntarism and private-sector involvement, raise the obvious questions about the future of federal funding of the arts.

As this debate continues, the controversy and debate of the period following the demise of the WPA, when the broad outlines of the new federal arts program were first sketched, once again invites analysis. Surprisingly, given the changes in the American cultural landscape since World War II, the philosophical underpinnings of the federal arts movement have remained largely the same. We are still treated, after all, to updates of Whitman's democratic vistas, a favorite theme of the New Deal years transposed in 1981 by the National Council on the Arts into a justification for its calling: ". . . the ability to respond to great art and to be enriched by it—in short the need for art—is everywhere." The arts, clearly, still incite grandiloquence, especially in the political arena; in 1981 the Presidential Task Force on the Arts and Humanities took it upon itself to "encourage the flourishing of the arts and the humanities, to open ways for future cultural achievements, and to diffuse the enduring benefits of American civilization." So, too, do the economics of the arts remain a burning issue, even when twisted by that same task force into a plug for New Federalism: "Inflation imperils America's economic vitality and the health of our cultural institutions. We recognize that the best remedy for the serious financial condition of the arts and humanities is the reestablishment of a sound non-inflationary economy."

Politics of a different stripe—the tense, boastful, whistling-in-the-dark politics of cold war—are also making their presence felt once again, if not with the explicit competitive thrust that marked the nation's cultural exchange efforts of the fifties, certainly with a distinct aftertaste of that era. Early in his administration, Ronald Reagan promised to revitalize the International Communication Agency (ICA, renamed the United States Information Agency in 1982); he appointed Charles Z. Wick, a zealous anti-Communist ("we are at war [with the Soviets], whether *de facto* or declared") to direct the agency. Project Truth, a campaign to identify and discredit Soviet "disinformation" was promptly launched, and with Project Truth in operation, can Project Beauty—another effort to combat Soviet propaganda with American art—be far behind?

The federal arts naysayers of the fifties bear reexamination, too, for their descendants are almost as numerous, if not so well organized, in the eighties. And here, too, the issues remain very much the same: the ubiquitous federal budget deficit, the state's rights issue (or "sibling rivalry," as a Presidential Task Force staff report described the Arts Endowment's so-called federal-state partnership), the threat of political control ("the creeping nationalization of culture," according to the Heritage Foundation's *Mandate for Leadership*, 1981), along with some good old-fashioned American small-town hysteria (the "National Endowment for Pornography" gasped the Heritage folks, much of whose commentary on the arts would be laughable did it not enjoy so much clout in the current Arts Endowment regime).

If there *is* anything new under the arts-and-government sun (which is doubtful), it is the heightened emphasis on federal "leveraging" of private-sector support for the arts. An old notion, really—arts legislation as early as 1954 included it as a facet—the renewed emphasis warrants attention for its implications for federal arts policy. Will the traditional beneficiaries of private-sector support—large institutions and glossy projects—profit in the new funding environment at the expense of less institutionalized, more experimental art forms? Indeed, does the increased reliance on the private sector presage a gradual return to an earlier era of cultural laissez faire?

In the thirties it was politics, of course, that killed the federal arts projects, bringing back laissez faire to the arts, and it is politics that pose the biggest threat to the federal arts program of the eighties. Conservatives cried "foul" in 1977 when Jimmy Carter appointed Livingston Biddle (an aide to Senator Claiborne Pell) to head the Arts Endowment, and subsequently grumbled about the "populist" drift of Biddle's administration. One hopes, certainly, that these critics of the "politicalization" of the arts will not have to renew their complaints in the eighties. More importantly, one hopes that these critics will be silent for the proper reasons, and not simply because they agree with the new politics of the new regime.

Prologue

Something Happened

Looking back over the landscape of federal arts support in America from the vantage point of the eighties, one is struck by the two conspicuous peaks of activity that rise up from the broad expanse of flatlands. The first, rising sharply out of the thirties and falling as precipitously when the nation turned to war, marks the initial experiment in federal arts support. The second, growing more steadily out of the Democratic administrations of the early sixties, reached a plateau in the seventies before dropping off in the early eighties. Despite their shared topography, far above the long tradition of federal indifference to the arts, the two peaks of government arts activity are distinct. The distance between the Works Projects Administration and the National Foundation on the Arts and the Humanities is far greater than the twenty-two years which separate those two experiments.[1]

The Federal Writers', Theater, Music, and Art projects of the thirties had about as much to do with federal support of the *arts*, after all, as the Civil War had with freeing the slaves. At best, the WPA arts agenda was mixed; the relief of white-collar unemployment was equally as important to the New Deal as the cultural products themselves. Nevertheless, the accomplishments of the New Deal projects are undeniable, and as the political controversy and the social turmoil of that era gradually faded, the record of the arts projects assumed a new significance. Even if they never served as models for the arts program of the sixties, the various cultural achievements of the New Deal—the state guides of the Federal Writers' Project, the "Living Newspapers" and other productions of the Federal Theater Project, the band and orchestra concerts of the Federal Music Project, and the paintings and murals of the Federal Art Project and the Treasury's Section of Fine Arts—did serve a spiritual function in gathering support for the later arts program. Indeed, during the expansive years of Kennedy's New Frontier, as more agreeable memories replaced the earlier charges of boondoggling and radicalism, the legacy of the New Deal projects became increasingly important to the drive for a new arts program.

The quest for a new federal program has been treated with the same neglect, unfortunately, that scholars have accorded the subject of government and art as a whole. Yet it is a topic rich in lessons from the past. The nation's self-perception comes into play, for example, especially as it attempts to define itself as something distinct from, yet related to, the Old World. (For years plans for a new arts program were regarded by many as a mere attachment to the nation's cultural exchange effort, a postwar necessity that only gradually called forth demands for a full-fledged domestic arts program.) While the nation used Old World models as a guide, even if only to reject the European tradition of state-run culture, it used American archetypes as well. Democratic visions, in particular, provided a standard theme for the federal arts debates, in which the dissemination of culture was optimistically placed as the crowning achievement of America's social and economic democracy. Every positive vision in America seems to have its menacing corollary, however. The fifties were full of such doubts and fears, from the visceral reaction to the supposed Communist threat early in the decade, to the more cerebral response to the military-industrial complex at the decade's close. The arts-and-government nexus played a part in both trends, moreover, distressingly so in the first case, as American art, especially that which was sent abroad by the State Department, was handled roughly in a series of congressional attacks. When culture was viewed at last not as a symptom of the nation's ills, but as a cure, it fared much better. Thus a new federal arts program, bolstered by the addition of the humanities, came to be seen as a mark of the nation's maturity, a rite of passage for American civilization, to counterbalance the nation's emphasis on science and technology.

The almost quarter-century quest for a new federal arts program is rooted in the hopeless legislative efforts of the late thirties to make the WPA projects a permanent fixture, and cuts through a variety of social and cultural concerns—the postwar conservatism and the origins of the cold war, the anti-Communist fears of the fifties, and the mixed national pride and self-consciousness of the sixties. Operating in both the public and private arenas, moreover, with legislative schemes interacting with private plans both for and against a new federal arts effort, the movement chronicles the growing organization of the arts community in America, a gradual coalescence of artists' unions and boards of trustees, arts associations and service organizations, eliciting in turn a response in the public arena. Cultural legislation, in fact, with all of its rhetorical trappings, became increasingly popular in the early sixties, reaching a peak in 1965 when the arts-and-humanities foundation bill was the single most popular legislative item in the House.

The federal arts story, however, is an unfinished one, and must remain so, even though pessimistic observers of the administration of Ronald Reagan have forecast the end of federally supported art in America.[2] It is also a story that is full of contradictions, exposed as it is to the yearly tug-of-war in Congress, where sectional rivalries and philosophical differences are apt to pull culture in any of a number of directions. The Ninety-seventh Congress (1981) offered a marvelous example of such tension. A bill was introduced to create the position of poet laureate of the United States at the same time that a Senate subcommittee was recommending the dissolution of the NEA's Literature Program. In Congress, verily, the left hand often knoweth not what the right hand doeth.

In any case, this particular study ends when the new federal program, the National Endowment for the Arts, begins, for the chronicle of that agency's rise and fall (if such be the case) is a separate story in itself, as yet untold. Covering the years 1943–65, from the death of the WPA to the birth of the NEA, the present study focuses on the years when, ostensibly, "nothing happened" in regard to government and the arts. In actual fact, a good deal happened during that period, not all of it conducive to the development of a future arts program, certainly, but all of it contributing in some way to the ultimate direction that program would take. Thus it is difficult to agree with Michael Straight, former deputy chairman of the Arts Endowment (1969–77), who points to the secretary of labor's landmark settlement of the Metropolitan Opera labor dispute in 1961 as the sole example of pre-Endowment federal arts policy. "Secretary Goldberg's principles," Straight declares, "were the closest that the government came to a concept of its role in relation to the arts."[3] While section three of Arthur Goldberg's decision ("The State of the Performing Arts") may have been the first official statement to make explicit the government's role in the public-private partnership of support for the arts, and while Straight points persuasively to subsequent federal and private-sector developments reflecting Goldberg's principles, he ignores the long series of events before 1961 that contributed to the Metropolitan decision, events that served, in effect, as the primary source material behind the secretary's thesis. He might not have annotated his decision, but the historical footnotes to Goldberg's settlement are as manifest as its impact on subsequent events.

Even a hasty survey of the seedling years between the end of the New Deal and the beginning of the Arts Endowment reveals a number of events—unfulfilled plans, false starts, unpassed legislation, even full-fledged disasters—all of which helped to shape the eventual federal arts program. While the "disasters" (most often involving congressional red-baiting) may have impeded progress, they were important in the long run, just as the WPA projects were important, in convincing public official and private citizen alike of the need for an "insulated" arts program, one divorced, that is, from the daily operations of the executive and legislative branches. Only the

most reactionary—or the most cynical—suggested a wall between art and government like the one that separates church
and state in America; but by the time that the arts legislation
was finally passed in 1964 and 1965, there was a clear need
for an independent arts agency, an agency operated by full-
time arts specialists and advised by private citizens who met
periodically in a public capacity. But while this administrative
principle may not seem surprising, given the vicissitudes of
the sundry federal arts efforts of the preceding three decades, the enthusiasm with which Congress finally embraced
the plan, after years of legislative foot-dragging, is nothing
less than stunning.

Three major trends need to be monitored over the twenty-
two-year period: (1) the growing level of organization within
the arts community, from the fragmentation of the forties to
the eventual formation of an "arts lobby" in the sixties;
(2) the structural evolution of the federal arts plan, moving
from the direct federal involvement of the New Deal, through
the arms-length sponsorship of the cultural exchange programs, to the highly rationalized framework of the National
Foundation on the Arts and the Humanities; and (3) the spirit
of the movement, both inside and outside of government,
reflecting a complex set of beliefs and theories ranging from
the extreme hands-off policy of reactionary legislators and
conservative artists, to the lukewarm position of those who
favored government recognition of the arts, to the activist
stance of the few congressmen and the many arts advocates
who favored an ambitious program of federal arts support.
The key to the movement, though, is the shift that took place
in the balance of power away from the spirit of laissez faire
that held sway after the exigencies of the Depression and
then World War II had subsided, to the federal renascence
of the New Frontier and the Great Society. It was the large
middle group uncommitted to either extreme, those who were
frankly indifferent as well as those who were mildly interested in the arts, who made the difference. This group's
movement to the side of the congressional activists—lured

more by the humanities than by the arts, it must be remembered—produced the sweeping victory for the cultural legislation in 1965.

The rationale for federal arts support, that ever-changing set of arguments designed to win converts from the middle camp, took a variety of forms, often far afield from the arts themselves, as advocates exchanged their aesthetic views for the more negotiable currency of the political marketplace. Following World War II, they stressed the arts as a means of winning friends for America abroad, in cultural exchange programs; and as the cold war intensified, the value of this argument rose accordingly. Those who resisted such cultural jingoism could always appeal to Old World values, the long tradition of public arts support in Europe that was one of the missing ingredients, or so the argument ran, in American civilization. On the purely domestic side of the question (although this, too, was grist for the propaganda mill), arts advocates invoked a long-cherished strain of democratic thought, calling for a chicken in every pot and fine art in every home. The drive to democratize the arts, in short, to make available to all Americans the art that tended to stockpile in large cities, was one of the most compelling of all arguments. Those who were suspicious of purely quantitative analyses of the spread of culture, meanwhile, expressed a concern for a more worthwhile (i.e., highbrow) use of the increasing amounts of leisure time that Americans had at their disposal. Taken one step further, this viewpoint blossomed into a statesmanlike concern for the future of American civilization, an absolutely irresistible theme for the orators in Congress, and one of the most popular items in the arts advocates' arsenal.

Finally, those whose commitment to the arts was less political, less ceremonial (those advocates who were not up for reelection), voiced a genuine concern for the future of the arts in America, based on a series of rather crude economic studies that cast doubts on the viability of the arts. Emerging in the early sixties from journalistic hearsay, union reports, government statistics, and, belatedly, economic research itself, these studies raised serious questions about individual artists and arts institutions alike. The former, it became apparent, by accepting low wages and irregular employment, were in fact subsidizing art in America, while the institutions, ostensibly more stable, employed crisis financing in a losing battle against spiraling deficits. Without government aid, it was believed, aid that not only helped pay the bills but stimulated increased private support as well, the arts in America were imperiled.

These were the arguments, a mosaic of beliefs, fears, theories, and hopes, that the arts advocates used in building support for their cause throughout the fifties and early sixties.

The arguments against federal subsidy, meanwhile, were much more straightforward. The antifederalists expressed their satisfaction with the status quo—which, in terms of growing attendance figures and the seeming popularity of culture, was quite rosy—and made four basic points about the proposed federal arts support: (1) it cost too much, considering the precarious state of the federal budget; (2) it was not within the province of the federal government to assist an essentially local, private concern like the arts; (3) such support could lead only to federal interference and control; and (4) even if one admitted the propriety of such support, more important items on the federal agenda warranted attention first.

These basic arguments, in their various guises, frustrated the arts-subsidy movement for nearly two decades, and the battle might very well have been a stand-off were it not for the entrance of a new set of reinforcements. In 1964 the Commission on the Humanities, a blue-ribbon academic panel, released a report calling for a National Humanities Foundation (including arts support within its sweep) and in an instant the deadlock was broken. Advocates acquired new, more practical, more politically appealing arguments—to restore the balance between science and culture in America; to foster a more well-rounded, better-educated electorate; to increase understanding of environmental and social issues—and the arts-and-humanities movement easily outdistanced the antisubsidy forces. Plaintive cries about the unbalanced federal budget and bleak forecasts of federal interference stood little chance against the new era in American civilization that the arts-and-humanities advocates promised. The proposed cultural program was perfectly tailored, moreover, to the expansive mood of Congress and the country. It was the time, after all, of the New Frontier and the Great Society, a time not for retrenchment or for doubt (although the latter was always a factor) but for putting the finishing touches on American civilization. And the arts-and-humanities bill, like the civil rights and anti-poverty and urban renewal legislation, was one of those finishing touches.

Despite the rush of progress in 1964–65 with the entrance of the humanists, the battle was not won overnight. It is necessary to look back on that period when "nothing happened," when the WPA was just a memory and a new arts program a mere pipe dream.

Even before the WPA projects became a memory, in fact, when they had only recently suffered defeat at the hands of a vindictive Congress before being obliterated entirely by World War II, the private sector was making plans—wildly optimistic plans, it turned out—for the next government arts program. But that program, emerging shortly after the end of the war, turned out to be an export business, sending American art abroad in an international public-relations campaign. An early effort in this regard, involving the State Department's purchase of modern art for exhibit abroad, was an unmitigated disaster, unleashing a McCarthy-style tirade against allegedly subversive art. Even in its failure, though, the program reintroduced the public-arts debate in Congress, in rather shrill, simple-minded terms, yet with sufficient intensity to rally the arts community in defense of itself. The Committee on Government and Art, an embryonic arts lobby, emerged, establishing a pattern in the arts community for collective activity designed to influence and initiate congressional action.[4]

Soon after, a more positive dialogue began in Congress. The first of the modern arts legislation was Representative

Jacob Javits's 1949 resolution for an arts assembly, followed later by Representative Charles Howell's more elaborate omnibus arts bills. Set against the background of the sporadic cultural exchange efforts, a concern for the presentation of art at home emerged. Unprepared for such attention, however, the arts community was initially ambivalent, unable to forget either the promise of the WPA projects or the reality of their unseemly demise. If any further evidence of the inherent problems in mixing art and politics was needed, Representative George Dondero's anti-Communist, antimodern art crusade or the discouraging attack on Anton Refregier's post-office murals in San Francisco provided enough to convince all but the most optimistic federalists. A cautious middle ground seemed the most plausible stance, calling for government recognition of the arts but not for actual subsidy, and this view received official endorsement with the Commission of Fine Arts' *Government and Art* report, a 141-page paean to the status quo.

About the same time, in 1952, the first of a series of congressional hearings on the arts began. Exercises in futility at the outset, at least as far as the chances for legislative success were concerned, these sessions did provide a rallying point for the still-fragmented arts community, helping to clarify the arguments both for and against a new federal arts program. Also emerging out of these hearings, with a surprising boost from President Eisenhower, was the plan for a federal advisory council on the arts, a phoenix-like scheme that rose out of the legislative ashes year after year for more than a decade. Along with plans for a national cultural center in the nation's capital and the continuing cultural exchange follies, the arts council concept provided the basis for the gradual development of a federal arts policy, around which the various elements of the arts community, one by one, could rally. The most hopeful of that group, encouraged by a handful of congressmen, began to speak of a national arts *foundation*, providing actual financial assistance to the arts, but for most the battle for an advisory arts council was a sufficient challenge.

While the federal arts debate was a narrow, special-interest issue throughout most of the fifties, by the end of the decade it had assumed larger, truly national proportions. Eisenhower's Goals Commission, by no means at the vanguard of American political thought, included American culture among its concerns. With the election of John F. Kennedy, the arts enjoyed their highest profile at the executive level since the presidency of Thomas Jefferson. Almost overnight, or so it seemed (for the issues had actually been simmering for over a decade), the arts seemed to *matter*. The Kennedys hosted artists, the secretary of labor intervened in the Metropolitan Opera strike, Congress held extensive hearings on the economics of the arts, and the president appointed a special consultant on the arts. Nor did this new cultural spirit cease with the assassination of Kennedy, for his successor proved to be no less ambitious (if perhaps less graceful) in adding the sparkle and prestige of the arts to the executive office. Congress, too, had by this time begun to respond with greater enthusiasm, and in northern Democratic circles, at least, the arts were fast becoming a cause. With the entrance of an organized force of scholars, finally, liberal-arts academicians who demanded their share of federal recognition and support, too, the federal arts movement developed into a more general concern for the nation's cultural maturity—for the future of American civilization—a lofty goal in the often prosaic affairs of Congress.

Such a whirlwind tour of almost a quarter-century of American cultural history does violence, admittedly, to the glacial pace of events in the realm of government and art following the feverish cultural activities of the New Deal years. This outline does suggest, however, the radical shift regarding the arts in American political life, from the disdain and disinterest of the forties and fifties to the "commitment to culture" of the sixties. Although the present study necessarily focuses on the arts debate in Washington, it identifies as well movements in the arts community at large (artists, administrators, critics, scholars, and that segment of the arts audience whose interests are as much participatory as spectatorial), movements both in response to and in anticipation of federal actions and policies, movements that ultimately helped define the cultural program established in 1965.

Government support of the arts is a field that has received only scant study to date. While the WPA projects have been (and apparently will continue to be) the subject of a number of scholarly investigations, later developments have fallen prey both to the mistaken assumption that "nothing happened" in the forties and fifties, and to that seemingly inescapable time lag that delays the scholarly treatment of such recent developments as the National Endowment for the Arts. With the unexpected return of the federal arts debate following the election of Ronald Reagan and with the recent appearance of a number of critical studies of the Arts Endowment, we can expect increased scholarly attention to the issue of government and art. This investigation must look to the interval between the WPA and the NEA, certainly, that period when, indeed, "something happened" in regard to government and the arts. Here were events that had a definite bearing on the arts program that was established in the sixties. And if one is to judge wisely the future operations and policies of that program, an examination of its historical antecedents is necessary.

Congress Vetoes Culture

In the throes of the Great Depression and with admittedly mixed intentions, the United States government launched an arts program unparalleled in the nation's history. At its peak, in 1936, the WPA arts projects counted more than 40,000 artists on their rolls, with unemployed painters, musicians, actors, and writers creating art for their fellow Americans and receiving a "living wage" for their efforts. Even as late as the end of 1937, nearly 30,000 artists were employed by the government. But the following year, 1938, was the beginning of the end.

"Whatever else may be said of the Government's flyer in art," *Fortune* magazine declared in 1937, "one statement is incontrovertible. It has produced, one way or another, a greater human response than anything the government has done in generations."[1] That "human response" was evoked, as Representative William Sirovich (D-NY) explained to his colleagues in the House in June 1938, by a unique federal program that brought culture to the masses as no other government program, anywhere, had ever managed before. It might be argued that no other country had so *needed* the reassuring effects of culture, nor possessed so many unemployed artists to fill that need, as the United States in the thirties. But that should not detract from the impact of the program. "During the past few years . . . ," Sirovich observed,

> a cultural transformation has occurred in our national life. Theater, music, painting, sculpture, literature, and the other arts have become the possession of millions of people in every section of the country who never before had the means or opportunity to enjoy the benefits of culture. Twenty-five million people in 22 States have witnessed the Federal theater productions; 65 percent of them had never witnessed a play

before. Federal musicians have played to aggregate audiences of 92,000,000 persons in 273 cities in 42 States. Eleven million people have witnessed art exhibitions or have been taught in art classes. The American Guidebook Series has been published in a greater number of states. This is but a brief résumé, but it serves to indicate what has been accomplished.[2]

Along with all of the praise and applause, however, was another aspect of that great "human response" cited by *Fortune*. Not all of the reviews of the federal arts projects were raves, after all. Tied as these projects were to a much larger work-relief program—the arts budget was only around 2 percent of the total WPA outlays—the projects were often found guilty by association. Nonaesthetic, political, often simply irrelevant criteria were used to pry open chinks in Roosevelt's armor, as conservative foes of the New Deal both in and out of Congress hoped to put a halt to the "ever-expanding" federal government.

Two of the most convenient venues for such attacks were the Federal Theater Project and the Federal Writers' Project, both of which felt the wrath of Congress early in 1938. With its controversial "Living Newspapers" and productions like *One Third of a Nation* (concerning the nation's housing problems), which had the audacity to quote members of Congress, the theater project was a prime target for opponents of the New Deal, while the writers' project, despite the obvious merits of its guidebook series, simply *looked* suspicious. Who *were* these federal writers, anyway, some congressmen wondered, and why had Sacco and Vanzetti received more attention in the Massachusetts guide than the Boston Tea Party? Unquestionably, some of the federal artists were Communists, but charges of a Workers Alliance conspiracy to gain control of the projects overlooked the federal proviso that forbade inquiries into the WPA applicants' political affiliations.

In any case, defenders of the arts projects were scarce. The futile effort by a handful of congressmen to incorporate the arts projects under a permanent Bureau of Fine Arts served only to highlight the vulnerability of this small but newsworthy corner of the New Deal. That vulnerability became even more apparent in the summer and fall of 1938, when federal arts suffered a second setback at the hands of Congress. Calling the Federal Theater Project a "hotbed for Communists," J. Parnell Thomas (R-NJ) demanded an investigation. Although the assorted cranks and well-intentioned patriots that the House Un-American Activities Committee called before it never really proved anything, Chairman Martin Dies (D-TX) persuaded many Americans in October that the theater and writers' projects were "doing more to spread Communist propaganda than the Communist Party itself."[3] If nothing else, HUAC raised enough questions in the mind of Congress—which took a giant stride to the right in the 1938 elections—to set the stage in 1939 for the third and final blow to the concept of federally supported arts.

Inspired by the HUAC inquisition, Clifton Woodrum (D-VA), chairman of the House Appropriations Committee, launched an investigation of the WPA that was calculated, by his own admission, "to get the government out of the theater business."[4] In June Congress accomplished that goal, voting to terminate the Federal Theater Project and place the remaining arts projects under state sponsorship and control. And what World War II failed to accomplish in phasing out those remaining projects, Congress completed in its repudiation of the New Deal in the forties, unceremoniously shelving the arts projects (with no concern for the safekeeping of their various creations), aborting a proposed Army "War Arts" unit, and launching a campaign that would reverberate into the fifties against a State Department exhibition program.

Ironically, under similar constraints of war, England inaugurated *its* program of government arts support during this period. Two private organizations in Britain, the Entertainment National Service Organization and the Council for the Encouragement of Music and the Arts (CEMA), had been established to provide music and drama for both military personnel and civilians. Created in 1939 "to prevent cultural deprivation on the home front," CEMA began receiving gov-

ernment funds in 1940, and following the war became
a permanent government agency, the Arts Council of Great
Britain.

The war had a far different effect on publicly supported
art in America, however, as the writers', music, and art projects, already weakened by the 1939 reorganization, soon became mere adjuncts of the defense effort. Such a merger had
been proposed as early as 1940, in fact, by none other than
Federal Art Project Director Holger Cahill, acting either out
of a recognition of the inevitable or in a final effort to regain
a measure of administrative control. The state projects had
already been turning their attention toward defense, deco-
rating service clubs and making posters for the military. In
July 1941 the chief of the Operations and Training Section
of the Army Corps of Engineers endorsed Cahill's plan for a
defense art project. While Cahill never did regain control, his
project, now including patriotic volunteers, became increasingly involved in the defense effort. In the face of the cam-
ouflage classes, contour maps, and instructional drawings that
now occupied the project workers' time, other, more creative
endeavors languished. Shortly after Pearl Harbor, when the
Federal Art Project (FAP) came under the WPA War Services
Subdivision, Cahill admitted that "there are now no art projects as such."[5]

The Federal Writers' Project suffered a similar demise,
and its fate seems all the more regrettable for the promising
works that could never be completed. Such ambitious projects as "Men at Work," a study of American occupations;
"Hands that Built America," a six-volume regional history of
the country's handicrafts; and "America Eats," a survey of
ethnic and regional cuisine, were all set aside in the transition
to defense-related publications. Placed initially under the
Community Service Program Division, the FWP launched a
National Defense Series that began with a guidebook to the
United States Naval Academy and included guides to other
military areas, along with air-raid manuals and various other
instructional materials. Following John Newsom's resignation
as director of the FWP early in 1942, the project joined the

FAP in the War Services Subdivision, in which only those state programs that "directly build morale or promote the public welfare" were allowed to continue operations.[6] Such morale builders as the Ohio unit's *Bomb Squad Training Manual* and Mississippi's *Our Army* reader for illiterate recruits were released, but in reality the Federal Writers' Project, like the other arts projects, was dead.

And once dead (the WPA formally closed its books on 30 June 1943), the arts projects were denied even a decent burial, as Congress made no provisions for the proper storage of the projects' legacy. The sale of New York City Art Project paintings by a junk dealer was an extreme case, perhaps, but none of the project material received adequate cataloguing and storage.

If federal art finally withered and died on the home front, it fared only slightly better on the front lines overseas, and even that limited success must be attributed as much to individual initiative as to government support. Ironically, the person responsible for setting up an art program for the army during World War II was Lt. Gen. Brehon Somervell, whose handling of the arts projects while WPA commissioner in New York City was generally less than cordial. He had ordered the destruction of a controversial FAP mural and once suggested that machine guns might be the most effective tool against striking artists. Taking a more humane approach on this occasion, however, and following the lead of Canada and Great Britain (both of which had extensive combat art programs), Somervell directed the Chief of Engineers on 13 November 1942 to form a select group of artists to be dispatched to "active theaters to paint war scenes," and instructed local commanders to employ competent soldiers to "embellish mess halls, recreation rooms, service clubs, administrative buildings, classrooms, etc., with appropriate decorations."[7] A War Department Art Advisory Committee was formed to assist the Chief of Engineers, and ultimately forty-two artists (twenty-three soldiers and nineteen civilians) were selected. "Our Committee expects you always to be more than a news gatherer," read a letter Leon Kroll received from the Art Advisory

Committee in March 1943. "The importance of what you have to say for the historian of the future will be the impact of the war on you, as an artist, a human being."[8]

Costing only $33,500 to set up and requiring $125,000 for 1944, the little art project hardly signaled a rebirth of the FAP. It probably would have escaped the watchful eye of Congress, too, were it not for a wire-service report that caught the attention of Representative Joe Starnes. The conservative Democrat from Alabama, a member of the House Appropriations subcommittee that reviewed the War Department's budget, was incensed to learn of an American artist who had his "easel set up," according to the report, "on a Cap Bon roadside facing a poppy-sprinkled wheat field strewn with wrecked cars and dead horses . . . calmly sketching the scene of death and destruction." Aside from the incongruity of the scene, the artist in question had two other strikes against him: he was a veteran of the New Deal art projects (as an accompanying photograph of one of his murals made clear), and he was the brother of Attorney General Francis Biddle. And it certainly did not help matters that the article, quoting George Biddle, described the army art project as one of the most liberal ever devised; the artist, he noted, works entirely without supervision or direction.[9]

Nor did it take Joe Starnes long to figure out that "this piece of foolishness" was another government boondoggle, and he prevailed upon the House to slash the $125,000 item from the War Department's budget. Although a more liberal (and less southern) Democrat, A. Willis Robertson of Virginia, defended the project on the floor of the House—"We can take photographs of what happens in Europe, but . . . it takes the vision and artistic skill of the artist to bring to us the inspiration which only the artist can put on canvas"—and although the Senate attempted to restore the item, the army's art project was sacrificed.[10] Once again Congress "vetoed" culture, as artist Pepino Mangravite expressed it in the title of a magazine article.[11]

It was not a devastating loss. The Army Corps of Engineers absorbed several of the civilian painters into a "Combat

Arts Section," and numerous military artists subsequently worked independently in conjunction with the Special Services and the historical divisions of the various theaters of operation. But the episode *was* important as a reminder that the spirit that killed the New Deal art projects was far from dead—Congress could *still* find the cultural needles in the haystacks of federal spending—and as a warning that the arts could expect similar treatment at the hands of Congress in the years to come.

"Veiled Plans for the Regimentation of Artists"

To George Biddle, temporarily stranded in Tunisia until *Life* magazine hired some of the civilian members of the War Arts Unit, the action of Congress must have seemed a cruel joke. He had witnessed such behavior before, of course, both when Congress frowned upon the arts projects in the late thirties and again when it literally laughed off legislative attempts to make those projects permanent, but like a lot of veterans of the New Deal, he remained convinced of the soundness of the public arts–subsidy concept.[12] Unlike a lot of other New Deal artists, however, who were eager to return to the distinctly private life of the artist, Biddle was prepared to put his ideas into action, or at least to make the effort, despite the slender prospects for success.

Biddle had prepared a memorandum on government and art for the National Resources Planning Board in 1942, a plan that was subsequently circulated among some seventy-five artists, museum directors, college presidents, and the like.[13] Believing that art would play an increasingly important role in postwar America, and that the government must be prepared "to do its share in the constructive planning which will gear the talent and scope of our 25,000 artists in the needs of 140,000,000 people," Biddle called for the creation of a single Bureau of Fine Arts to organize the various government art activities. Specifically, Biddle wanted to see the three former art projects—the Treasury's Section of Fine Arts, the

Federal Art Project, and the art education program of the National Youth Administration (NYA)—combined under a single bureau. In this way, the three major thrusts of the federal arts effort of the thirties—quality, availability, and training—would be maintained. With its focus on securing art of the highest standard for new federal buildings (generally involving murals obtained through anonymous competitions), the Treasury's Section was committed to quality. The FAP and the NYA, meanwhile, much more broadly based relief efforts, followed a more democratic course; the former, for example, employed thousands of artists to create murals, sculpture, easel paintings, photographs, posters, and lithographs, and operated over a hundred community art centers.

Biddle's new agency would not only foster cooperation between programs that were too often competitive in the past, joining the diversity of the FAP with the high standards of the Section, but it would add an important new element of promotion. Recalling the two federally sponsored "Art Week" campaigns of the early forties, designed to bring art to the people and funds to the artist, Biddle sketched an "art week" functioning fifty-two weeks of the year: "a Federal employment and help-wanted agency which would tell artists of their opportunities and of the varying conditions for work throughout the country on the one hand, and, on the other, would inform people in industry how they could effectively use art for given purposes and how they could obtain qualified artists."[14]

Among those who saw Biddle's proposal, the response was generally quite favorable. Artist Thomas Hart Benton called the memorandum "an excellent job and one with which I am in complete accord," while historian Charles A. Beard declared that it deserved "careful consideration and popular support." Historian Samuel Eliot Morison and literary historian Van Wyck Brooks, along with several museum directors, also expressed support for the concept of a Bureau of Fine Arts. One of the most skeptical, surprisingly enough, was Holger Cahill, who was well aware, after his years with the

FAP, that not all observers shared Biddle's enthusiasm for publicly supported art.

Even among those who agreed with Biddle that the government should have an arts program, three criticisms came up repeatedly, echoes from the WPA years, yet with implications for future subsidy plans. First was the notion of "relief," which either had no place in an arts program or which, according to others, should at the very least be segregated from genuine efforts to foster "quality" art. Robert Moses, New York park commissioner, was of the former school. "God forbid that we should have another gigantic relief program," he fumed. "If there is a gap to be filled by public works . . . then let us have a genuine works program and not a make-shift make-work affair."[15]

Beyond the relief question, the advocates of a federal program expressed their fears about two other aspects of the partnership between government and art—the potential negative effects of centralization, of a bureaucracy imposing cultural standards from above, and second, of political influence playing too large a role in the proposed bureau's decisions. While the relief question faded in the face of postwar prosperity, the other two concerns, over the potential federal domination and the "politicalization" of the arts, grew increasingly important in the coming years. These issues, moreover, tended to divide the arts community itself, with traditional and modern art factions, for example, fearing each other's potential for gaining control of a federal bureau.

Thus even the hypothetical selection of a chairman of Biddle's proposed bureau was viewed as a critical point. Harvard professor John M. Gaus finally declared himself in favor of an informed layman, "chosen primarily for general human qualities. . . . I am fearful of tying the position to a particular professional group or a particular craft or art," Gaus observed, "because I think this invites a possible clash between technical schools within the art or craft, or the tendency to select a person acceptable to conventional or formal standards of a particular group."[16]

But while artists and museum directors continued the old modernist-traditionalist debate, making fine-line distinctions in the administration of a federal arts program that would not really come into play for another two decades, others were raising objections that would loom much larger in the immediate future. The whole issue of federal arts support, discussed so optimistically by Biddle and others in the early forties, made certain assumptions, after all, about the *right* of government to engage in activities that before the Depression had been left to private initiative in America. In view of the dismal record of the WPA arts projects in Congress, moreover, and the determination of a growing number of congressmen to prevent any postwar versions of the New Deal, such assumptions were rather dangerous.

Speaking firmly on behalf of private initiative, Dr. Henry Allen Moe, secretary general of the Guggenheim Foundation, expressed doubts about Biddle's claims for the need of a federal art program:

> I do not myself see that government has any more duty to "artists" than it has to plumbers when "artists" are reckoned in the thousands as was done by WPA and as George Biddle apparently proposes to reckon them. For the plain fact is that there never were five thousand artists (in the sense of original creators) in any one country at any time and there are not anything like that number in the United States now. Apart from a relief program, when the "artist" is entitled to the same help that a plumber needing help is entitled to, but no more ... helping artists as artists is justified only when it adds to the creative power and output of the United States. This, WPA never seemed to realize.[17]

According to Moe, then, American culture, with its limited number of "original creators," was best served by discriminating private patrons like Carnegie, Rockefeller, and Guggenheim, whose wealth had been placed in special philanthropic agencies. A federal program, in contrast, by lowering standards and artificially stimulating the arts market, could only produce that kind of cultural "inflation" that plagued the WPA.

There were other plans for federal arts support besides Biddle's during the post-WPA years, and even a couple of timid legislative proposals, but they all faced the same two stumbling blocks—sweeping questions such as Moe's about the very *premise* of public subsidy, and the more intricate points raised by arts advocates, citing the possible abuses of such support.[18] The first served the congressional critics well (although the legislators' motives were more broadly political than Moe's elitist position), while the latter served to fragment an arts community that for years was unable to mount an effective campaign for government support as a result.

"Regardless of who will be President or which party may be in power," declared the conservative American Artists Professional League in a typical early criticism of federal subsidy, "such ventures can not escape the political driver in the back seat. . . . It is for this reason," the AAPL explained in 1945,

> the League opposed the Fine Arts Bureau Bill previously offered and also opposed the Coffee-Pepper [arts bureau] Bill. After the high and lofty preambles had been stripped from these proposals, there remained nothing but veiled plans for the regimentation of artists and especially all the pseudo artists, and some highly artistic person like John L. Lewis would have been director of fine arts.[19]

As it turned out, however, American artists need not have feared a labor leader like John L. Lewis—not, at least, when they had congressmen like Fred E. Busbey and George A. Dondero to worry about.

"Advancing American Art"

It all started innocently enough. During World War II the United States had carried on a modest cultural information and exchange program under the auspices of the Office of War Information (operating in the eastern hemisphere) and the Division of Cultural Cooperation of the State Department (operating in the American republics). In June 1940 these projects were consolidated in the State Department's Office of International Information and Cultural Affairs, with the goal of demonstrating, according to Assistant Secretary of State William Benton, "to all those abroad who thought of the United States as a nation of materialists, that the same country which produces brilliant scientists and engineers also produces creative artists."[20]

With this in mind, the State Department put together two exhibition programs in 1946. One of them, conceived in the summer of 1946, reflected the essence of the State Department message. Entitled "American Industry Sponsors Art," it was designed to display the best of both American worlds— the world of culture as contained in the art collections of the business world. Thus when Egypt requested a selection of nineteenth- and twentieth-century American paintings for a 1947 international exhibition in Cairo, the State Department turned proudly to the art collection of the International Business Machines Corporation. Thomas J. Watson, IBM president, had purchased more than 30,000 art items for the company over the preceding ten years, and a permanent museum was being constructed in Endicott, New York, to house some of these works. From that collection the State Department's art expert, J. Leroy Davidson (a former assistant director of the Walker Art Center in Minneapolis), selected works for the "60 Americans Since 1800" exhibit to be sent abroad. Following the Cairo showing, the exhibit was supplemented by paintings from other corporate collections (including Standard Oil of New Jersey, Pepsi Cola, and the Container Corporation of America) for further touring in Europe.

That project, it turned out, was the noncontroversial half of the State Department's art plans. For also in 1946 the department allocated funds for the *purchase* of American art, which would be exhibited in both Europe and Latin America before being installed in American outposts abroad. The explanation for the purchase was quite practical—the impossibility of borrowing art for long periods and the expense of borrowing it for short ones. But what the department could never satisfactorily explain, to its critics, at least, was the predominance of modern works among the seventy-nine items Davidson purchased.

That explanation was quite simple, too, although apparently not convincing enough for some members of Congress. Several foreign governments, it seems, had requested examples of modern American art and thus Davidson, working with less than $50,000, put together a collection representative of then recent trends in American art.[21] Included were some of the same artists as those in the corporate collections, painters like John Marin, Max Weber, Stuart Davis, Ben Shahn, Byron Browne, and Phillip Evergood, along with a number of other fairly prominent American painters, including William Gropper, Philip Guston, Robert Gwathmey, Marsden Hartley, Yasuo Kuniyoshi, Jack Levine, Georgia O'Keeffe, Anton Refregier, and Charles Sheeler. By design, then, the collection, entitled "Advancing American Art," lacked the balance of the IBM exhibit. It was, as *Newsweek* put it, "frankly weighted on the experimental and creative side"; and in reference to the "canvases belonging in the categories of extreme expressionism, fantasy, surrealism and abstraction . . . ," *New York Times* critic Edward A. Jewell asserted that "Mr. Davidson, who took great pains in gathering together the material purchased by the State Department, made no attempt to present a rounded report on contemporary painting in America."[22]

When it opened at the Metropolitan Museum of Art in the fall of 1946, before touring in two sections to South America and Europe, "Advancing American Art" received generally favorable reviews from the critics.[23] Although there was some quibbling about a few of the selections and a few of the artists represented, almost all agreed that for $49,000 the State Department had acquitted itself quite nicely.[24] Among those concerned with the larger issue of international cooperation, moreover, the two State Department projects were hailed collectively as a cultural landmark, carrying the ideal of "one world" to thousands of Europeans and South Americans. "At a time when the world is trying so desperately to be 'one,'" the *Magazine of Art*'s John D. Morse observed,

> such unanimity of feeling in our own country is, to put it mildly, most encouraging. And the fact that the paintings in these exhibitions were bought by so many different agencies, for so many different purposes, yet hang so harmoniously together, is surely an answer to those uninformed and inexperienced critics of modern art who find in it only confusion and chaos.[25]

Morse vastly underestimated those critics, however, both in and out of Congress, who in their attacks on the State Department's exhibition program created a fair amount of confusion and chaos of their own.

"Definitely New Deal in Various Shades of Communism"

It is not clear who fired the first salvo against "Advancing American Art," but by the end of the year the art world's biggest controversy since the close of the New Deal had begun. Like the WPA, the State Department art program was vulnerable to attack from a variety of quarters—from Republican congressmen in search of an easy Democratic target, from conservative newspapers ever on the lookout for federal extravagance, from academic painters opposed to modern art, and even from disgruntled artists who were upset, quite simply, that they had been overlooked by the State Department's program.

The conservative American Artists Professional League (AAPL) was probably the most effective in its attack. Rallying the troops in its monthly *Art Digest* column, and aiming straight for the top with a letter to Secretary of State James Byrnes, it protested "the one-sided representation of American Art" by the State Department. Speaking for the league, Vice President Albert T. Reid cautioned the government against creating a monopoly for one "school or fashion in art," noting that the league had already fought the modernists on other fronts, in the vanguard's effort "to create a monopoly in museums and otherwise control criticism and galleries." In language that would soon echo through Congress with even less restraint, Reid raised the specter of foreign radicalism in American art: "Our associated groups question the cultural value of any exhibition which is so strongly marked with the radicalism of the new trends in European art. This is not indigenous to our soil."[26]

These were mild complaints, though, compared to the attacks that appeared regularly in the Hearst newspapers, with their references to "junk," "lunatic delight," and the collection that "concentrates with biased frenzy on what is incomprehensible, ugly, and absurd." When the Hearst press tired of outrage, it employed sarcasm, as in this caption to a photograph in the *New York Journal-American*: "GIVING US THE BIRD . . . This is a t-u-r-k-e-y. A t-u-r-k-e-y is a b-i-r-d. It is an impressionist turkey, by Everett Spruce, an abstract turkey, maybe, or even a cubistic turkey. It is not good for eating. Is it good painting? The State Department says, yes."[27]

If the AAPL lacked some of the flair of Hearst's yellow journalism, it more than compensated with the thoroughness of its campaign. Gathering support from other conservative art organizations like the National Academy of Design, Salmagundi Club, Society of Illustrators, Allied Artists, Fine Arts Federation, and the Municipal Art Society, the AAPL organized a letter-writing campaign that made a distinct impression on Congress, which considered the State Department's appropriation in the spring of 1947. When Secretary of State George C. Marshall, who had replaced Byrnes in January, appeared before a House Appropriations Subcommittee in March, for example, he acknowledged that he had "received notice of this affair from every direction. I think I have already had some 50 to 100 letters on the subject, with some oral discussions back and forth, from the President all the way down."[28] Although he deferred to Assistant Secretary William Benton for the particulars, he seemed to indicate that the State Department had already decided at that point to close the exhibitions.

This fact became evident two weeks later, when the lengthy hearings turned their attention once again to the art program. Assistant Secretary Benton informed the subcommittee that the State Department had decided to halt the art tour after the current exhibitions in Haiti and Prague, when the collection could be evaluated by a "panel of leading American art specialists."[29] But even this concession was not sufficient for some members of the subcommittee, most notably Chairman Karl Stefan (R-NB), who badgered Benton with exchanges like the following, involving an unidentified abstract work:

> Mr. Stefan: What is the picture?
> Mr. Benton: I can't tell you.
> Mr. Stefan: I am putting it about a foot from your eyes. Do you know what it is?
> Mr. Benton: I won't even hazard a guess of what that picture is, Mr. Chairman.
> Mr. Stefan: How much did you pay for it? You paid $700 for it and you can't identify it.[30]

By this time, the "Advancing American Art" episode had become a *cause célèbre*. Letters of protest poured into Congress, and a skeptical spread in *Look* magazine, "Your Money Bought These Paintings," added fuel to the fire.[31] Not surprisingly, in May, when the House Appropriations Committee made its report citing the "many hundreds of letters received in protest to this program," it rejected funds for the exhibitions. "It would seem," the committee noted, "that if we are going abroad to impress people, we should try to impress the average individual rather than a certain segment of the art colony."[32]

But even after such congressional censure, and even with the collection safely packed away, the fray was only beginning. For the little collection of modern art had been transformed into a symbol of the larger ills of America—of moral laxity, of government profligacy, of Communist infiltration, of all those sins of the thirties, in short, that were being visited on the children of the forties. Art, neither wholly necessary nor completely comprehensible, and already tainted by its associaton with the New Deal, would often serve during the next several years as a political scapegoat, judged not on its own merits but on its alleged political associations.[33]

Just a week after the Appropriations Committee issued its report, Representative Fred Busbey opened the reactionary floodgates with the first of a series of congressional disquisitions on art that would continue into the fifties. Calling the exhibit a "disgrace to the United States" but typical of an administration "infected by Communists," the Illinois Republican described the "sinister aspects" of the "alleged art exhibition." "The Circus Girl Resting and other trashy paintings sent on tour by the State Department," he declared in Congress, "with the taxpayers footing the bill, have done our country harm abroad. Foreigners must be wondering what kind of crackpots assembled such a jumble of paintings."[34]

More to the point, many conservatives saw the collection as part of a larger threat, as an example of the New Deal–Communist continuum that grew out of fifteen consecutive years of Democratic rule. Thus it was not Davidson's knowledge of art that Busbey questioned, but rather the company he kept: "It is my opinion that Mr. Davidson, in acting as the art arbiter for the United States, has been moving with very fast company in the new dealers' world—that radical band who would uproot all that we have cherished as sacred in the American way of life." Disputing the State Department's claim that foreign governments had requested the exhibit and taking one more blast at abstract art, Busbey finally got to the heart of the matter with his assertions (backed up by several pages of standard guilt-by-association furnished by the House Un-American Activities Committee) about the politics of the artists: "The records of more than 20 of the 45 artists are definitely New Deal in various shades of Communism. Some we found to be definitely connected with revolutionary organizations."[35]

Busbey's trend-setting attack was a potpourri of conservative fears, one part academicist objection to modern art, one part HUAC conspiracy theory, and one part Republican revolt against lingering New Deal politics. It might not have been completely logical, but, in its buckshot approach, the attack was shrewdly designed to attract a number of followers:

> The movement of modern art is a revolution against the conventional and natural things of life expressed in art.
>
> The artists of the radical school ridicule all that has been held dear in art. Institutions that have been venerated through the ages are ridiculed.
>
> Without exception, the paintings in the State Department group that portray a person make him or her unnatural. The skin is not reproduced as it would be naturally, but as a sullen, ashen gray. Features of the face are always depressed and melancholy.
>
> That is what the Communists and other extremists want to portray. They want to tell the foreigners that the American people are despondent, broken down or of hideous shape— thoroughly dissatisfied with their lot and eager for a change of government.
>
> The Communists and their New Deal fellow-travelers have selected art as one of their avenues of propaganda. Their game is to use every field of information and entertainment in an effort to shatter all that conflicts with despotic communism.
>
> When the taxpayers' money is used to buy pictures painted by Communist artists we not only distribute their propaganda, we also put money in their pockets and thereby enable them to influence their efforts to make America Red Communist.

While Busbey and his allies kept things stirred up in Congress, the Republican National Committee exploited the episode in the summer of 1947 by distributing a garish pictorial spread to newspapers across the land.[36] Put together by William C. Murphy, publicity director of the committee, it featured unflattering black-and-white reproductions of seven works, complete with references to wasteful Democratic spending and program notes courtesy of HUAC. "Fellow-traveler 'artists' with State Department connections . . . were able to sell their 'art' and gain prominence . . . ," the editorial taunted. "We hope you taxpayers like it—you bought it!"[37]

In the face of such publicity, the State Department soon decided to liquidate its art holdings, in a manner only slightly more dignified than the disposal of the New York FAP paintings a few years earlier. Declared "surplus property" by the State Department, the entire collection (including the original seventy-nine paintings along with thirty-nine watercolors) was put up for sale by the War Assets Administration (WAA), following a final showing at the Whitney Museum of American Art. Although the American Federation of Arts attempted to obtain the collection intact, WAA regulations gave a priority to veterans and public institutions, granting the latter a 95 percent discount on the fair market value. Thus while the collection (purchased at $55,800) was appraised at $79,658.50, it brought the government a return of only $5,526.68. As a final ironic note, moreover, eighty-two works from the exhibit ended up in the collections of three institutions not known for their radical activity—the University of Oklahoma, Alabama Polytechnic, and the University of Georgia.

"Abstract Red Herring"

The biggest irony of all was the haphazard use by Busbey and his colleagues of the "Communist" tag, attributing it wholesale to works of modern art that would have been even less welcome in the Soviet Union. Indeed, the Communist press had panned the "Advancing American Art" exhibit in Prague, and at the very same time that Busbey was attempting to banish the State Department modernists, Soviet censors were attacking similar trends in their country. Thus in an effort to reduce the influence of Picasso, *Pravda* declared that his "debasing and formalist art represents man as a monster deprived of feeling and thought . . . and serves the selfish interest of the bourgeoisie, catering to their decadent and perverted tastes. . . ."[38]

Nor did the sale of the State Department collection—and the stipulation of Congress that future official displays of American art abroad would require its prior approval—end the assault on modern art. In Busbey's absence (he failed in a reelection bid in 1948), the position of leading congressional art critic was assumed by George Dondero of Michigan, the arch-conservative Republican who had suffered through Democratic administrations since his election to the House in 1932. Now, however, it was Dondero's turn in the spotlight. Armed with his own anti-Communist predilections and some choice, ghost-written harangues provided by the American Artists Professional League, he launched a campaign against modern art that made Busbey's attack seem almost logical in comparison.[39]

Dondero, in short, went after *everything* associated with modern art—from an exhibit in a New York hospital to the ranks of Artists Equity, from a tiny Fifty-seventh Street gallery to the host of "foreign isms" that he loved to disparage. It was all part of Dondero's larger campaign against communism. If he never accomplished what he set out to (which was never very clear in any case), Dondero, like Busbey, can at least be credited with helping to close the ranks of American artists. For in the very act of defending themselves against the often absurd charges of the two representatives, artists were laying the groundwork for the more positive efforts in the fifties to secure government support. In the meantime, though, artists and their advocates (especially museum directors and critics, also targets of Dondero's wrath) were fully occupied in warding off the attacks emanating from Washington.[40]

Dondero's first blast was issued on 11 March 1949, when he warned his colleagues in Congress that the radical art episode of 1947 was not yet closed.[41] Noting that such art could never survive on its own merit, he charged that its creators "are constantly scheming to get their hands on public funds, and even private philanthropies, in order to grow." The latest scheme, according to Dondero, was an innocent-looking project entitled "Gallery-on-Wheels," in which art and artists had visited a naval hospital in St. Albans, New York. But upon closer examination (and with the assistance of the same HUAC files that Busbey had used), it turned out that several of the twenty-eight artists represented in the portable exhibit had also been part of the State Department show.[42]

Dondero was not concerned with the nature of the art presented; nor did he bother to determine that no public funds were used and that only two painters participated directly in the event.[43] The mere *idea* of radical artists spreading their lies to a captive audience was sufficient to send the congressman's imagination reeling. "I do know," he charged, "that these individuals—radicals all—spending two weeks in an important naval hospital explaining their theories to an audience who could not get away from them, had a great opportunity not only to spread their propaganda, but to engage in espionage, if they were inclined to do so." Not everyone present was persuaded by Dondero's claims—Representative Gordon Canfield (R-NJ) wanted to know if perhaps one of the paintings was of a red herring. But the reaction must have been favorable enough to encourage Dondero to deliver more of the same. For two weeks later he was back in the pulpit for a second sermon on radical art, warning this time that "we have been neglectful of the knowledge that communism is a hydraheaded serpent that attacks the true democracies on all fronts, political, social, economic, scientific, cultural."[44]

Red-baiters like Dondero and his mentors on HUAC were notorious for simultaneously rejecting the "lies" of Communist ideologues while accepting their boasts at face value. Thus when Communist Party Chairman William Z. Foster spoke of using art as a "weapon in the class struggle" in a *New Masses* article cited by Dondero, the congressman read sinister intentions into the plans of all left-wing artist associations. (And because such groups tended to favor government art support, Dondero concluded that such assistance, too, must be a part of the larger radical plot.) In this particular instance Dondero's target was the recently formed Artists Equity Association, "arisen from the ashes of other dead and dying" organizations "cloaked in the disguise of legitimacy." Once again the congressman's investigatory technique involved a close reading of political pedigrees, noting the leftist connections (usually from the thirties) of such artists as Ben Shahn, Max Weber, and Robert Gwathmey.

"If it were possible to show examples of the output produced by these artist politicos," promised Dondero (and the closer his comments came to art criticism, the more apparent was the influence of his AAPL informers), "I am sure most of you would agree that they are enemies of true art, instead of artists. . . . Through the aid of Marxist evaluators in the cultural sphere, leftists in art are attempting to break down the standard to which artists of the past adhered—to be worthy of the calling of art."[45]

The two March speeches and another in May (exposing the ACA Gallery in New York as a hotbed of Communist art) were mere warm-ups, however, for Dondero's August treatise, "Modern Art Shackled to Communism," in which he ranged over the entire scope of modern art in an effort to ferret out subversive activity. Dismissing the seeming contradiction between the work of Communist artists in America ("the human art termites, disciples of multiple 'isms' that compose so-called modern art, boring industriously to destroy the high standards and priceless traditions of academic art . . . ") and that of Soviet realists—"one is the weapon of destruction, and the other is the medium of controlled propaganda"—Dondero offered a brief "history" of modern art while railing against the Harvard-trained "effeminate elect," those museum directors who promote this "hog-scrapple of art."

"Not only do they persist in jamming this art trash down the throats of the public," Dondero raged, again revealing his AAPL sources, "but they have effectively aided in excluding the works of our real American artists from exhibitions and competitions. . . .

"Communist art, aided and abetted by misguided Americans, is stabbing our glorious American art in the back with murderous intent."

If Dondero was sincere in his anti-Communist beliefs, and there is no reason to suspect that he was not, it is nevertheless doubtful that his speechwriters were quite so ingenuous. Their attack on "Communist art," after all, was at least as much motivated by the economic threat posed by abstract expressionism in the domestic art market as by any alleged international conspiracy to overthrow American democracy. "Behind the aggrieved cry of dispossessed traditionalists in the conservative art organizations," Jane De Hart Mathews has theorized, "was the impending reality of vanguard triumph. Understandably threatened economically and stylistically, they made common cause with other Americans to whom modernism in any guise was perceived as threatening."[46] Thus the ongoing battle between academic and modern artists, on purely aesthetic grounds, cuts through much of the smokescreen of Dondero's wild suspicions.

Still, that battle only begins to explain the confusing state of art and politics of the late forties, so strange were the bedfellows of the period. "Only a great, generous, muddling democracy like ours," concluded Alfred Frankfurter in an article aptly titled "Abstract Red Herring," "could afford the simultaneous paradox of a Congressman who tries to attack Communism by demanding the very rules which Communists enforce where they are in power, and of a handful of artists who enroll idealistically in movements sympathetic to Soviet Russia while they go on painting pictures that would land them in jail under a Communist government."[47]

Despite such confusion, American art was able to withstand, happily, *both* the Communist "threat" and Dondero's stirring defense. And while Dondero and Busbey resurfaced as congressional art critics a few years later, perhaps the most important and lasting effect of their campaign in the late forties was the reaction it elicited from artists and art organizations. Although not nearly so well organized as Dondero imagined, and certainly not at this stage as effective as the conservative groups in influencing Congress, artists and arts advocates did rally in response to the attacks from Washington. "Indeed," Museum of Modern Art curator James Thrall

Soby declared in response to the State Department art squabble, "almost the only encouraging factor in the current witchhunt is that it has united American art circles in protest as I have never seen them united before."[48] Groups as diverse as Artists Equity and the Audubon Society gathered in New York to protest the cancellation of the State Department exhibitions, while the art press, spurred by Dondero's barrage and led by editors Peyton Boswell of *Art Digest* and Alfred Frankfurter of *Art News*, rallied support for the artists' cause.

Equally important, two youthful congressmen (one who was shortly to emerge as a leading arts advocate in the House) rose to counter Dondero's assault. On 18 August 1949 the *other* McCarthy of the era (Gene, D-MN) spoke in protest of Dondero's "oversimplified analysis" of modern art:

> The gentleman from Michigan does not leave us much. Is America to be made safe for and by Norman Rockwell, James Montgomery Flagg, Petty, and Varga? Is America to be made safe by the suppression of every expression of social criticism by the smothering of every new approach either to the understanding of problems or the presentation of them? Let us judge each work of art in itself, rather than in terms of [the] school in which it is classified, or in terms of our feelings about the artist.[49]

And five days later, Representative Jacob Javits (R-NY) protested Dondero's campaign in even stronger terms:

> In seeking to discredit modern art by its wholesale condemnation as communistic my colleague—I am sure unwittingly—falls into the trap of the same propagandistic device the influence of which we have all decried in the Soviet Union, Nazi Germany, and Fascist Italy, for it is condemnation by class and broad-scale labeling without individual evaluation and, beyond everything else, without a patient confidence in the ultimate judgment of our people and their capability for discerning the good from the evil, the artistic from the progagandistic and the true from the false.[50]

Even liberals like Javits had to draw the line somewhere in the question of artistic freedom, and for Javits and many other congressmen that line was crossed by the Library of Congress that same year, when it awarded its Bollingen Prize for Poetry to Ezra Pound, then under indictment for treason and recently committed to an institution for the insane. With none of the thunder-and-lightning of Dondero's crusade, Congress handled the matter with dispatch, promptly canceling such awards, including similar prizes for music and art, in August.[51]

Congress still didn't know what art was, perhaps, but it was becoming clear that it knew what it didn't like. As in the thirties, when federal art proved to be such a convenient target for opponents of the New Deal, Congress became increasingly active in speaking out on the arts, criticizing those efforts judged to be offensive or politically suspect. Artists, too, were becoming more willing to speak out, if not with the intensity of the WPA artist union strikes, at least with an increasingly organized, more politically astute, approach. They were beginning to speak out, moreover, not only in self-defense against congressional attacks, but in a more positive manner as well, with visions of a new program of federal support.

The Committee on Government and Art

Lloyd Goodrich, art historian and curator at the Whitney Museum, emerged as the leader of the groundswell of opinion concerned with the relationship of government and art. It was Goodrich who became the unofficial historian of the American government's unsteady relationship with the arts, citing in a number of articles the three major historical impediments to federal patronage—the pioneer/puritan spirit that viewed art as a luxury rather than as an essential, the decentralized federal system that delegated authority over educational and cultural affairs to state and local governments, and the phenomenal growth of private capital, which since the nineteenth century had supported the arts. And it was Goodrich who was elected chairman of a new consortium of arts organizations that set out in 1948 to alter that traditional pattern of cultural laissez faire.

Goodrich first proposed the new arts organization in the spring of 1948 at a panel discussion in Washington sponsored by the American Association of Museums. The Committee on Government and Art (CGA), as the organization would be known, had, according to Goodrich, three broad objectives—the reactivation of a federal arts program; the inclusion of private, professional advice in such a program; and the elimination of government censorship. It was this last point, especially, underscored by the recent attacks on modern art in Congress, that fueled the movement, and twelve of the thirteen organizations that Goodrich approached agreed to name representatives to the new committee.[52] "Ever since the end of the federal art projects in 1943," Goodrich told the members of the committee at its first meeting in New York on 14 February 1950, "there has been a growing feeling that our federal government lacks any planned consistent policy in relation to art."[53]

As a first step toward developing such a policy, the committee passed a resolution, favorably received by arts organizations across the country, requesting President Truman to commission a study of existing government facilities and procedures:

> We . . . respectfully urge that the President appoint a commission to consider the whole question of the Government's relation to art, to study existing governmental agencies and methods, and to submit recommendations for their improvement. Such a study, we believe, should be related to the general social and economic position of the American artist. We suggest that such a commission be made of leaders in the art world—museum officers, art educators, architects, painters, sculptors, graphic artists, designers, and informed laymen—and that its membership should be broadly representative of all leading tendencies and schools of thought.[54]

That investigation, as it turned out, was conducted by the government's own Commission of Fine Arts, a low-profile agency that had been looking after Washington architecture and planning since 1910, without attracting much attention in the process. The CGA's own report did not appear until 1954, but the committee, thanks largely to the efforts of Goodrich, helped keep the issue of federal arts support alive; and once congressional hearings began in the fifties, it was an important advocate for a moderate federal arts program.

Another organization active during the period, the National Arts Foundation (NAF), served more as a model for subsequent government efforts than as a lobbying group. Formed in 1947, the NAF was a nonprofit agency dedicated to stimulating interest and participation in music, literature, drama, dance, and the visual arts. Endowed by anonymous donors, the agency worked very much like the arts wing of the Rockefeller Foundation (which may have been, in fact, one of its benefactors), with an interest in improving America's image abroad. Indeed, Carleton Smith, a former music critic and management consultant who directed the foundation, called it a "quasi-governmental organization," designed to interpret American thought and culture to the world and to stimulate public interest in art in the United States. Secretary of Defense James Forrestal, Smith pointed out, had requested such a plan for presentation to the Hoover Commission for government reorganization and to Congress. "We are winning the economic and military conflict, but losing the war of ideas," Smith emphasized. "While we feed the Europeans, the Russians poison their minds."[55]

To counter that trend, Smith proposed channeling the country's best artistic resources through the State Department, while disseminating creative ideas through the schools in this country, leading eventually to a permanent agency like the National Science Foundation. Yet despite such ambitious plans, and despite international advisory panels that included the likes of T. S. Eliot, Jean Sibelius, Jascha Heifetz, John Huston, and the presidents of Finland and Ecuador, comparatively little was heard from the NAF. Whether it simply failed to achieve what it set out to, or whether, like Rockefeller (and the CIA), it succeeded in covering its tracks, remains unclear.[56]

In the meantime, interest in public arts support was developing in other areas as well, including the state level, where in New York legislation for an art program had been introduced.[57] More importantly, musicians and actors, comparatively silent on the subject of government support during the State Department fiasco, began discussing federal aid. For both groups, moreover, it was a growing sense of economic urgency that provoked the discussions. Addressing the National Music Council in 1948, for example, Roy Harris, speaking as president of the Fellowship of American Composers, noted the impossibility of competing with the "entertainment music" industry and called for public support of "serious music." The following year, Serge Koussevitzky made a similar plea, but the retired conductor, like Harris, was outnumbered. Most musicians, it seemed, were still wary of government aid.[58] Citing the demise of the WPA projects and the ensuing State Department debacle, *Musical America* concluded that the risks of federal support far outweighed the possible benefits. "Any Congressional vote to award funds to orchestras or opera companies," the magazine noted, "would carry with it an implicit carte-blanche to inaugurate political witchhunts at any moment.[59]

Not surprisingly, the theater community, which had served its political apprenticeship during the WPA skirmishes of 1938 and 1939, was more favorably disposed toward government support. Theater leaders, led by Actors Equity president Clarence Derwent, made plans in 1948 to lobby for a federally subsidized national theater and discussed as well the possibility of a new cabinet office for the fine arts. At its annual meeting in New York in December, Actors Equity made plans to lobby for Congress to set up a mind-boggling $100 million theater program with two repertory theaters (one for children and one for adults) in each state. More realistic were the plans discussed at a three-day meeting in New York by the American National Theatre and Academy (which had good reason to be realistic, having endured fifteen years of government neglect after receiving a congressional charter in 1935 to encourage and develop theater in the United States).[60]

Unlike the thirties, when plans to make the federal arts projects permanent were laughed out of Congress, or the forties, when even the State Department's temporary arts programs were rejected, the fifties promised a more receptive, if comparatively small, audience in Congress. Led by a young Republican representative from New York, a handful of congressmen were about to introduce the first of what would be countless arts proposals over the next fifteen years. Almost all, of course, would fail, but each one had a part in shaping the eventual arts legislation that passed in 1964 and 1965.

The Artist and the Politicians

Jacob Javits did not enter the House of Representatives until 1947, but had he been around ten years earlier, when another New York representative introduced a bill for a Bureau of Fine Arts, the young Republican might not have been in such a hurry to sponsor an arts bill of his own. William Sirovich, the earlier New Yorker, was a physician-playwright turned politician whose first effort to civilize America actually predated the WPA arts projects by several months. Sirovich secured a hearing for his fine arts bill before the Committee on Patents in the spring of 1935, although nothing came of the proposal—an odd plan for a "single department of the Government of the United States dealing wholly with science, the beaux arts, and the arts utile"—until 1938, when House and Senate hearings launched a revised version of the bill. The congressional critics closed the show overnight.

Sirovich's visionary proposal, thirteen lofty "Whereases" anchored by a rather bland resolution to establish a Department of Science, Art, and Literature, joined forces with a much shrewder proposal sponsored by Representative John Coffee (D-WA) and Senator Claude Pepper (D-FL). Inevitably dubbed the Coffee-Pepper bill, this plan had called for the incorporation of the WPA arts projects into a Bureau of Fine Arts, to be established within the Department of the Interior. As such, the bill became the natural target for enemies of the New Deal, who zeroed in on two aspects of the plan. First, and most obvious, were the relief aspects of the measure, assuming the burden, as it did, of the WPA's unwashed masses, the federal artists who "shall continue in such employment without interruption of time or salary under the jurisdiction of the Bureau of Fine Arts." Second, and more nefarious, according to some readers of the fine print of Coffee-Pepper, was the threat of union control of the proposed fine arts bureau. Both the commissioner of that bureau, along with the five other members, were to be "selected from a panel of names to be submitted . . . by organizations representing the greatest number of artists employed in each of the arts under the bureau," organizations like Actors Equity, the American Federation of Musicians, or the American Artists Congress, in other words, to the exclusion of the much smaller taste-making cliques like the American Academy of Design and the National Sculpture Society. Such a setup, according to one witness before an Education and Labor subcommittee chaired by Senator Pepper in 1938, would "pave the way to Government control and regulation of the arts and artists throughout the country . . . furnish the Government the most powerful medium of subversive political propaganda, . . . and officially introduce into our Government labor union domination supported by Federal funds."[1]

When it resurfaced in the spring of 1938, the revised Sirovich-Coffee-Pepper plan (H.J.R. 671) appeared to have answered the two major objections, leaving it to the president's discretion to appoint whomever he wanted to the bureau, and making optional as well the transfer to that bureau of any or all of the federal arts projects' activities. Nevertheless, the mere *mention* in the bill of the Works Projects Administration sealed its fate in Congress, where, despite the stirring plea of Representative Sirovich—"Let us through the Department of Fine Arts become the greatest and mightiest Nation in the world in cultural and artistic development that will be a monument to our genius in the centuries to come"— the bill was swept aside in a sea of laughter. There were jesting complaints about acrobats and milkers being left out of the bill, along with questions about the inclusion of "puppeteers" (a "man who raises puppies," according to Minnesota's Harold Knutson) and the apparent absence of a provision for the puppet Charlie McCarthy himself. Representative Dewey Short (R-MO) treated his colleagues to a mock ballet on the floor of the House, while demanding to know how "anybody can feel comfortable or enjoy listening to the strains of Mendelssohn with the seat of his pants out."[2]

Discouraged by such levity, a sympathetic Adolph Sabath (D-IL) recommended the withdrawal of the resolution "until such time as it may receive the merited consideration that it deserves." The bill's opponents demanded a vote, however, ("let us give it at least a decent burial," quipped Wisconsin's Gerald Boileau) and the proposed fine arts bureau fell by an overwhelming 195 to 35 vote. In the wake of such a defeat, not surprisingly, Sabath's call for "merited consideration" went unanswered for years. Aside from a couple of ill-fated bills relating to surveys of arts education in 1941 and 1943, a full decade elapsed between the last attempts to make the WPA projects permanent and the new era of arts legislation that began quietly in 1949. In the interim, as we have seen, the little attention that the arts received in Congress was more often than not of the wrist-slapping variety, with art alternately regarded as a needless frill or a radical plot.

That narrow viewpoint began to widen somewhat in 1949, however. After extensive consultations in 1948 with several arts advocates (who had been aroused, ironically, by recent congressional attacks), Representative Jacob Javits introduced on 24 January 1949 a joint resolution aimed at the eventual creation of a National Theater and a National Opera and Ballet. Cosponsored in the Senate by Irving Ives (D-NY) and Elbert Thomas (D-UT), the resolution was admittedly a modest proposal. But in its larger implications, initiating the first positive congressional dialogue on the arts in years and raising the expectations of the arts community in the process, H.J.R. 104 set an important precedent.

Citing both the failure of the federal government to promote the arts ("almost alone among the great powers") and the large number of Americans who lacked direct access to professional performing arts ("especially outside the great centers of population"), Javits introduced a resolution that would permit the *consideration* of federal arts support. It was a tentative first step, to be sure, and one that frankly recognized the potential opposition to such support, both in and out of Congress. Javits chose to meet that opposition head-on by anticipating its arguments, stealing its thunder, in effect. "I realize full well the dangers of the paralyzing hand of Government control of the arts, of the use which can be made of them to control thought," Javits told his colleagues in the House,

> hence my bill calls for a constitutional convention to be called by the President representative of all branches of theatre, opera and ballet—performers, workers, writers and audience—to draft and propose plans—but not WPA schemes of unemployment relief—which will deserve government support while providing for the democratic control of a national theatre and a national opera and ballet by the constituent elements so called together.[3]

While the references to the government's "paralyzing hand" and to the "WPA schemes," like the resolution's small ($25,000) price tag, were his way of acknowledging the opposition's strength, Javits's personal vision for the arts was not nearly so limited as his bill suggests. For at the same time that his colleagues were introducing legislation for a "national theater" to be housed in a refurbished Washington landmark (the Belasco theater), Javits's plans were far more expansive.[4] In 1949, for example, he urged Americans to "think of a national theater not in terms of a physical structure but as an integrated, country-wide organization aided by the Federal Government" to expand the "theater arts to every section of the U.S." Speaking to the National Music Council (NMC) the following year, he stressed the possibility of a "National Theatre and Music Foundation" being developed, to be patterned after the Smithsonian Institution, with an independent board of trustees.[5]

As it turned out, however, Javits may have been moving too fast even for his allies in the arts community. For after Javits addressed an American National Theatre and Academy conference in March 1949, that body opted for a more traditional approach to legislation, lobbying (unsuccessfully) for a million-dollar rider to the federal aid-to-education bill. Nor was the NMC, meeting the next year, ready to follow Javits's lead. It desired, in a typical fashion of the time, "more information" before it could support either the foundation or the assembly plans that the congressman had described.

Even with the backing of such organizations, however, it is unlikely that Javits's resolution would have been reported out of committee, for at that time there was still little visible enthusiasm in Congress for arts support. As one of the more sympathetic congressmen observed in 1950, a national theater, however laudable an idea, could not be considered during the "grave international situation" that faced Congress and the nation.[6] One got the impression during the early cold war years that there would always be some "grave" situation somewhere that would forestall the consideration of a purely domestic program like arts support—until arts advocates learned to stress the international implications of American culture. In any case, despite its quiet demise (without even being considered by the House Administration Committee), H.J.R 104 can be credited as being at least partly responsible for the new era of arts legislation that followed in the fifties.

And it *was* a new era for the arts in Congress, if not in terms of the success of the legislative proposals—large-scale federal support was still fifteen years off—at least in the number and variety of such proposals. Every session brought forth new schemes for the arts, often duplicate measures destined to become mere campaign fodder, but including some sincere, novel approaches as well. Novelty seemed to be the key, in fact, as congressional arts advocates, led by Javits and Charles Howell (D-NJ), along with Emanuel Celler (D-NY) and Stuyvesant Wainwright (R-NY), sought alternatives to the direct federal subsidy approach of the 1937–39 arts bureau bills, which would have been equally out of place in the conservative fifties. The new crop of arts legislation was far more tentative, even devious, calling for admissions-tax exemptions, or for a new arts commission or an academy of fine arts or a capital arts center, or for plans to bring college performing arts groups to Washington or to send the arts abroad. All of these measures flirted with the crucial issue of government subsidy, but only rarely was such support made explicit.

Nor was it simply the presence of the Donderos and the Busbeys in Congress that produced such circuitous routes to federal support, for the arts community itself was still divided on the question of federal aid. Not until a consensus of opinion in favor of such support emerged in that community several years later would more ambitious legislation be proposed in Congress. In the meantime, arts advocates were still uncertain about that "paralyzing hand" of government.

"We Live in the Great Paper Age"

Even George Biddle, whose visions of government art had preceded the New Deal projects, was beginning to have second thoughts about the relationship of government and art. The plan for a Bureau of Fine Arts that he sketched in *Art Digest* in 1950 seemed less ambitious than his proposal of 1943 that advocated consolidation of Roosevelt-era projects and active promotion of art. The 1950 model, streamlined in deference to the recent attacks in Congress, sounded more like an agricultural extension unit dispensing information than a New Deal project creating art. "It could be essentially a bureau," Biddle noted, "for channeling information and services between artists and industry, between government and the artist, between American artists and foreign nations." He recommended that the Truman administration investigate the techniques and shortcomings of the Depression art projects, as well as the British Arts Council and similar experiments in Latin America, before formulating the new arts bureau. But in the end, Biddle conceded, American art must look to the private sector for support: "I believe that the vitality of our art is, in the long run, dependent on the initiative of private organizations and individuals—not on Federal relief and Federal subsidies."[7]

Biddle's cautious middle position accurately reflected the divided arts community of the early fifties, unable to declare itself firmly either for or against government support. Even those in favor of such support were unable to decide precisely what form it should take, ranging in their opinions from mere "recognition" of the arts to outright "subsidy," with a variety of terms like "encouragement" and "stimulation" falling in between.

For some observers, at least, the matter was simple: government meddling could only hurt the arts. Jacques Barzun was of that school, urging in a *Magazine of Art* symposium on government and art that the two spheres were incompatible. Even a "good plan" of the kind Javits had envisioned, carefully worked out to insure adequate citizen participation, would eventually sink into a bureaucratic mire. "The 'good plan'," Barzun warned,

> will breed red tape, investigations by the Civil Service Commission and the FBI, queries whether a given style or statement of belief is not subversive, and senseless infuriating specifications of place, time, materials and whatever other features of artistic work the new administrators may earn their salaries by meddling with. We live in the Great Paper Age— we must never forget it—and paper means petty rules framed in advance of facts, as well as the substitution of verbal description for performance.[8]

If Barzun's complaints about red tape seem both querulous and shopworn today, his other reservation about government art, based on the question of "democratic taste," was more profound. Indeed, the fundamental issue of the *kind* of art that might be produced in a government program— which in the thirties had run the gamut from the potpourri of WPA art to the rather narrowly defined "American Scene" of the Treasury's Section—was an issue that most subsidy advocates avoided. The presumption, of course, was that subsidized art would be no different from any other American art, with the exception that it would reach more people. That a *selection* process would be necessary, and that as a consequence some art would be "vetoed" while other art "passed," was a less attractive topic than a Whitmanesque vision of a new cultural democracy.

To Barzun's way of thinking, such a vision was a pipe dream. Calling into question the notion that subsidized art would serve to raise the general standards of taste, Barzun envisioned the "senator from Maine or Idaho" demanding academic art for the local post office, and the "potato growers of East or West" similarly rejecting modern art. (For the very reason, he shrewdly noted, that "you wouldn't find artists patronizing an 'experimental' farmer whose potatoes tasted like an eau de cologne, however much he might argue that the new product was rich and rare and would in time become palatable.") Nor could Barzun fault the patron-taxpayer for insisting on his simple preferences. "Because of its legitimate habits as a consumer . . . ," Barzun explained, "a democracy does not want advanced, pioneering, experimental art. Not wanting it, a self-governing people cannot be asked to pay for it, directly or indirectly."

Another symposium participant, *Architectural Forum* editor Douglas Haskell, was equally skeptical about the kind of art that would spring from a government-sponsored program. Painting a negative view of the government's relationship with art based on the architect's experience with restrictive building codes and Federal Housing Administration regulations, Haskell found the political and aesthetic worlds to be at cross-purposes:

> Government seeks ever to console the people with the security of law, in other words the security of the *expected*. The purpose of art, on the contrary, is always to shock people out of their sleep, and into life, by the surprise of the *unexpected*. Therefore when government intervenes directly in art matters, it is almost always in order to veto expressions that are new and consequently disturbing to the people's peaceful slumber.

Haskell was reacting to the State Department episode, clearly, and while his definition of art seems unduly skewed toward the avant garde, he raises the same important questions that Barzun did regarding the nature of government art. Given the continuing battle between modern and traditional painters, for example, would government art necessarily turn out to be a bland compromise between the two camps? Indeed, was such a compromise even possible? Or might a federal program, as some artists feared, fall into the hands of one group, to the detriment of the other?

The musical and theatrical communities, meanwhile, if no more unified than the visual artists on the question of federal support, were at least less troubled by the bitter academic-modernist debate. Like the visual artists, both actors and musicians had felt the wrath of Congress during the forties—with HUAC's initial investigations of Hollywood and five separate hearings on musicians union activities—but both groups had taken the offensive, too, lobbying for Congress to repeal the 20-percent admissions tax. Both groups, moreover, had strong unions (Actors Equity and the American Federation of Musicians [AFM]) and national organizations (American National Theatre and Academy [ANTA] and the National Music Council), distinguishing them from the more fragmented visual artists and providing a forum for the discussion of such issues as government subsidy.

Thus the theater community, as noted in chapter 1, was the first segment of the arts world to lobby actively for federal aid, although by 1951 plans were being made for a private-support structure to operate in the absence of government funding. Meeting under the auspices of ANTA in New York in January 1951, the National Theatre Assembly studied a proposal for a privately funded National Theatre Foundation to aid nonprofit projects and institutions across the land. Such an effort, however, did not preclude eventual government support, and the planners emphasized that funds would be sought from all possible sources.[9] Two years later, in fact, Javits introduced legislation for a similar plan to be supported by federal funds.

The music community, too, was well-prepared to discuss the subsidy question on its merits. No strangers to the public arena after numerous court battles, congressional investigations, and even a bill directed squarely at the labor activities of the AFM (the Lea Act of 1946), musicians were thrust into the struggle for public support by the very language of their union's constitution: "The international executive board is instructed to do all in its power to persuade the Federal Government to create a national subsidy for music in this country."[10] Led by their fiery union leader, James C. Petrillo, whose stunts in the forties had included a fifteen-month recording ban and who had taken on at various times not only the radio, recording, and motion picture industries but Congress itself, musicians were uniquely prepared for the legislative debates of the fifties. It is not surprising, then, that when the musicians formed a political task force in 1950, its very name—Musicians Committee to Promote Government Subsidies for Music—got right to the heart of the matter. Organized by former New York Philharmonic cellist Joseph Malkin, the new committee boasted an all-star cast, including such well-known names as Stokowski, Krenek, Monteux, Piatigorsky, Gould, Rubinstein, Koussevitzky, Bernstein, and Mitropoulos.[11]

If less intimidated by Congress and more politically experienced, musicians were also probably the most desperate of all artists. They had suffered not only the setback of the Depression, which all artists felt, but were doubly vexed by technological advances—radio, phonograph recordings, and sound movies—which sharply reduced employment opportunities.[12] "It is common knowledge that music as a profession is shot to pieces," wrote Malkin, overstating his case in a letter to the *New York Times* in 1950. "The machine is the indisputable master of the situation." Making a similar claim the following year, Petrillo called for both government subsidy and an end to the 20-percent admissions tax.[13]

Yet many musicians, like other artists of the period, were uncomfortable with the prospects of a new federal arts program. Most supported the tax repeal, of course, but many opposed a more active program under a Department of Fine Arts. "Many of us are disturbed by this proposal," declared Paul Carpenter, director of the University of Oklahoma's School of Music. "No one can be particularly happy while wearing bureaucratic shackles."[14] Others, like New York Philharmonic conductor Dimitri Mitropoulos, favored government subsidy, but only at the state level. The whole range of opinions—from direct subsidy to the tax repeal to a firm preference for private funding over government support—was presented at a panel discussion on the subsidy question at the December 1950 meeting of the National Music Council. The six participants offered six different versions of the ideal state of affairs.[15]

But if there was no consensus in the early fifties, at least the issue was being actively discussed. More importantly, unlike the earlier discussions, this time the issue was not merely theoretical. For the wheels of Congress were beginning to turn, however fitfully, in the direction of federal support for the arts.

"The Nation Wants to Hear About That Far Greater America"

Having run smoothly for several years, the British Arts Council was seized upon by arts advocates and their allies in Congress as an example of government support of the arts. Neither the regimented art of Nazi Germany or Soviet Russia nor even the blunders of the State Department need be the only products of government subsidy, or so the argument ran.[16] But however admirable the British system appeared, no congressman was willing to come forward to propose such a plan for America. Instead, there was a flurry of piecemeal proposals, foot-in-the-door legislation designed to ease the federal government back into the arts business after a ten-year hiatus.

The Eighty-first Congress, 1950, saw the introduction of the first of a series of legislative window-dressing—bills designed to bring the arts to the culturally deficient capital—in an effort that appeared to be as much concerned with improving America's image abroad as with initiating a federal arts program.[17] The two were related, of course, but while the latter was merely a timid first step (the initial bill would have authorized the secretary of agriculture to bring to Washington the theater productions of land-grant colleges), the former was a grave concern of the cold war years. What other capital in the world, it was often asked during the fifties, could boast of so few cultural events as Washington, or so few suitable buildings to house such events?

Thus while the plan to bring the arts to Washington went through numerous guises before finally getting a formal hearing in 1952 (after which it quietly faded), more ambitious plans—short of outright subsidy—were also being proposed.[18] New York's Representative Celler, for example, who earlier in 1951 had introduced legislation to exempt nonprofit performing arts organizations from the 20-percent admissions tax, expanded the concept of tax relief to include assistance from the executive branch as well in the form of an assistant secretary of the interior for fine arts. If such a plan sounded too much like the decidedly un-American ministries of fine arts in Europe, Celler included an explicit disclaimer in the bill itself. He explained in May to the annual meeting of the NMC: "Paragraph 2 of section 102 of this bill provides that the Assistant Secretary of the Interior for Fine Arts will 'encourage and assist but not dominate or control nonprofit organizations in the presentation, perpetuation and development of the fine arts in the United States.'"[19]

While that plan was dying in committee, another, more ambitious scheme was being launched, calling for the creation of a new National Arts Commission and the construction of a theater and opera house in the capital. Representative Arthur Klein (D-NY) introduced a resolution to this effect in April (H. R. 243), followed six months later by the Senate version (S.J.R. 105), cosponsored by Senators James Murray (D-MT), Paul Douglas (D-IL), Hubert Humphrey (D-MN), Herbert Lehman (D-NY), and Estes Kefauver (D-TN). The president himself expressed his support for a *privately* financed arts center in Washington, although neither bill managed to get out of committee.[20] Nevertheless, their two-pronged approach, calling both for an advisory body to encourage the growth and development of the arts in America and for a capital structure to showcase those arts, established the pattern for numerous proposals in the years ahead.

Another approach, which like Celler's assistant secretary sounded perhaps too European to be adopted, was Javits's 1952 proposal for an American Academy of Music, Drama, and Ballet to be established as a branch of the Smithsonian.[21] While Javits's plan was wedded to another empty legislative vision, a National War Memorial which would include a theater and opera house, at least part of his bill was realistic, recognizing the limitations of Congress' commitment to culture: the academy was to be supported by private funds. That, too, would become a feature of later arts legislation, most notably the long-delayed National Cultural Center (subsequently renamed the John F. Kennedy Memorial Center for the Performing Arts).

If such visions of arts centers and academies were destined to failure in the early fifties, a far more modest proposal to encourage art in America—and liven up the Washington scene—nearly succeeded. One of a number of bills designed to bring college performers to Washington, Charles Howell's H.R. 7494 not only managed to get a subcommittee hearing—the first such exercise for a positive arts proposal since 1938—it actually passed in the House.[22]

The bill's success, such as it was, should perhaps be attributed as much to its author—who chaired the subcommittee which held the hearings—as to the merits of the bill itself. Howell, a New Jersey Democrat, served three terms in the House before running unsuccessfully for the Senate in 1954, and, as a member of the Committee on Education and Labor, emerged as one of the leading congressional spokesmen for federal arts support. Initially, Howell's bill authorized the commissioner of education to facilitate the appearance of college "fine arts productions" (including both performances and exhibitions) in Washington and elsewhere. But even before the hearing was held on 5 May 1952, the scope of the proposal had been narrowed to include only the nation's capital, and the full committee subsequently limited the commissioner's role to *assisting* the making of arrangements for such presentations and offering the use of government buildings where feasible. As the Senate Committee on Labor and Public Welfare made explicit in its report for the Senate version (S. 2300), the measure was clearly a "hands-off" arrangement: "In providing such space neither the Federal Government nor the government of the District of Columbia would be authorized to incur any expenses or assume any responsibility whatsoever for the business management, promotion, or other services or arrangements for such proceedings."[23]

However watered down in its final version, the *spirit* of the bill, at least, was promising. Representative Celler, who had introduced similar legislation, noted the broadly democratic aspects of the measure, developing culture, as it did, "from the roots." And the full Education and Labor Committee, borrowing freely from the language of drama critic Richard Coe's testimony, spoke similarly of the potential of such legislation to meet a basic need of the nation:

> There seems to be no doubt to the committee that there is a great need in this country for the fresh voices of the very young non–New York, non-Hollywood people to be heard. But, for them to be heard, they must be encouraged. There is a need for these young people to feel that the Nation wants to hear about that far greater America of their native states and regions, to hear about the legends of their past and the hopes they have for the future. With the encouragement this bill gives the youth from all over the country to be seen and heard in the Nation's Capital there may be uncovered creative talents of which our own country might well be proud, and which may contribute to a better understanding of our Nation throughout the world.[24]

On the strength of such rhetoric of grass-roots culture and international understanding, Howell's bill passed in the House on the Fourth of July, appropriately enough. It did not fare so well in the Senate, however, where similar legislation had been tabled the day before. Referred to the Senate Committee on Labor and Public Welfare on July fifth, the Howell bill died quietly two days later when the Eighty-second Congress came to a close.

While it had failed to enact any art legislation in 1952, Congress had at least succeeded in opening up the debate, holding the first of several hearings on the arts. Unfortunately, the Eighty-second Congress renewed an older debate as well, dragging American art into American politics once again, and damaging the reputation of both fields in the process.

"The Vaporings of Half-Baked, Lazy People"

"It is unendingly strange . . . ," wrote *Art News* editor Alfred M. Frankfurter in 1953, "that some of the very same men and their colleagues who planned the Federal art projects—and, above all, those who have continued the same government—have shown themselves to be among the most ardent congenital enemies of art."[25] In view of the attacks on art in Congress and the fate of the early arts legislation of the fifties, Frankfurter's perception was accurate. It betrayed, however, an oddly *British* point of view—that the twenty years of Democratic rule from Roosevelt through Truman somehow amounted to the "same government," ignoring shifts in both popular and congressional thought which by 1950 had almost entirely rejected the New Deal ideology. Postwar America, back on its feet economically and facing new responsibilities abroad, was simply not the same as the thirties' variety, when desperate circumstances permitted wholesale social experimentation like that of the New Deal. America in the fifties, with its conservative mood fully entrenched, was even less likely to approve arts programs that smacked of either radicalism or the welfare state. Translated into more narrowly aesthetic terms, the conservative viewpoint that opposed government patronage was apt to cite the Soviet example of controlled art, claiming in turn that given America's diverse culture, government art would necessarily be of a compromising, mediocre nature. Popular culture did not require such support, the argument ran, while "modern" art did not deserve it.[26]

Perhaps the one justification for government patronage

that even conservatives could favor was the use of art in international exchange programs, using American culture to spread the gospel of American democracy abroad. Even this effort was risky, as the "Advancing American Art" episode had demonstrated, and when the State Department made plans for another art program in 1950, it quickly reversed itself and canceled the project.[27] With America's commitment to cultural exchange limited to the movement of scholars abroad under the Fulbright Act and the comparatively small cultural component of the International Information and Education Exchange Program (the Smith-Mundt Act of 1948), the assistant secretary of state for public affairs, Edward W. Barrett, declared in 1951 that the United States was losing the "cultural war" with the Soviet Union, which had sent 39,000 athletes, scientists, writers, artists, musicians, and dancers abroad in 1950. The Soviet program in France alone was estimated at $150 million a year, more than the entire U.S. effort.[28]

The issue of government patronage for international cultural exchange, an admittedly limited concept of arts support, was nevertheless of vital importance during the cold war years, and became by the middle fifties an entering wedge for the more ambitious art programs that followed. In the vacuum created by those "congenital enemies of art" in the early fifties, however, American culture was more likely to be presented abroad under private auspices such as the Rockefeller Brothers Fund, which made a five-year, $625,000 grant to the Museum of Modern Art (MOMA) in 1953 for an international cultural exchange program.[29] The CIA, too, as part of its covert effort to fight communism abroad, sponsored intellectual and cultural programs, including, as Thomas Braden recalled in 1967, an orchestral tour and a cultural magazine. "I remember the enormous joy I got," Braden wrote in response to recent exposés of CIA cultural activities,

> when the Boston Symphony Orchestra won more acclaim for the U.S. in Paris than John Foster Dulles or Dwight D. Eisenhower could have bought with a hundred speeches. And then there was *Encounter*, the magazine published in England and

dedicated to the proposition that cultural advancement and political freedom were interdependent. Money for both the orchestra's tour and the magazine's publication came from the CIA, and few outside the CIA knew about it.[30]

Eva Cockcroft has noted the similarity between the CIA and the MOMA programs for exporting American art. "Freed from the kinds of pressure of unsubtle red-baiting and superjingoism applied to official governmental agencies like the United States Information Agency (USIA)," she explains, "CIA and MOMA cultural projects could provide the well-funded and more persuasive arguments and exhibits needed to sell the rest of the world on the benefits of life and art under capitalism."[31] Such circuitous means of promotion were necessary, too, for those unsubtle red-baiters, Dondero and Busbey, were back in action in 1952, warning the nation once more of radical art organizations and subversive State Department programs.

Dondero, who had not expounded on Communist cultural infiltration since 1949, was at it again in March 1952, claiming to have received "an overwhelming response from artists from coast to coast asking that I further expose the throttling dictatorship of this Red cultural monopoly." What all of that meant, of course, was that the National Sculpture Society (NSS) was up in arms again (over a recent competition at the Metropolitan Museum this time), and that some conservative artists had prepared for the Michigan Republican another art-hysterical broadside against abstract expressionism.[32]

Dondero's attack focused on allegedly radical art organizations, all of them rivals of the NSS and the American Artists Professional League factions, and, as before, the congressman relied on episodes in the thirties to uncover subversion in the fifties. Beginning with the famous 1930 Kharkov conference of artists and writers and laboriously making his way through such groups as the League of American Writers (1935), the American Artists Congress (1936), United American Artists (1938), the Artists League of America, and finally Artists Equity, Dondero declared that "the sinister conspiracy conceived in the black heart of Russia has become a threat to the standard of art in America." The goals of this conspiracy, he noted, were threefold—control of the artist, infiltration and control of the museum, and "the usual plan for a government art program on a permanent basis." That last point was especially important to Dondero's 1952 harangue, as it represented the latest thrust in the radicals' quest for "socialized art." Like the already tainted museums (he cited biased competitions held at the Metropolitan in 1950 and 1951), a federal art program would be another source of artistic treason by this "cultural fifth column."[33]

A few weeks later it was Representative Busbey's turn, and he, like his colleague, had little that was new to offer. His remarks concerned a State Department exhibition of contemporary American prints in Paris that he judged to be "even more communistic" than the infamous 1946 collection. Busbey's method of analysis, once again, involved the use of HUAC files to expose the radical artists included in the exhibition. In this instance, only eight of the fifty-odd artists in question were suspect (including Alexander Calder and Robert Gwathmey), but apparently that was sufficient to trigger the Illinois Republican's conservative outrage.[34] As it turned out, however, the exhibit was more of a private venture than a government project. Selected by the curator of MOMA and funded by Nelson Rockefeller, the exhibit was displayed at the American embassy in Paris at no government expense. The State Department had learned from its prior experience as art exhibitor, clearly, and served only as intermediary in the present case.

The final irony, though, was that an exhibit designed to fight Communist propaganda abroad was itself attacked as communistic at home. For the moment, at least, the emerging American foreign cultural policy was at odds with the conservative spirit of Congress. Caught between the quasi-official Rockefeller-MOMA efforts and the reactionary trend in Congress, the State Department had at the very least to pay lip service to the Dondero-Busbey viewpoint. "Our government should not sponsor examples of our creative energy which are non-representational," the USIA's A. H. Berding told the American Federation of Arts in 1953. Nor would the USIA send "works of avowed communists, persons convicted of crimes involving a threat to the United States or persons who publicly refuse to answer questions of Congressional committees regarding connection with the Communist movement."[35]

Thus the bemused art world faced the paradox of official art critics in Russia and self-appointed censors in the United States who denounced the same brand of modernism in their demand for realistic art. Even President Truman, never known for his tact, decried the art that was fast becoming, as one historian put it, America's chief weapon of the cold war. "I do not pretend to be an artist or judge of art," the president growled, "but I am of the opinion that so-called modern art is merely the vaporings of half-baked lazy people."[36] By removing the president's initial disclaimer and substituting "decadent capitalist bourgeoisie" for "half-baked lazy people," one has a fair approximation of the official Soviet position toward abstract art of the period. Such criticism was reserved for art, moreover, that had long been rejected by American radicals as apolitical and devoid of social meaning. And even if they escaped such censure, the artists in question were often embraced by the left for all of the wrong reasons: because of the status of the artist—as Picasso was embraced in Moscow—or for a foothold in the intellectual community, a ploy dating back to the Communist party's "popular-front" activities of the thirties. Thus the artist, as Ben Shahn explained it in a 1953 *Art News* essay aptly entitled "The Artist and the Politicians," found himself "caught midway between two malignant forces." On the one side stood the "forces of reaction," the Donderos and the National Sculpture Society watchdogs, for example, "who will oppose reform or progress with whatever weapons [they] can lay [their] hands on, including slander and calumny." Pressing the artist from the other side, meanwhile, was "the Communist contingent, ever alert," according to Shahn, "to move in upon his good works, always ready to supply him with its little packages of shopworn dogma, to misappropriate his words, his acts and intentions."[37]

In the fifties, surely, the arts faced a greater threat from the far right than from the far left. While the blusterings of Dondero and Busbey might seem merely amusing today, the reactionary marksmen, given a large enough target, could prove potentially destructive. Such was the case in 1953, when the target was a collection of government-sponsored murals in a San Francisco post office. The battle had begun in 1949, actually, soon after Anton Refregier's twenty-nine panels depicting the history of California were unveiled at the Rincon Annex post office. One of the Treasury's Section of Fine Arts projects, the award to Refregier had been made in 1941, but work was interrupted by the war and not completed until eight years later.[38] Local citizens' groups like the Veterans of Foreign Wars and the Daughters of the American Revolution had voiced complaints about the murals at the time, protesting especially the depiction of racial and labor violence, and even the 1906 earthquake and fire, along with Refregier's stylized figures which, while realistic, were too grim to conjure up happy pioneer memories. As an astute young congressman named Richard Nixon recognized, the times were not ripe for a full-scale attack on such subversive art. "At such time as we may have a change in the Administration and in the majority of Congress," Nixon wrote a former commissioner of a California American Legion post in 1949, "I believe a committee should make a thorough investigation of this type of art in government buildings with the view to obtaining removal of all that is found to be inconsistent with American ideals and principles."[39]

In 1953, finally, with a new Republican administration and a Republican majority in Congress—and with George Dondero as chairman of the House Committee on Public Works—such an investigation could be launched. Dondero appointed a subcommittee to hold hearings on the matter, while California Republican Hubert Scudder introduced a joint resolution, H.J.R. 211, calling for the removal of the murals.[40] Citing the Russian-born Refregier's seven-page HUAC files and calling his creation an insult to California, Scudder told his colleagues in the House that the murals "cast a most derogatory and improper reflection on the character of the pioneers, are controversial in design, and tend to promote racial hatred and class warfare."[41] Painting an even blacker picture of the murals at the hearing on 1 May 1953, Scudder declared that Refregier's works "are ill-advised and slanderous to the American people and endeavor to belittle the United States of America and its history and its institutions."[42]

That the murals were really that powerful is doubtful, but aided by the exposure of Scudder's resolution they were sufficiently unorthodox to stir up the already fractured art community. Conservative artist organizations like the Society of Western Artists (formerly the "Society for Sanity in Art") lined up with like-minded political and social organizations (including the Republican Women's Council of San Francisco and the American Legion) in opposition to the murals, while an even more impressive array, ranging from local arts and museum groups to the American Federation of Arts, Artists Equity, and the American Section of the International Association of Art Critics, rallied in defense of Refregier's work.[43]

The collective response of artists in mutual defense against attacks in the political arena was the most important product of the Rincon Annex episode. For while Scudder's joint resolution failed, the congressman unwittingly succeeded, just as Dondero and Busbey had succeeded before him, in providing the cultural "assembly" that Javits had vainly sought in 1949 with *his* resolution. In rallying artists in self-defense, moreover, the conservative critics helped prepare the arts community for a more positive campaign, for that long legislative battle for government arts *support* that was just getting underway in the early fifties.

The outcome of these various battles was still very much in doubt, of course, and most interested observers at the time correctly predicted that government subsidy was still a long way off. Certainly the two presidential candidates of 1952 offered arts advocates little reason to be optimistic. The popular favorite, a military man who rarely took a definite stand when he could avoid it, allowed as how the matter of federal subsidy would require "a great deal of study" before he could arrive at a decision. His opponent, possessed of a more critical mind, *had* studied the matter, but did not like what he saw. Stevenson opposed the creation of a new executive department with authority over the arts "because such a department might eventually subject the arts to unwholesome controls. In the hands of an unscrupulous or reactionary administration, our cultural life would be threatened and perhaps even the most basic freedom of expression would be stifled."[44]

No one ever claimed that the election of Eisenhower would bring an "unscrupulous or reactionary" administration into the White House, certainly, but even before the new president had taken office there were indications that the battle *against* art would have to be completed before the legislative battle *for* art could hope to be successful. That preliminary bout took a discouraging turn in January 1953, when the Inaugural Concert Commission decided to drop Aaron Copland's *Lincoln Portrait* from the upcoming concert at Constitution Hall. Representative Busbey, ever on the alert for subversive art, it seems, had objected to the composer's alleged Communist associations.[45]

The president-elect himself, fortunately, was still undecided on the question of federal arts support. It remained to be seen how that battle would fare under the new administration.

3

The American National Arts Act

If President Eisenhower was uncertain about the arts, as he suggested during the 1952 campaign (and that assumes that he gave the arts any thought at all), the arts community was equally unsure of the new president. It was true that Ike himself was known to dabble in paint, but then his predecessor had been a pianist; and "one who paints," as Alfred Frankfurter wryly noted, "may do as little for a national school of painters as one who played the piano did for a national music."[1]

In all likelihood, the arts would not have received much attention at all in the new administration were it not for some unfinished business from the Truman years—the report to the president on government and art prepared by the government's own Commission of Fine Arts after a two-year study. George Biddle and David Finley, representing Lloyd Goodrich's Committee on Government and Art (CGA), had met with the president early in 1951, informing Truman of the committee's 1950 resolution, which called for an investigation of the "whole question of the Government's relation to art." Biddle and Finley—members as well of the Commission of Fine Arts—conveniently forgot to tell the president of the CGA's request for an *independent* body of arts leaders to conduct such a study, and of course neither objected when Truman appointed the Commission of Fine Arts to perform this task. "What the president was doing," Goodrich later grumbled, "was appointing a commission to investigate itself."[2]

Under the best of circumstances, self-examination is a difficult, problematical affair; and given the slender tradition of federal art in America and the doggedly businesslike personality of the fine arts commission, the prospects for this particular study were not favorable. Part of the problem was purely mechanical. Even the most energetic, independent blue-ribbon panel would have been frustrated in its effort to get beneath the surface of the government-and-art relationship by the absence of funds for travel and other expenses of witnesses. On the other hand, Chairman Finley did not seem to mind that his commission would be limited to what was essentially an in-house review of existing government art activities. Only at the urging of the Goodrich committee did he agree to consider outside testimony, and even that was limited to a single day of consultation with an advisory committee made up of members of the CGA. In stark contrast, the Canadian Royal Art Commission issued a five-hundred-page report in 1952 after a two-year study that included 114 public hearings for over twelve hundred witnesses.

The investigatory effort was also hampered by the nature of the fine arts commission itself—an advisory body whose scope of operation had traditionally been limited to Washington architecture, "especially in carrying forward the work begun under the L'Enfant Plan of 1791," as the commission explained its role. Nor did the composition of the commission in 1951—museum director Finley and painter Biddle along with five architects and urban planners—lend itself to a challenge of that antiquarian perspective.

Art and Government, the modest 141-page document that the commission released in 1953, was characteristically bland.[3] Reflecting the commission's fundamental belief in private support of the arts, its recommendations were more concerned with the continuation of existing governmental arts activities (primarily involving exhibitions, education, cultural exchange, and art in public buildings) than with the initiation of any new programs. "Here we have had no centralized control of art activities on the part of the government, such as exists in many other countries," the commission noted at the outset of its report. "For that reason the Commission is opposed to efforts to create a Ministry of Fine Arts or to combine in a single bureau art activities carried on effectively in a number of government agencies." But if the commission opposed the creation of a new arts agency (or even an expanded arts role for the Administrator of General Services, as recommended by the Committee on Organization of the Executive Branch in 1949), Finley's group could not be accused of attempting to feather its own bureaucratic nest. In regard to the function of the commission, that body recommended that "no change be made in its basic character," declaring that "the special role for which it was created would be compromised and, perhaps, destroyed if it should be given large sums of money to administer."

Despite its conservative bent, the commission did make some positive recommendations, none of them revolutionary, perhaps, but all of them designed to quicken the pace of federal arts activity in America. *Art and Government* called for the creation of an office for cultural exchange in the National Gallery of Art; for an expanded role for the National Collection of Fine Arts ("to promote understanding of American art and artists and to bring American art into a closer relationship with the life of the community"); for a new program of art education; for an expanded program of cultural exchange in the State Department, including a program coordinated by the Library of Congress's Music Division (despite its testimony that it was ill-equipped for such a task); for increased use of art in public buildings by the General Services Administration; and for a music center in Washington. All of these plans had been raised before, of course, but in the opinion of George Biddle, the lone painter on the commission, they would never be effective until the government called on the advice of a "qualified body of experts" to assist it in its fundamental arts-related task—selecting public art. "As long as these selections are made through political agencies or individual caprice, as has often been the case in the past," Biddle warned, "the Government will continue to get adequate work by second-rate artists."[4]

If George Biddle had doubts about the report (while agreeing with its emphasis on decentralization and the limited role of the commission), the response in the arts community was even less favorable. Many were appalled at the stand-pat nature of the report, citing in particular the commission's desire to protect its own territory, and its almost total disregard for the performing arts.[5] If the commission's report proved anything, the critics declared, it was the necessity of a new federal agency to give strong direction to the government's role in the arts, direction that the fine arts commission seemed both unwilling and unable to provide. *Art and Government* might have been quickly forgotten, in fact, had it not served as a catalyst for those in the arts community who demanded much more from the federal government.

"Man Cannot Live by Bread Alone"

Arts advocates had grumbled about government action (and inaction) before, of course, but on this occasion, at least, the critics had an important ally in Congress, Representative Charles Howell, the New Jersey insurance broker turned politician who adopted the arts as his personal cause. After the work he had done in this area over the past three years, setting the stage for the ensuing federal arts debates, Howell must have felt betrayed by the commission's report, and he openly expressed his misgivings at a meeting of the National Music Council early in 1954. "The Commission is looking through the wrong end of the telescope," Howell declared, noting that the commission's preoccupation with Washington architecture ignored the multifaceted cultural needs of the rest of the country. "The Federal Government," Howell complained, "has now been without a comprehensive art program for over 160 years."[6]

To remedy that situation, Howell had introduced in 1953 a bill to establish a National War Memorial Arts Commission, a federal agency that would oversee a new theater and opera house in the capital, award scholarships and graduate fellowships in the fine arts, and generally formulate that "comprehensive art program."[7] It was the kind of precedent-setting measure, Howell explained to the NMC, that was beyond the ken of the Commission of Fine Arts and which would, surely, elicit that body's firm opposition. "There is a philosophical

difference in viewpoint which must be considered in the evolution of the measure I have sponsored," Howell explained.
"The debate is between the proponents of the belief that the
arts are living and must be encouraged with every resource
at hand, and those who regard the arts basically as the product of a past age, which must be preserved rather than encouraged."

Those two forces, of innovation and preservation, running roughly parallel to the modernist-traditionalist split in
the art world and underscored by the lingering New Deal–
conservative schism in the politics of the period, met head-
on five months later when Howell secured a hearing before
a special subcommittee of the House Committee on Education and Labor for thirteen pieces of arts legislation, including his own H.R. 9111, the "American National Arts Act."[8]
Like its predecessor, this bill would establish an arts commission to "develop and encourage the pursuit of a national policy for the promotion of, and for education in, the fine arts
by all age groups," erect a capital theater and music center,
and award fellowships. Additionally, the new version included an important new section designed to "assist the several States in developing projects and programs in the fine
arts," and to "assist financially and otherwise in the preparation and preservation of professional and amateur fine arts
productions and programs," items that would be incorporated into subsequent arts legislation.

Equally important, Howell's measure contributed to the
philosophical underpinnings of the arts advocacy movement,
a movement that depended ultimately on a nonaesthetic rationale, on political and utilitarian (and even ceremonial) justification, in its effort to gather sufficient support to secure
passage of the legislation. Thus the American National Arts
Act addressed the contribution of the arts to the "morale,
health, and general welfare of the Nation." And in an act of
sheer prophecy (in view of the sudden and decisive emergence of humanities legislation in 1964), Howell's bill described the crucial link between cultural legislation and the
political life of the nation. "The Congress, recognizing the

fact that man cannot live by bread alone," the bill's Statement of Findings and Policy read,

> . . . finds that an education which includes the humanities is essential to political wisdom, and that in the world of today, as we face the persistent problems of man and defend and attempt to add stature to the ideals and principles of free men and free institutions, the relevance of the humanities to our task is unquestionable, for it is the humanities, more than science or statistics, which provides the real answers to communism.

The bill itself was a hectic, grab-bag affair, ranging from efforts to make the arts accessible to urban renewal, from arts programs for children and the elderly to the destruction of the "Communist myth that Americans are insensitive, materialistic barbarians." But in its very size, teetering through Congress like an overladen pack horse, Howell's H.R. 9111 was a useful compendium of early-fifties arts advocacy.[9]

Howell's bill and the other twelve measures were not treated to an impartial jury, however, for the three-man Special Subcommittee on Arts Foundations and Commissions included one ardent arts advocate (Howell himself) and two fiscal conservatives who were almost certain to look askance at "welfare" programs like federal arts support. Both subcommittee chairman Albert Bosch (R-NY) and Clarence Young (R-NV) were freshmen congressmen eager to demonstrate their mastery of the congressional purse strings.

But if that minority of one ultimately triumphed at these first full-scale hearings on arts legislation, the testimony collected in 1954—overwhelmingly in favor of some form of government arts support—should not be overlooked. For the newly organized pro-subsidy forces (and their organization was not nearly so complete as it would be a few years later) were helping to establish the vocabulary, the rhetoric, of public funding, which would evolve over the next ten years. The early arguments might be broken down into five logical categories, five clusters of thought, revolving generally around European standards, the cold war, the state of the arts in

America, the dissemination of culture, and the economics of the arts. Those who held these views did not always distinguish among them, however, for the language of the arts advocates, like that of most others in the political arena, was often more elegant than precise.

"Let Us Not Neglect Our Own Soul"

One of the underlying forces in the drive for federal arts support was the long-held notion that America, in its laissez faire approach to culture, had somehow failed to measure up to European standards. Mark Twain might have scoffed at the Old World's preoccupation with the past in *The Innocents Abroad* (while he delighted in the U.S. Patent Office's subsidy of the *future*), but many more Americans were impressed with the Europeans' sense of priority that insured the transmission of culture to future generations. Nor was this attitude reserved to Boston Brahmins.

Speaking in 1852 on behalf of proposed governmental commissions for two painters, Emanuel Leutze and George Healy, Senator James Cooper of Pennsylvania emphasized the duty of Congress to encourage the development of native talent, to enhance America's reputation in the arts, and to elevate the public taste.[10] In trying to justify his claim, Cooper managed to bridge that gap between aesthetics and industry that would trouble Mark Twain a few years later. "In other countries the fine arts are the objects of the patronage of the government," Cooper declared. "They are encouraged, not only for their refining influences, but likewise with a view to the perfection of the more useful arts. . . . Heretofore we have been obliged to resort to Europe for designs for . . . articles . . . produced by our artisans. But by encouraging painting and the kindred art of design, we would soon cease to be dependent on Europe for our patterns."[11]

During the thirties (when, incidentally, the federally sponsored Index of American Design perfectly filled Cooper's "useful arts" prescription), the call had been made, as we have noted, both in and out of Congress, for a permanent federal arts program, lending an element of Old World stability to Roosevelt's emergency projects. Nor did the envious references to European practices cease with the eventual establishment of the National Endowment for the Arts. During the Arts Endowment's early years, when its budget remained tied to a seven-figure level, the complaint was often made that the United States government spent less on the arts than a single European city—Vienna.

It is not surprising that Representative Javits, author of the "U.S. Arts Foundation Act" (H.R. 5030), emphasized in his testimony at the 1954 subcommittee hearings that "we are almost unique in the world as a government which has no part" in public arts support. The implication was that American civilization lacked an essential humanizing element. "In our country," Javits continued, "we deal with the grim realities of war and spend enormous sums for defense, but somehow or other we do not seem to pay attention to the happier side of life which this represents, and I think that it is high time that we should." [12]

For Milo Christianson, superintendent of recreation in Washington, D.C., and the first to offer testimony before the subcommittee, public subsidy was, quite simply, a national obligation, especially for a nation whose citizens "have more leisure time than the people of any other country in the world." [13]

Senator Murray of Montana, cosponsor in 1951 of S.J.R. 105, which would have created a National Arts Commission, raised another facet of the international argument, pointing out that America was *already* engaged in cultural subsidy, an effort directed, ironically, solely at European culture. "If you will inspect our Economic Cooperation Administration program in Europe," Murray explained in a statement that was reproduced at the 1954 hearings, "you will find that this government is investing in the preservation of the culture of the Old World. This is sound business because it recognizes that man does not live by bread alone.

"But while we carry out our responsibilities as missionaries to a foreign land," the senator warned, "let us not neglect our own soul."[14]

It was more than a spiritual matter that concerned most Americans, however. Far more immediate than a desire to emulate certain European practices was the fundamental issue of the cold war—the ideological struggle with Russia for allies in Europe, Asia, and the Middle East. This struggle was reflected, not surprisingly, in the cultural debates of the early fifties, when the connection was made, long before the cultural exchange hearings of 1955–56, between American culture and the nation's prestige abroad. Again and again in the fifties, the plea for federal patronage was made, not on the intrinsic value of the arts or their inherent benefits to American society, but on their propagandistic value—on the role they might play in America's effort to win friends and influence nations.

"The Greatest Sales Campaign in History"

"I believe that the fine arts, in their broadest sense," declared New York's Senator Herbert Lehman in May 1954, "provide one of the most effective ways of transmitting to the peoples of the world the true essence of democracy. We can help destroy the Communist myth by encouraging cultural interchange of representative American artists with others in the free world."[15] Lehman was speaking on behalf of his Arts Commission bill, and his comments exemplify one of the major selling points used by arts advocates in building support for public subsidy. The arts, far from being a mere decorative element, became (along with athletic and industrial displays) one of the major "cultural weapons" of the cold war.

Senator James Murray had put the matter even more bluntly three years earlier: "We are presently engaged in the greatest sales campaign in history: we are striving to convince hundreds of millions of people around the world that the American way of life is superior to the slave existence that the totalitarian aggressors would thrust upon them. And our very existence as free men may well depend upon the success of our sales effort."[16] Drawing on that theme at the hearings in 1954, Javits viewed America's cultural efforts as a matter of self-defense in the worldwide struggle with communism:

> There is an enormous propaganda weapon which the Russians are using against us, with the most telling effect, all over the world. They are posing, and getting away with it, as the people of culture, as juxtaposed to us who are painted to the world as the people who don't care for culture. The Russians are doing an enormous job in that. They have sent traveling artists, violinists, pianists, whole ballet companies, theater companies, into the big world centers, and they have made an impression.[17]

One of the cultural battle cries of the fifties, then, was a call for the United States to match the propaganda efforts of the Soviet Union. It was the impetus for the president's $5 million emergency fund of 1954 (with the money divided between cultural and industrial exhibits), and it sparked a series of subcommittee hearings later in the fifties on the need to incorporate the so-called ideological offensive as a permanent part of American foreign policy. Such an effort, clearly, included the export of examples of American culture. Less clear, however, were the implications of such a policy for American culture at home. Javits and Lehman and a handful of others in Congress made the vital connection between the two—that even a modest State Department program of cultural exchange demanded that more attention be paid to culture in America, if only to make certain that the nation's cultural resources were sturdy enough to compete with the Soviet arts offensive.

In any case, the cultural debates of the early fifties, even if largely concerned with cold war politics, admitted a discussion of American culture that helped pave the way for a more serious examination of federal arts subsidy in later years.

"One of the World Centers of the Fine Arts"

Proponents of federal patronage in the early fifties seemed undecided as to the most effective arguments to use in presenting their case. On the one hand, they could speak, as did Javits, of an endangered American culture, one that needed the helping hand of government if art were to reach the masses. Javits painted an especially bleak picture in his testimony before the subcommittee, speaking of a "singular dearth, as you get out in the broad expanses of the country . . . in the art field." While culture might be flourishing in a few of the major cities, Javits warned that "it has been dying off in the rest of the country at an alarming rate, and at a rate which I think is harmful to our national cultural pattern and hence is a proper area for the interposition of the Federal Government."[18]

It is not clear just what evidence Javits had for his assertion of a dying cultural scene, although he referred vaguely to the competition between live art ("more than entertainment") and television, radio, and motion pictures, and to the economic problems of the arts (an issue that would loom much larger in the sixties). Regardless, Javits's line of reasoning was never a popular one. It was too pessimistic a view for an enthusiastic arts community that was reluctant to place American art on an endangered species list, and it was too vulnerable, moreover, to that variety of latter-day Social Darwinism that opposed propping up failing enterprises with public funds.

More attractive was the American Renaissance argument, citing an American culture that flourished *despite* government neglect. Thus the Whitney Museum's Lloyd Goodrich waved the banner of American creativity before the subcommittee. "The United States today is one of the world centers of the fine arts," Goodrich proclaimed, "and there is greater creative activity in our country than at any time in our history. Yet our federal government gives little recognition to this important aspect of American life."[19]

The American Renaissance argument was just as vulnerable as Javits's pessimism, of course, to a similar brand of conservative logic, one that in this instance questioned the need to support the arts if they were already flourishing. This issue became especially important in the early sixties, when notions of a "cultural explosion" were often touted in the press, raising doubts about the necessity of a new federal arts program. Thus the proponents of federal subsidy could expect stiff opposition to either the feast or famine argument, and so they stressed the foreign affairs angle—the need to bring American culture to Europeans and Asians—and its domestic corollary—the need to bring American culture to Americans.

"A TVA for the Arts . . . A Caravan of Culture"

The drive to democratize the arts in America had been a constant thread running through the nation's history from Jefferson's educational scheme to Whitman's poetic masses, and reached a fever pitch during the WPA years before finally becoming institutionalized in the Arts Endowment's "Federal-State Partnership" and its nervous preoccupation with geographic distribution. In the fifties the democratic argument was viewed as perhaps the only means of justifying arts funding to tight-fisted, isolationist legislators. (Howell tried unsuccessfully, for example, to win Representative Young's support for an arts center in the capital by suggesting, rather lamely, that "people from all over the country . . . come here, even from Nevada.") The democratic viewpoint, in fact, was the primary reason that the Committee on Education and Labor favorably reported the college-art legislation of 1952. Even in amending the teeth out of the bill, the committee voiced its concern for decentralizing the arts. It called, as noted earlier, for the "fresh voices of the young non–New York, non-Hollywood people to be heard," and for the exposure of this talent, not only for our own benefit but to "contribute to a better understanding of our Nation throughout the world."

Here, then, was the old spirit of the WPA arts projects tempered by a new concern with foreign affairs—democratic art exhibited on the global stage—and if Congress was not yet ready to finance such endeavors, it was at least willing to consider them. Predictably, the democratic-art argument came up repeatedly at the 1954 hearings, often with a WPA twist. In his testimony in support of H.R. 9111, for example, Patrick Hayes, past president of the National Association of Concert Managers, called for federal patronage to extend beyond the mere construction of an opera house in the nation's capital. "We need a veritable TVA for the arts . . . ," Hayes declared. And to make the democratic thrust of his vision explicit, he offered this gem of WPA-style alliteration: "We need a covered-wagon caravan of culture to cross the nation to its utmost horizons."[20]

Representative Javits, too, spoke of encouraging a populist movement in the arts. Javits's own bill favored the more ambitious arts council plan over the capital cultural center scheme. "It seems to me," Javits told the subcommittee, "that [the arts council] would distribute the benefits of whatever was done the most widely throughout the country in the most grassroots way. A war memorial [opera house and theater] might easily be a structure without a soul."[21]

While Javits doubtless knew that his bill stood little immediate chance of passage, he was not acting solely as a visionary in his quest for democratic culture. He spoke as well of dollars-and-cents issues, anticipating subsequent discussions of the economics of the performing arts, including major hearings on the subject in 1961–62. Indeed, if only to fend off the fiscal conservatives, who were wary of increasing governmental expenditures, Javits liked to view the proposed arts subsidy in economic terms, as "leverage money," citing $5 million as a base figure that would get the program off the ground, lending the "prestige of the Federal Government" to the arts and yielding increased private support in turn.

In the face of opposition to even that initial figure, Javits was not reluctant to point out its comparative insignificance in the larger scheme of federal spending. "You spent $100 billion a year to fight World War II," Javits scolded Representative Young, "and we are spending $50 billion a year to fight the cold war." In light of such figures, Javits insisted, "we can afford to spend some millions in order to enhance life in our own country, and give us an even greater superiority over the Communist way of life."

One way or another, it seemed, the arts debates of the early fifties always got back to that issue, to the cold war, with its political rhetoric and cultural displays taking the place of more conventional means of battle. But for others involved in the debates, those who were closer to the arts than to politics, there were economic issues other than cost-benefit analyses of the cold war to be considered. The economic problems of the arts in America began to get exposure at the 1954 hearings, anticipating by more than a decade the major economic studies of the arts that served as ammunition for arts advocates seeking increased support from both the public and private sectors.

"They Are the Forgotten Men and Women"

If the economic woes of artists were heard during the thirties, it was only because *everyone's* economic woes were being discussed. In the prosperous postwar years, however, comparatively little was said, outside of the small-circulation professional arts journals, about the financial status of the arts. Like most other businesses, the arts business, it was generally assumed, was booming. And like other businesses during the Korean War years, it was taxed, to the tune of 20 percent on admissions.

Senator Murray was something of an exception in his frank recognition, as early as 1951, of the economic plight of artists. If the tone of his remarks in the *Congressional Record* seems slightly shopworn, the thrust of his comments was prophetic:

> High taxes have all but eliminated the contribution of our erstwhile wealthy private patrons of the arts; mechanical reproductions of cultural artistry without continuing reward for those who performed has decimated the ranks of artists and discouraged would-be newcomers to these pursuits. They are the forgotten men and women who need desperately the help

that our Government can give them through the agency of a
National Arts Commission.[22]

During the 1954 hearings, a few witnesses offered similar
testimony, bleak reports on the economic conditions of the
arts, which, if failing to persuade the subcommittee, were at
least suggestive of future trends in arts advocacy. The composer Howard Hanson, for example, appearing as president
of the National Music Council, warned the subcommittee that
the American symphony orchestra "is today in real economic
peril" and thus in need of public support. And Lawrence
Tibbett, former president of the American Guild of Musical
Artists, made a similar plea on behalf of the individual performing artist.[23] Although lacking the impressive statistical
evidence that would be marshaled in the sixties, a number of
arts advocates began building the case for the special nature
of the arts—a part of American life beset by inherent economic problems that could not be solved without outside
support.

"The Fine Art of Balancing the Budget"

If the five clusters of opinion—concerning the European
model, the cold war struggle, the status of American culture,
and the issues of decentralization and economics—were
suggestive of long-range trends in the rhetoric of federal patronage, of more immediate interest were the arguments of
those who opposed such support. It was a loose-knit group,
to be sure, consisting of Republican and southern Democratic
legislators, Commission of Fine Arts members and their allies, old-line arts establishment figures, and assorted lone-
eagle artists, and they were not nearly so vocal as the prosubsidy forces. But then they did not have to be. Riding a crest
of fiscal conservatism and anti–New Deal thought, these
spokesmen for the status quo were in the ascendancy in the
fifties. Nor did they have to make the logical leaps of their

opponents in the arts debates, those who attempted to balance Old World models and Communist threats, economic arguments and democratic visions, in their pleas for government support. The conservatives could assume a much more consistent position, which, again for the sake of convenience, might similarly be divided into five categories, but which in reality all added up to largely the same thing.

The favorite question of Chairman Bosch and Congressman Young during the subcommittee hearings, one they asked repeatedly, was the one that no one could satisfactorily answer: "How much will it cost?" That question seemed to cut through all of the talk about prestige and propaganda, culture and democracy. And regardless of the answer to that simple question—answers that ranged from $50,000 to more then $20 million—a second question invariably followed: "Can we *really* afford such an expense?" That was the kind of question that did not require an answer, that summed up, in fact, the mood of a large segment of the country.

"You feel, even as painful as the present appropriations bills are," an incredulous Representative Young asked Javits, "that we would be justified in voting additional millions for this purpose?" Javits, it turned out, *did* feel that way, and he said as much. But few other witnesses could respond in kind to the incontrovertible logic of Young's rhetorical question. "One of the fine arts my people are concerned with," Young shrewdly observed early in the hearings, "is the fine art of balancing the budget."[24] And as if that fundamental truth were not sufficient to discourage the spendthrift rascals, Young and Bosch had other truths at their disposal as well.

"We Are Forever Encroaching upon the Rights of the States"

One of the reasons that the European role-model argument was not entirely persuasive was that it savored too much of the political intrigue of the Old World, of a state-imposed culture that had little to do with America's laissez faire tradition. It sounded, too, like another New Deal scheme, an effort by Washington to tell Charleston or Boise or wherever the proper way to live. Representative Young wondered, for example, whether federal arts support was not yet another "invasion" of the states' proper authority. "Here certainly is something that the States could do if they would," he observed. "I have been alarmed at the tremendous growth of the Federal Government during the past 40 or 50 years."[25]

Bosch was equally concerned with the state's rights issue, fearing that the so-called pump-priming measure proposed by Howell might turn into another full-fledged federal waterworks, overextending an already strained federal budget and further reducing the states' sphere of authority. "I am somewhat disturbed about the government getting into any more of these problems," Bosch declared.

> I mean, we are forever encroaching upon the rights of the States and the citizens of the States, and I just wonder. If I could be sure that in doing a thing like this we would, so to speak, pull up the bootstraps of the States, so that they would really get in and do a job, I might go along. But . . . the initial investment is not the thing that worries us; it is the continuance of that over a period of years. How long can we stand a thing of that kind?[26]

The arts, according to Bosch and Young, were not something that belonged in the long-range plans of the federal government. For one thing, they were too expensive an undertaking, and even overlooking cost considerations, they were too much a private matter, beyond the pale of what governments were supposed to be doing. However reactionary such views may or may not appear today (and the "may not" would seem to have the edge), they were persuasive in the fifties. They had, moreover, logical corollaries, axioms tied to dim memories of the WPA arts experiment, which attracted a variety of supporters from beyond the ranks of stand-pat conservative legislators.

"Pawns in a Centrally Managed, Nationalistic Program"

George Biddle, a member of the Commission of Fine Arts from 1950 to 1955, helped establish the tone for the conservatives' specific objections to the proposed arts legislation. While he found some of the provisions of the American National Arts Act admirable (those, in particular, that merely underscored the ongoing work of the commission), Biddle was disturbed by the political implications of the bill. He objected especially to "such provisions in the organizational setup and in the enormous, highly centralized, and quasi-political power granted the proposed Commission, or implicit in the wording, which might make it a very grave threat to the free and healthy development of American art."[27] Education and Labor Committee staff director John Graham echoed this concern during an exchange with Javits. While the congressman discounted the threat (citing adequate protection both in the trusteeship system as employed by the Smithsonian Institution and in the arts council format of Great Britain), the issue proved to be a thorny one for the arts advocates. The specter of the WPA arts fiasco (as it was most often regarded at the hearings) was brought up in this connection—"PWA theaters and that sort of thing," as Graham put it. The arts advocates were never completely successful in their attempt to distinguish their arts commission plan from the earlier relief effort.

Nor were the advocates united in their defense of the new proposal. There was a fair amount of "friendly fire" at the hearings, as several members of the arts community shared some of the conservatives' mistrust of government activity in the arts. While they might desire government "encouragement" or "stimulation" of the arts, many were wary of the implications of outright subsidy. Lloyd Goodrich, for example, expressed his concern that H.R. 9111 granted too much power to the secretary of Health, Education, and Welfare (HEW), that it tended to centralize authority in the arts, and that even with the 50-percent matching requirement of the proposed grants, the bill might upset the delicate balance of the existing arts economy. "In a field as underfinanced as the fine arts," Goodrich reasoned, "this can amount to a considerable power."[28]

But by far the most effective in warning about the dangers of federal patronage was the American Symphony Orchestra League (ASOL), whose executive secretary, Helen M. Thompson, came to the hearings fully prepared to defend the status quo. One of the best organized of the performing arts service agencies, with a membership of over six hundred symphony orchestras across the country, the ASOL had been prompted to survey league members by an earlier Howell bill (H.R. 5397). This survey was not exactly an impartial plebiscite of string players in the United States but more of a campaign, a campaign that began with Thompson's "Report on Proposed Federal Government Participation in the Fine Arts," presented before the league's June 1953 national convention in Elkhart, Indiana.[29] By the time Thompson finished her lengthy report, which ranged from discussions of European arts programs to domestic industrial subsidies to the proposed arts legislation of Representative Howell, it was hardly necessary to tally up the response. But for the record, Thompson reported to the subcommittee the startling figure that 91 percent of the ASOL members (i.e., orchestra executive boards) opposed federal subsidy.

Thompson's report was a shrewd one, painting a fairly grim picture of the British Arts Council experience, skimming over other foreign programs, and then treating Howell's proposals to a ruthless Socratic dialogue. Is the federal arts plan designed to initiate and establish arts activities and groups? Fine, but private, local action has already created an abundance of cultural activities. Is the federal government going to pay for art in America? Fine, but how would that affect private, local support? Thompson answered that question with another: "Will the fact that the Federal Government establishes an amount which it will contribute to your pro-

ductions be interpreted by your community generally as a
tacit recommendation by the government that that amount
is all you really should need by way of subsidization?" If the
conventioneers could follow Thompson's argument this far
(and even if they could not they all received copies of the
report to take home to their fellow board members), they
learned that the government would have a $25 million mo-
nopoly on arts subsidy. That, at least, was what it would cost
each year to keep American culture afloat, according to
Thompson's calculations. As she meticuously pointed out, no
single operation (aside from railroads, shipping, air trans-
port, and dairy production) had ever been granted a federal
subsidy in excess of $10 million a year. Twenty-five million
dollars for the arts? Why, that was more than the apple, beef,
coffee, egg, peanut butter, sugar, and wool industries had
collectively received.

However impressive such figures were, the keystone of
Thompson's attack was the issue of control, the rules and
regulations that would be clamped upon art in America if
Uncle Sam suddenly decided to play Medici. Hazy standards
would be applied, perhaps insisting on only English-language
opera or demanding that only American compositions be
performed.[30] "Is it possible," Thompson wondered, "that the
arts, the thousands of people contributing time and effort to
them might become mere pawns in a centrally managed, na-
tionalistic program whose control could be so buried in bureaucracy as to give little hint of its ultimate purpose?"

In all fairness to Thompson and the ASOL, whose position was doubtless influenced by the congressional investigations of the WPA arts programs and the State Department
fiasco, Orwell's *1984* must have seemed closer to 1954 than it
does today.[31] In the era of Joe McCarthy, after all, it must
have seemed plausible that "we would have to check composers and musical works not only with the lists of licensing
agencies but also against lists of people ruled O.K. on loyalty
and security considerations." In any case, Thompson insisted
that the federal government could do little that would truly
help the arts in America. If there was to be a federal arts

commission, it should serve only as an information clearinghouse, serving "to strengthen and expand all the arts fields
through research, counseling, exchange of information, etc."

In the face of such a thorough attack, Howell was understandably disheartened, although he held out hope for
the nonsubsidy aspects of his bill—the capital cultural center
and the arts commission plan. Still, the issue of control seemed
inescapable, the threat, as HEW Secretary Oveta Culp Hobby
put it, "of centralized dominance or control in the aesthetic
and cultural fields." Howell received equally bad tidings from
the Executive Office, where the Bureau of the Budget expressed doubts about the "comprehensive character and wide
scope of the bill and the drastic change from past activities."
Here, too, the question of control arose, the degree to which
the government "should attempt to evaluate and influence
the cultural and artistic development of the Nation."[32]

Although the antisubsidy forces may have been outnumbered at the hearings—except on the three-man subcommittee itself—they obviously had clout. Administration officials,
cabinet officers, the Commission of Fine Arts, and, of course,
the self-proclaimed legislative watchdogs of the federal budget, all made an impressive showing against the scores of
"civilian" witnesses and letter-writers that Howell had rounded
up. Nor were the opponents of federal patronage mere nay-
sayers who had no concern for culture, citing budget constraints, states' rights, and the threat of federal domination
to defeat the arts proposals. On the contrary, many were actively involved in artistic pursuits, and all paid tribute to the
existing federal programs for the arts.

"The Commission . . . Has Rendered
Distinguished Service"

The two-year survey by the Commission of Fine Arts on government art activities certainly created the illusion of a federal arts policy. There *were* numerous art activities, after all,
and there was an arts commission; thus the report made it

easy for a legislator like Young to dismiss the proposed arts bills with a vague reference to the "15 departments and agencies now that stimulate art in the government." And those witnesses, like the Special Committee on the Institute of Art (American Council on Education), who were wary of Howell's more ambitious arts commission plans, could similarly refer confidently to the work of "existing Federal agencies."

The biggest booster of the status quo, not surprisingly, was David Finley, director of the National Gallery of Art and chairman of the Commission of Fine Arts, who used both roles to take shots at Howell's proposal. Writing to the Education and Labor Committee in May 1953, Finley the museum director lent his support to plans for buildings to house the arts in Washington, but firmly rejected the arts commission proposal. The tasks of such a body, he was convinced, were already being accomplished. "The Commission of Fine Arts," Finley reminded the committee, "was established in 1910 for the purpose of providing expert advice to the President, the Congress, committees of the Congress, and government agencies on questions relating to the fine arts. The Commission, whose members serve on a voluntary basis, has rendered distinguished service during its existence." Six months later Finley the commission chairman reiterated this view:

> Many of the duties to be assigned to the [proposed] Commission are now being carried out efficiently by existing government agencies. It would be a mistake, therefore, in the opinion of the Commission [of Fine Arts] to attempt to concentrate so many of these duties in one agency with the responsibility for the expenditure of large amounts of government funds, as provided in the bill.[33]

Finley, then, touched lightly on all of the major objections to an expanded, centralized federal arts program—the expense, the violation of established spheres of authority, the threat of control, and the simple fact that the status quo was satisfactory. When all of those arguments were added up—and it was the singular strength of the antisubsidy position that they *could* be added up—the final truth became manifest. The federal government, quite simply, had better things to do with the taxpayers' money than to support the arts.

"Under a Heavy Public Debt"

Representative Young offered the most poignant examples in defense of his opposition to federal subsidy. His words conjured up homespun themes, small-town post offices and one-room schools, both sturdy American institutions threatened by the federal government's newfangled ways of spending money. Young scoffed, for example, at a plan to include art centers in public works projects in order to decentralize American culture. "You know," observed Young, "we have not been able to build the post offices for the last 14 or 15 years, and I can see some people throughout the country raising their eyebrows to see public art centers going up, if they cannot have a post office." Young lost patience, too, with an opera promoter from North Carolina who offered a plan to bring art to children in the schools. "I hate to see us spend money for this kind of thing when there is a need for so many schoolrooms," Young declared, recalling the dismal test scores compiled by the U.S. Army during World War II, "and some American boys and girls aren't even learning to read and write. And you are talking about bringing opera to others."[34]

Still, there were more effective, if less colorful, ways of announcing that America had higher priorities than support of the arts. Edward T. Mansure, administrator of the General Services Administration (GSA), informed the Bosch subcommittee of his department's position with bureaucratic precision. While recognizing the appeal of a measure such as Howell's, the GSA could not recommend favorable action on the bill: "The compelling problems of national defense with which the government is presently confronted make it desirable that action upon the proposals embodied in the bill be deferred until less parlous times when defense requirements no longer weigh heavily upon the economy." And Lindsay C. Warren,

U.S. comptroller general, had similar reasons for his opposition to federal subsidy. Like Mansure, Warren recognized the desirable qualities of Howell's plan, but he, too, cited more pressing needs. "It seems open to serious question," Warren stated, "whether the matter is sufficiently urgent or sufficiently important to justify the Federal government undertaking such activities at a time when it is operating under continued deficit financing and under a heavy public debt."[35]

No one dared suggest, of course, that the Roosevelt administration had managed to take on arts activities—and a dozen other normally "private" concerns—precisely when times were most "parlous." For the New Deal was out of fashion in the fifties, and the arts had to find justification other than the specter of mass unemployment.

The arts advocates, in this early round of legislative inquiry that would occupy the next ten years, came up with another means of support, with a hodgepodge of ideas, really, as foreign affairs, American political theory, and economics all came into play. But a streamlined package of conservative thought confronted such notions in the spring of 1954, and it was hardly necessary to wait three months for the subcommittee's decision.

"A Matter Better Suited for
State, Local, and Private Initiative"

The subcommittee's report was released on 21 September 1954, and the arts lost by a two-to-one margin on all thirteen counts. Representative Howell, nevertheless, claimed a moral victory of landslide proportions. The victory, in fact, was unanimous, according to Howell. "The majority report . . . ," he noted, referring to Bosch and Young's statement, "rejects the viewpoint of all witnesses at the hearing who, without exception, endorsed in some degree the concept of Federal aid for the encouragement and promotion of the fine arts."[36] Howell's statement was a little misleading, though, for the testimony on his measure included some severe critics. A rough poll of the hearing's participants shows a tally of about 120 to 12, still an impressive margin of victory for the prosubsidy forces.

Realistically, though, it was impossible in 1954 to measure with any precision the feelings of the arts community regarding federal support. Neither the ASOL survey nor the subcommittee testimony—both of which showed 90-percent unanimity, but on opposite sides of the question—can be trusted as accurate samples, and a fifty-fifty split is doubtless closer to the truth. If the board members and the trustees of the arts world were generally opposed to federal support, as the ASOL poll and the numerous Commission of Fine Arts supporters suggest, many rank-and-file artists and especially union members favored government subsidy. The National Music Council, a federation of forty-five nationally active music organizations (totaling about one million members), called a meeting to discuss the Howell legislation in December 1953, and after much discussion passed a resolution in support of the bill. And a 1953 survey of eight "music leaders" by *Musical America* found only two who opposed federal subsidy, while AFM president James Petrillo, as noted earlier, successfully rallied support for government aid among the members of his vast organization.[37]

Among architects and visual artists, on the other hand, the split was based not so much on economics as on aesthetics and politics. Conservative arts groups like the American Artists Professional League, the National Academy of Design, and the National Sculpture Society, as we have seen, regularly opposed proposals for federal support, fearing the undue influence of "modern art" organizations on any new government program, while the more liberal Artists Equity Association favored federal support. Speaking for architects, meanwhile, Henry H. Saylor, editor of the *Journal of the American Institute of Architects*, glibly assumed that members of his profession would unanimously oppose the establishment of a government bureau that would inflict "more PWA projects" on "our defenseless post offices." But Christopher Tunnard, professor of city planning at Yale, promptly contradicted Say-

lor, throwing his support behind Howell's plan and predict-
ing that numerous artists and architects would do likewise.[38]

And so it went in the early fifties. Fears of government
control of the arts were balanced against pleas for federal
support, and the old WPA projects alternately described as a
boondoggle or a boon to American art. Perhaps the wisest
words of these early years of the debate were those of *Art
Digest* in August 1953, criticizing both the "toothless plan" of
the Commission of Fine Arts and the "rigid provisions" of
Howell's H.R. 5397. "We drag politics into the realm of aesthetics," the magazine observed, raising a complaint that continues to be voiced today, "expecting our cultural agencies to
be models of proportionate representation. In the name of
democracy, we submit our culture to the whims of the uncul-
tured. We spread it thin and support it indiscriminately in a
feckless attempt to satisfy 150,000,000 people." The point of
the editorial was that there were inherent problems in American culture—the split between "high brow" and "low brow"
and the concomitant philistinism and distrust—that were beyond the cure of the economic injections of a government
bureau. "The fact of the matter is that we will never be able
to legislate culture as we legislate agriculture," the magazine
continued.

> How can questions of aesthetics be resolved quantitatively?
> proportionately? representatively? How can we even have an
> American culture if we fail to distinguish between significant
> and insignificant? And why do we give blanket encourage-
> ment? Because it's more democratic? Or because we won't as-
> sume responsibility for making our own intelligent choices,
> and don't believe that it's democratic to let others with the
> proper qualifications make those choices for us?[39]

Choices. Qualifications. These remained the unanswered issues in the federal arts debate, the troubling details
beneath the comparatively simple structure that had been
proposed for a federal arts program. Even though Howell's
plan was more complex than most, the structural issue, at
least, tended to be viewed in blacks and whites. Either

one favored a federal presence in the arts or one opposed it, but this glaring contrast obscured the ultimately more important gray issues that lay beneath the structure, involving the actual operation of such a program. Here was a debate, too, that was destined to continue even after the establishment of the federal arts program. In the harrowing fifties, twice vexed by the threat of Communist infiltration and the reality of reactionary outrage, the federal arts issue was clouded by doubts about how a new government arts agency would look and feel. The handy metaphors of the period, moreover, were not encouraging.

For Emily Genauer, art critic for the *New York Herald Tribune* and no mere antifederalist crank, Howell's plan conjured up an organization that could reach, "octopus-like, into every corner of our national art life and, under certain conditions, strangle it like an octopus, too. I shudder to contemplate," Genauer continued, "the judgment of the behemoth art commission consisting of political bigwigs and citizens whose qualifications and judgment must first be approved by the Senate, on such questions as who will paint a mural—and how—for public buildings, and should the ladies of Keokuk Corners who paint as a pastime be awarded a subsidy and how much."[40]

Bosch and Young did not have to trouble themselves with such details, however, as the two Republican congressmen stated their case against federal arts support with campaign-slogan simplicity. "We do not believe this is a proper area for the expenditure of Federal funds," the subcommittee report flatly stated. "It's a matter better suited for state, local, and private initiative." Bosch and Young went on to reiterate their earlier objections, that the true cost of such measures could not be ascertained and that federal support might discourage private giving to the arts. They were not even certain of the value of the arts to America's foreign policy: "We are dubious, to say the least, of the contention that people abroad are drawn more easily to communism because we have failed to subsidize or nationalize the cultural arts in the United States."[41]

Bosch and Young's primary objection, however, was economic, and their report bristles with the kind of fiscal outrage that still wins elections today:

> Cognizant of the fact that almost one-third of the American worker's wage goes for taxes to support government, we cannot conceive it our duty to dip even further into his threadbare pocket to indulge in the luxury of subsidizing an endless variety of programs and projects supposedly related to the so-called finer arts. Neither do we believe that Federal money should be spent to subsidize the arts in order that aspiring young people will have the opportunity to succeed in their chosen field. We think instead, that young American artistic talent will overcome the hardships it encounters, just as outstanding engineering, medical, and related talent surmounts the obstacles in its way to success. Aside from the highly questionable economics of the matter, we feel that such a subsidy would make mediocrity the standard where excellence ought to prevail. We are convinced that the programs under the WPA clearly support this conclusion.[42]

Howell was not willing, however, to accept any of the majority report's conclusions. Reviewing the testimony in support of his bill and offering some new material as well, Howell attacked both the economic objections to the arts legislation and the alleged WPA parallel. "The majority is not consistent," Howell complained,

> voting one way on business and farm subsidies while at the same time urging "self-reliance" on the smallest and least strong of the many links in our national economy. They do this with impunity, no doubt, since our country's cultural leaders . . . have not yet demonstrated the same prowess at the polling booths on election day that is characteristic of the American businessman.[43]

Howell went on to chide Republicans in Congress for their "campaign oratory," citing the capital opera house legislation that had fifty-three "cosponsors" in the Senate, yet never reached the Senate floor for a vote. Nor would he accept the specter of the WPA as a plausible reason to withhold support from the current arts legislation, which "could by no stretch of the imagination be considered to bear even the

slightest resemblance to the WPA arts projects."[44] A joint
statement signed by eight representatives had made the same
point, which, in fact, had been written into the arts legislation
itself.[45] Thus the proposed arts commission would be instituted

> to facilitate the formation of plans for the preservation, en-
> hancement, and further development of the fine arts in time
> of war, depression, or other national emergency, in order to
> prevent our cultural institutions from shrinking in impor-
> tance or passing out of existence and to avoid the often de-
> plorable standards exemplified by art projects of Federal
> agencies at such times in the past.

But even though virtually no one in Congress dared to
defend the WPA projects, and few others were willing to propose a new arts program, the battle for arts legislation did
not end with the unfavorable report of the Education and
Labor subcommittee. The arts community was still buzzing
with talk about federal subsidy—both for and against such
assistance—and Howell had already introduced yet another
bill (H.R. 9881, followed shortly thereafter by Representative
Lee Metcalf's H.R. 10223), calling for $100,000 matching
grants-in-aid to the states and a maximum $1 million for a
National Arts Commission, based on the National Science
Foundation Act.[46]

Howell launched the new campaign, too late in the session to serve as anything more than a prelude to the next
year's battle, with a brief lesson in economics for his tight-
fisted colleagues. Using figures supplied by the Library of
Congress, Howell pointed out that the proposed arts program would cost the individual taxpayer, on the average, about
eleven cents a year. And as if to remind us how much we
really needed the finer things of life, Howell noted that the
average expenditure per taxpayer for tobacco was $100.07,
and $167.05 for alcohol. "It is to be seriously doubted," How-
ell offered as a parting shot, "that the expenditures of the
minor sums called for would contribute to the impoverish-
ment of the richest nation in the world."

4

Ike Likes the Arts

"We have come a long ways," concert manager Patrick Hayes told a House Education and Labor subcommittee early in 1956, "a long ways . . . from the days of June 8 and 9, 1954, when I had the privilege of sitting at this same table." Hayes had been a witness at the hearings chaired by Representative Bosch, and his sense of progress was based not so much on events within Congress, where arts legislation still faced an uphill battle, as on activities outside of government, in the arts community itself.

Another witness, Ruth Reeves, testifying before the new subcommittee at its initial hearings in July 1955, offered a vivid, if somewhat confusing, example of those activities. "As chairman of the committee on government in art of Artists Equity Association, the committee which spearheaded the formation of the committee on the arts and government, and as an alternate delegate to the United States Committee of the International Association of the Plastic Arts which is part of UNESCO . . . ," Reeves went on to offer her support, not surprisingly, for the new crop of arts legislation. The real point of her testimony, whether she knew it or not, was the mind-boggling array of committees on government and art to which she belonged, an illustration of the organizational activity that had taken place in the art world in response to the interest in a federal arts program shown by a few congressmen.

Such organized responses were also part of a defensive reaction against governmental attacks on the arts, attacks that began, as we have seen, during the WPA years and continued sporadically throughout the forties and fifties. The American Federation of Arts (AFA) adopted its "Statement on Artistic Freedom" late in 1954, a well-circulated document, but it was unable to prevent yet another round of government attacks on art in 1956. "In view of the current threats to artistic freedom," the statement began,

> the Trustees of the American Federation of Arts have adopted the following statement of principles to guide the Federation's activities in relation to contemporary art:
>
> Freedom of artistic expression in a visual work of art, like freedom of speech and press, is fundamental in our democracy. This fundamental right exists irrespective of the artist's political or social opinions, affiliations or activities. The latter are personal matters, distinct from his work, which should be judged on its merits. . . .

The AFA statement went on to urge the symbolic importance of artistic freedom in the United States, as "the most effective proof of the strength of democracy. . . . We believe that in opposing anti-democratic forces throughout the world," the AFA declared, "the United States should do so by democratic methods, and give no cause for accusation that it is adopting the methods of its opponents."[1]

In the face of the government's cultural activities—those exchange programs that proved so vulnerable to reactionary attacks—artists were forced to recognize the unavoidable political implications of art. It was not simply "social protest" art, which had long been put to political use, but all art that was presented under public auspices. Such art might range from string quartets to Broadway plays to painting and sculpture, with all manner of styles represented. But in passing from the private into the public realm, from traditional means of support to experiments in government funding, it all became "political" art, or at least subject to political pressures, both domestic and international. Ironically, in making its vain plea for immunity, the AFA invoked "democratic" principles, and found itself in the curious position of defending American art—which had been selected to counter anti-American forces abroad—from charges of "un-Americanism" at home. And yet the artists never really had a choice in the matter. Their art, like it or not (and those who were participating seemed to like it a lot), had become a vital part of the cold war struggle.

Perhaps emboldened by the new importance granted to art on the world stage, the arts community increasingly took the offensive in its relations with the government in the middle fifties. Several speakers at a Columbia University conference on the arts in March 1955, for example, called for the establishment of the office of secretary of fine arts, while the Committee on Government and Art, active since 1948, had finally released its report on the relations of government and art in the fall of 1954.[2] The report had been sent to President Eisenhower the previous May, but as was often the case in the fifties, such efforts attracted more attention outside of Washington. Called the "Goodrich Committee Report," it was hailed by some as a useful alternative to the tepid recommendations of the Commission of Fine Arts, while reviled by others for being "un-American in its challenge of all tradition."[3]

The committee's report did not challenge *all* traditions, certainly. It recognized, for example, the long tradition of private support of the arts in America, calling plans for another large-scale government art project "unrealistic." The primary aim of government art activities, according to the report, should be the use of art for "public purposes," including the design and decoration of federal buildings; official portraiture and historical paintings; design of stamps, currency, and coins; conservation and exhibition of national collections; educational activities; and international cultural exchange. None of these were new concerns, after all, and the only real innovation was the call for advisory commissions, independent panels of experts without administrative powers as an alternative to both the vacuum created by the limited perspective of the Commission of Fine Arts and the all-encompassing, single-bureau approach of Representative Howell.[4]

Despite the National Sculpture Society's hysterical cry that such a proposal was a scheme for nonartists to control artists— "it would be the end of all freedom of expression and the biased and ruthless shackles of modern art would make conformity to that point of view absolute"—Goodrich's sober appraisal of the report was surely closer to the truth: "Based on the economics of the American art world, it proposes no radical expansion of the government's role in art but rather an extension and reform of essential functions. It is built on existing agencies and procedures, and recommends no large-scale central agency or extravagant appropriations."[5]

The president himself never responded directly to the committee report (he had not said much about the Commission of Fine Arts' report, either), but it quite possibly served, along with the urgings of Nelson Rockefeller, as one of the catalysts that prompted the Eisenhower administration to take a surprisingly active interest in the arts. The president may have lacked the daring of FDR in providing for domestic arts support, but he made great strides in the area of international cultural exchange. And if his own tastes were conservative, he at least avoided the kind of if-that's-art-I'm-a-Hottentot rhetoric of Harry Truman.

"The Federal Government Should Do More"

It was on the occasion of the Museum of Modern Art's twenty-fifth anniversary in 1954 that Eisenhower made his first major statement on the arts. Without direct reference to either the unfortunate State Department episode or to the other Dondero-Busbey attacks (and Dondero had blasted MOMA five years earlier), the president took a firm stand on the issue of artistic freedom:

> To me, in this anniversary, there is a reminder to all of an important principle that we should ever keep in mind. The principle is that freedom of the arts is a basic freedom, one of the pillars of liberty in our free land. For our Republic to stay free, those among us with the rare gift of artistry must be able freely to use their talent. Likewise, our people must have unimpaired opportunity to see, to understand, to profit from our artists' work. As long as artists are at liberty to feel with

high personal intensity, as long as artists are free to create with sincerity and conviction, there will be a healthy controversy and progress in art. Only then can there be opportunity for a genius to conceive and to produce a masterpiece for all mankind.[6]

If such words gave hope to American artists, the president's concluding remarks made it all too clear that he was not sounding a warning to the reactionary critics of modern art in America, those who read radical plots into abstract expressionism and who sought to clamp down on "Communist" artists. Indeed, the president's message to MOMA was in large part an aerogram to Europe, yet another cold war missile designed to distinguish American democracy from the ruthless Soviet system. "How different it is in tyranny," Eisenhower declared. "When artists are made the slaves and tools of the state; when artists become chief propagandists of a cause, progress is arrested and creation and genius are destroyed." But even if the president's words had diplomatic implications far removed from the affairs of art, they concluded with a promise (three days before the AFA adopted its statement) that served the arts community well in its ensuing battles with political censors: "Let us resolve that this precious freedom of America, will, day by day, year by year, become ever stronger, ever brighter in our land."

Even before issuing this statement, the president performed what turned out to be an even greater service to the arts when he persuaded Congress to pass a $5 million Emergency Fund for International Affairs. The measure was an effort to shore up the country's sagging cultural exchange program, which was still suffering from the attacks of the late forties, and the fund proved to be one of the most important contacts that the worlds of government and art managed to forge in the fifties. "Ike Likes the Arts," glowed a *U.S. News and World Report* headline early in 1955; an article noted that the emergency measure (which became a permanent fund two years later) had assisted the export of such attractions as *Porgy and Bess*, the José Limon Dance Company, and violinist Isaac Stern.[7] It was a small step, perhaps—half of the money went to trade fairs and part of the rest went to athletic events in addition to the arts—but it was an important step nevertheless. For cultural exchange was a fundamental part of the government's concern for the arts in the fifties, a concern that only gradually grew to include a full-scale domestic arts program.

The Eisenhower administration, as it turned out, was instrumental in that long process, too, midway through the president's first term of office. Addressing Congress in the annual State of the Union message early in 1955, Eisenhower made the first significant presidential pitch for the arts since the New Deal. "In the advancement of the various activities which will make our civilization endure and flourish," the president observed,

> the Federal government should do more to give official recognition to the importance of the arts and other cultural activities. I shall recommend the establishment of a Federal Advisory Commission on the Arts within the Department of Health, Education, and Welfare, to advise the Federal government on ways to encourage artistic endeavor and appreciation.[8]

Here, then, along with Javits's original 1949 resolution and the various Howell bills, was another element in the foundation of the eventual federal arts program, even though it was rejected at the time. The curious history of the proposed Federal Advisory Commission on the Arts, in fact, captures perfectly the on-again, off-again relationship between government and the arts, as the proposal eluded congressional approval for several years before finally bearing fruit in the Johnson administration. At the same time, Eisenhower's call for "offical recognition" of the arts was hailed as a breakthrough, as indeed it was.

Nor can the Eisenhower administration be faulted for neglecting to carry through on the proposal, despite its failure to secure legislation. Less than a month after Eisenhower's address, Secretary of Health, Education, and Welfare

Oveta Culp Hobby sent a draft on an Advisory Commission bill to House Speaker Sam Rayburn. Nelson Rockefeller, at that time undersecretary of HEW, was one of the chief architects of the bill which, if nothing else, established the "three essential governing principles" of the new federal arts plans:

> (a) that the growth and flourishing of the arts depend upon freedom, imagination, and individual initiative;
> (b) that the encouragement of creative activity in the performance and practice of the arts, and of a widespread participation in an appreciation of the arts, promotes the general welfare and is in (the) national interest;
> (c) that the encouragement of the arts, while primarily a matter for private and local initiative, is an appropriate matter of concern to the United States Government.[9]

This statement declared at once the need for a federal arts program as part of the "promise" of American life as well as the need to insure personal freedom and private initiative—another, often conflicting, part of that promise. It was as close to a definitive "official" arts policy as the country would have until the Secretary of Labor's Metropolitan Opera decision of 1961 and the report of the president's special consultant on the arts the following year. And while the three points may seem like fairly commonplace truisms today, their importance can be surmised from their incorporation into nearly all proposed arts legislation that followed.

In her letter accompanying the draft legislation, moreover, Secretary Hobby touched upon three of the five basic arguments for federal involvement in the arts that had emerged from the 1954 hearings. If the economic argument was too subtle for HEW—and the Communist-propaganda argument too ubiquitous—Hobby was masterful in her use of the other three points. "Throughout the great epochs of history," Hobby declared, invoking the Old World role-model argument, "civilization has been importantly exemplified by masterworks of art and architecture, music and the dance, drama, and literature. Achievements in these fields represent, of course, one of the enduring criteria by which history appraises every nation." And in her inventory of the nation's cultural achievements, Hobby showed her appreciation of the American Renaissance argument as well:

> The United States, despite its relative youth, is rich in artistic achievement. We have contributed new power in design in architecture, created new rhythms in music, and developed a literature which commands worldwide attention. In the theater and film, and in the ancient form of the dance, we show a creative vitality. Our great museums, art galleries, and orchestras are a source of pride for our people.

The final point, of course, was that despite our various cultural triumphs, much remained to be accomplished, especially in bringing the arts into the mainstream of American life. "There are many respects in which we lag behind other nations," the secretary observed, "in the general position we accord the arts in our society." Most important for the democratization of culture, according to Hobby, "new ways should be sought to bring the enjoyment of and participation in the arts to more of our people."

It was nine years before the kind of advisory commission that Eisenhower called for and Hobby proposed would come to pass, but the president's first term was not without its legislative successes in the arts. Although the arts had lost a strong supporter in Congress in 1954 when Representative Howell failed in his bid for a Senate seat, his replacement in the House, Frank Thompson (also a Democrat), proved to be equally devoted to the arts.[10] It was due largely to the efforts of Thompson and James Morrison (D-LA) that a bill was passed in July 1955 creating a "Federal commission to formulate plans for the construction in the District of Columbia of a civic auditorium, including an Inaugural Hall of Presidents and a music, fine arts, and mass communications center." That project, as it turned out, moved as slowly as the advisory commission plan, dependent as it was on private funds and lacking any real impetus until it subsequently became a memorial to President Kennedy. As a concept, however, and as another tentative step easing the government back into the arts business, the passage of the cultural center commission bill was another important victory for the arts in the Eisenhower administration.

Like other arts projects of the period, however, this one, too, was tied to other concerns, to political issues largely irrelevant to the arts but curiously linked to the future of arts subsidy in America. "Making Washington the cultural center of the world would be one of the very best and most effective ways to answer Russian lies . . . ," Thompson observed, without the grace of Secretary Hobby, perhaps, but with the political "relevance" that the arts needed if they were to be taken seriously by Congress in the fifties.[11]

"Fighting Culture with Culture"

For his New Year's Day broadcast of 1956, Edward R. Murrow called together three American correspondents who had spent the previous year abroad, including Daniel Shorr (in Russia) and Robert Pierpoint (in the Far East). The program, aptly entitled "Year of Crisis," was given over to the discussion of weighty international political matters (which always seemed a little more weighty when Murrow was around). When asked to select the most significant diplomatic event in their respective areas during the past year, however, Shorr and Pierpoint offered answers that must have pleasantly surprised more than a few Americans. In Shorr's opinion, it was the appearance of *Porgy and Bess* in Russia, while Pierpoint cited the visit of the Symphony of the Air. Such government-sponsored cultural efforts, it seems, had attracted far more attention than the standard diplomatic fare.[12]

Members of the arts community and a handful of congressmen had been calling for cultural exchange for several years, of course, but aside from sporadic State Department efforts—which always ran the risk of offending Congress—little official effort had been made in this area. Even the warnings of the United States Advisory Commission on Educational Exchange, in one of its 1952 semiannual reports to

Congress, failed to elicit much response. "The emphasis on the fine arts in the cultural phase of the Soviet peace offensive," the commission noted,

> creates a special problem for the United States.
>
> First, the Soviet's emphasis on the fine arts capitalizes on the fact that certain areas of the world, particularly Europe and Latin America, have always underestimated the level of American cultural achievements. This prejudice has affected the attitudes and judgments about American policies and foreign relations. . . .
>
> Second, the Soviet drive in the fine arts field finds the U.S. at present without a counteroffensive. Fine arts programs per se are not included in the Department of State's information and educational exchange program.[13]

When it came to recommending a counteroffensive to the Soviet's cultural drive, however, the commission proved as timid as the State Department itself, advising that the program "should be undertaken under private auspices. . . . The Department of State's activities in this field should be limited to the awarding of a modest number of grants in the fine arts field and to the facilitation of certain worthwhile private projects."[14]

Thus most of the early State Department collaborations with the American National Theater and Academy during the Truman administration, projects like the Barter Theater's appearance in Denmark, and the European tours of the Howard University Players and *Porgy and Bess*, were privately financed. Even after the government became more heavily involved in the arts-export business during the Eisenhower years, the biggest event of the period, the "Salute to France" (which included tours by the Philadelphia Orchestra, New York City Ballet, and *Medea* and *The Skin of Our Teeth*) was privately funded. The hero of the hour, clearly, was ANTA, whose advisory panels made the artistic decisions that the State Department was ill-equipped to make, even had it possessed the temerity to make them in the first place.

Still, government involvement in cultural diplomacy increased dramatically during Eisenhower's first term, especially after the creation of the United States Information Agency in 1953 and the launching of the International Exchange Program the following year, fueled by the $5 million Emergency Fund. "The purpose of the United States Information Agency," explained the president in his 1953 directive, "shall be to submit evidence to other nations by means of communication techniques that the objectives and policies of the United States are in harmony with and will advance their legitimate aspirations for freedom, progress, and peace."[15] Included among such "communication techniques" were the arts, an element that took on increasing importance with the establishment of the Emergency Fund.

The "emergency" that prompted the president's request for $5 million for cultural exchange was, of course, the Soviet cultural offensive. Even after two years of increased cultural activity under Eisenhower, the Russians were sending out eight times as many cultural delegations as the Americans. "It is ironic," observed Robert Breen, director and coproducer of the *Porgy and Bess* company that had toured internationally, "that Communist activity in the field of the arts exchange really awakened the official United States to the need for our involvement in such a program. Unfortunately," Breen continued, getting to the heart of the cultural exchange issue, "arts exchange is not yet officially viewed here as being intrinsically desirable or necessary. It is used, as it were, in 'combat,' as a tactical arm—fighting culture with culture—a new but not-so-secret weapon for use in various, everchanging 'target areas'."[16]

Breen was right in his perception of the government's use of the arts. Again and again the arts were valued chiefly for their use as an element of propaganda. Even such an outspoken advocate of the arts as Representative Thompson drew occasionally on the rhetoric of the cold warriors in building support for his legislative proposals. "One of the major ways in which we might turn reluctant and uneasy military allies and the millions of uncommitted peoples into friends," declared Thompson in 1955, "is to earn their respect for our culture." The time had come, he continued, "for the United States to mount an important counter-offensive against the huge Soviet cultural drive which includes everything from violinists and ballerinas to athletes and chess players."[17]

The time had also come for another round of congressional hearings, for if the arts were winning friends for America abroad, that particular use of culture was gradually winning new friends for the arts themselves at home. In the House and Senate hearings of 1955 and 1956, finally, the question became not so much whether to spend money on the arts, but rather how much to spend, and how to spend it.

"An Orderly, Step-by-Step Procedure"

"Our thinking about the relation of government and the arts has matured," observed Lloyd Goodrich early in 1956. "There is less irrational opposition to any government role in art, based on fears of "socialism' or 'government control,' and on the other hand, less of the naive belief in wholesale government support."[18] Although events later in the year would prove that irrationality had not left the realm of art and government altogether, Goodrich's observation about the climate of the federal subsidy debate was generally correct. Certainly the second major arts hearing, conducted by another subcommittee of the House Committee on Education and Labor in July 1955 and January 1956, was a more orderly affair than the 1954 hearings under Representative Bosch. Like its predecessor, the new Subcommittee on Distinguished Civilian Awards and Cultural Interchange and Development included the leading congressional arts advocate, in the person of Frank Thompson on this occasion; but it also benefited from its new chairman, Representative Lee Metcalf (D-MT), who had introduced arts legislation of his own.

If the 1955–56 hearings lacked the ground-breaking quality of the 1954 session—which had so neatly laid out the several arguments both for and against federal subsidy—and if they lacked as well the fireworks of the earlier hearings, the 1955–56 event shared a certain legislative grandeur with its predecessor. For in the footsteps of Howell's "American National Arts Act" came something even more elaborate, Thompson's "American National Arts, Sports and Recreation Act" (H.R. 6874), a five-pronged attack on the tradition of cultural laissez faire in America. That attack began with a "Statement of Findings," an eleven-part litany of anti-Communist fears, global aspirations, cultural beliefs, and spiritual proclamations. The statement attempted, in a word, to dress up arts support in the trappings of democratic obligations and international good will. The bill itself, ranging all the way from cultural exchange and arts grants to medals of honor and tax relief, threatened to pull apart at the seams; but the message at its core—which eventually would prove successful in providing the impetus for a federal arts program—was consistent with a whole set of American values. To connect such values to the arts might have seemed novel at the time, but the values themselves, especially the anti-Communist zeal and the rhetoric of peace and freedom, were solid fifties Americana:

> (a) The Congress hereby finds that the program of building armed strength should be widened into a more flexible and imaginative strategy for competitive coexistence with the Communists in every field and on every front. The Congress further finds that (1) the Communists have taken sports and culture and the impressionable years of youth and transformed them into arenas of cold war; (2) the Russian athletes are not really amateurs, but are professionals trained under government guidance with government help, bonuses, and prizes; (3) ballet, the theater, and literature are all shaped toward aiding communism's long-range scheme of world domination, and from Moscow there radiate troupes of athletes and artists, circulating through the Soviet world, the satellites, Red China, India, and the West with their gospel of communism; (4) America is proud not only of its material achievements but also of its athletes and artists and its cultural achievements; (5) the whole global scene should be surveyed and plans developed for getting the peoples of the world on our side through maximum use of sports, the theater, and

educational exchanges, and indeed no field should be neglected; and (6) it is through cultural interchange and development, more than superhighways, science, and statistics, that the real answer to communism must be sought.

(b) The Congress, approving and endorsing the statements recently made by the President in support of the cultural arts, further finds that (1) in the advance of the various activities which will make our civilization endure and flourish, the Federal Government should do more to give official recognition to the importance of the arts and other cultural activities; (2) there is an important principle which we should ever keep in mind—the principle that freedom of the arts is a basic freedom, one of the pillars of liberty in our land; (3) there is no aspiration, no dream on the horizons of man's hopes and beliefs and faith, that is so strong and so vivid as the dream of lasting peace; there are many things that must be understood and many things that must be done if we are to make progress toward the realization of that dream, but there is one thing that educators cannot afford to forget, and that is this element of understanding as opposed to mere knowledge; (4) we must make the effort to understand something of the culture of other peoples; their history, their tribulations, and the trials through which they may have passed, for unless we understand these things we will never comprehend why our motives are so often misunderstood; (5) peace is not primarily in the hands of the elected political leaders; it is in the hands of the family and the home, the church and the school.[19]

The five titles of the bill, each at various times before and after the Eighty-fourth Congress separate legislative proposals themselves, called for (1) a program of cultural and athletic exchange; (2) grants to the states for cultural projects; (3) a Federal Advisory Commission on the Arts; (4) medals for distinguished civilian achievement; and (5) a reduction of the admissions tax on arts events to 5 percent.[20] Although that last title, a technical measure designed to provide further tax relief for the arts, was generally ignored at the hearings, the other provisions were explored at length, with most of the attention going to the cultural exchange and the medal of honor schemes.

The "Medal for Distinguished Civilian Achievement" was something of an odd bird, only marginally connected to the arts (Jonas Salk and the late Albert Einstein seemed to be the major candidates for citation); it was doubtless included in Thompson's bill because the plan had been linked to the proposed advisory arts commission in Eisenhower's 1955 State of the Union address. "I shall also propose," the president had declared in his reference to culture, "that awards of merit be established whereby we can honor our fellow citizens who make great contributions to the advancement of our civilization and of this country." The plan, at least, was something on which most of the participants at the 1955–56 hearings could agree.[21] Only a few (including Librarian of Congress L. Quincy Mumford, probably recalling the Ezra Pound incident) expressed the concern that awards based on "matters of taste" might create a "hornet's nest of opinion" in the already divisive art world.

Far more important to the future of the arts—and far more controversial—were the state grants and the advisory commission plans. The former was the hottest potato, setting off the same fire alarms that Howell's H.R. 9111 had the year before. "It appears to me, in title II . . . ," observed Representative John Rhodes (R-AZ), "that we may well be getting into a situation in which the Federal Government, by assisting the States, may well be kind of preempting the field."[22] "Kind of preempting the field" was hardly vintage Dondero, but it was sufficient to express the dominant mood of Congress, a mood that was still sensitive to any possible violations of the traditional bounds of private and public action. In defense, Thompson pointed out that the model for the proposed state grants was the Hill-Burton Hospital Construction Act, an ostensibly noncontroversial federal aid program. But even such well-meaning programs, Representative Metcalf pointed out, could engender controversy. "We have learned to shy like a yearling colt," the Montana Democrat declared, "from any questions of Federal control in the question of school construction programs and any like programs in this committee."[23] Nor did he have to remind his colleague that arts subsidy was in itself a good deal more controversial than hospital or school construction.

But if government spending for the arts still sounded ominous to Congress in 1956, government *talking* about the arts—a Federal Advisory Commission, that is—seemed much more attractive in comparison, especially after getting the president's blessing in 1955. The plan ultimately took several years to be realized, but even in its formative stages it served, along with cultural exchange, as a marvelously useful "buffer zone" between Congress and outright arts subsidy. Luke-warm legislators—always a majority when the question of arts support was raised in the fifties—adopted a gradualist posi-tion, one that stipulated the advisory commission as a neces-sary first step before more aggressive action could be taken, and which then succeeded in delaying that first step for the next eight years. The Federal Advisory Commission on the Arts odyssey is a separate story in itself (see chapter 5), but the congressional one-step began at the 1955–56 hearings.

The chief means of dismantling Thompson's omnibus bill was not the blitzkreig approach used on its predecessor by Bosch and Young in 1954, but rather the delaying tactic of the advisory commission concept itself. "If upon careful objective statistical studies and evolution of the present status of the organization and support of the arts throughout these United States," declared the American Symphony Orchestra League's Helen Thompson, archenemy of federal support at the 1954 hearings, "if through such studies it is found that the citizenry of the United States desires its Federal govern-ment to expand arts activities of local groups, then let us bring that governmental activity into being in an orderly, step-by-step procedure devoid of compromise and hysteria."[24]

Nelson Rockefeller, Eisenhower's special assistant and primary arts tutor, emerged at the hearings as the leading spokesman for the gradualists, stressing the need for an ad-visory commission to be established before other projects could be considered. "Rather than try to spell out the program in detail . . .," he advised, dismissing four-fifths of H.R. 6874's provisions and nine-tenths of its force, "it is better to move into this more gradually on an evolutionary basis, with Congress feeling its way, the Administration and the people interested, and find out how we can more effectively move into this field."[25]

The basis for such advice, clearly, was the old issue of the limits of federal authority, of the need to protect certain areas of American life from the encroachments of the federal government. It was not the same shrill "Hands off!" cry of Bosch and Young, perhaps, but it was concerned with preserving the same tradition. "It just seems to us, from our studies made in the Health, Education, and Welfare Department," Rockefeller concluded, "that this thing should be slow and move step by step, and that it should not do something that will interfere with the already vital growth and culture and great forces which are already in existence on a purely private sponsorship basis."[26]

In the face of such amiable, well-meaning opposition, there was little that Thompson could say. "I do not think anyone wants to move into this precipitously," he explained to Rockefeller, "but do you not agree that in the cold war, that the sooner we can implement a program of selling our culture to the uncommitted people of the world as a weapon, the better off we are?"[27] Thompson's sense of timing may have been off, as the one-step-at-a-time forces easily outdistanced the sooner-the-better camp; but he was correct in his emphasis on the cold war. For questions of immediacy or delay aside, that issue was at the heart of the 1955–56 hearings.

"We Can't Afford to Do Less Than the Russians"

Senator Herbert Lehman (D-NY) was on the right track in 1954 when he introduced the Senate version of Howell's omnibus arts package. "Perhaps the most important part of the act," he told his colleagues, many of whom would find it the *only* important part,

> is that section which provides for cultural international interchange with other countries of the world. We in the United

States have fallen into the habit of letting the rest of the world believe in the myth that there is no real cultural base in the United States—that the creative artists of the United States have little to contribute to the cultural growth of our civilization. The Communists have exploited this myth by propagandizing the peoples of the world with the story that we in the United States are materialistic barbarians.[28]

The latest official response to that dreaded myth was title I of H.R. 6874, developed, according to Thompson, by the State Department and the USIA, the country's chief counter-mythologists, whose cultural programs had subsisted the previous year, 1954, on an emergency appropriation. The new plan called for the secretary of state, working in conjunction with the U.S. Advisory Commission on Educational Exchange and the proposed Advisory Commission on the Arts, to provide for the exchange of American and foreign athletes and creative and performing artists. Granting a permanent status to the operations of the president's Emergency Fund, then, title I of H.R. 6874 had the following purposes:

(1) to provide specific means for strengthening the social and cultural ties which unite us as a people with the free nations of the world, with our allies and with other nations inspired by the same ideals and animated by a like determination to resist aggression; and
(2) to authorize programs and projects on a basis of cooperation with peoples of other nations to demonstrate the social and cultural developments and achievements of the people of the United States and the people of such other nations for the purpose of promoting mutual understanding and respect.[29]

Lest anyone conclude that the government had fundamentally altered its policy on cultural exchange, the bill also included a statement declaring that, to the maximum extent feasible, "private agencies shall be encouraged to participate in carrying out the purposes of this title." ("That simply means . . . ," explained Thompson matter-of-factly, "that we do not want the United States of America to have a symphony orchestra of its own.") The exchange program would continue, in other words, as a supplementary funding source to assist private organizations in meeting their expenses from expanded tours abroad.

The need for such an effort became increasingly apparent in 1955 and 1956. Congressmen were repeatedly reminded of the Soviet's extensive program of "cultural propaganda," and its threat to America's position in the world. At the Metcalf subcommittee hearings, for example, Willard Swire, executive director of ANTA, reported the striking (and dubious) figure that Russia had spent more than $2 billion for cultural exchange over the past two years, far outstripping the American government's $2.5 million a year.[30] Two separate hearings were conducted early in 1956 to discuss America's response to the Soviet effort.

The Senate Foreign Relations Committee met in February to consider two versions of the International Cultural Exchange and Trade Fair Participation Act of 1956. Although both Hubert Humphrey's S. 3116 and Alexander Wiley's S. 3172 would make the president's Emergency Fund permanent, Humphrey's bill showed a particular concern for culture, creating an Advisory Committee on the Arts to advise and assist the government in its effort. Such a committee had been recommended by the Advisory Commission on Educational Exchange every year since 1951, Humphrey pointed out, and although Theodore Streibert of the USIA and Russell Riley of the State Department protested that such a committee was unnecessary because a similar body would soon be formed under the provisions of the Smith-Mundt Act of 1948, Humphrey was adamant. "This goes on and on," he snapped. "The only reason I included it in my bill was that I figured that, after five years of recommendations and nothing yet being accomplished, it might be better if we made it mandatory. . . . We frankly have not done the job we should in the field of fine arts."[31] Although the testimony of the five officials from the Departments of State and Commerce and the USIA supported the administration bill (Wiley's S. 3172), letters from various arts organizations favored S. 3116. The

Foreign Relations Committee, surprisingly enough, favorably reported Humphrey's bill.[32]

The question of cultural exchange was raised the following month in the House, March 1956, when the Committee on Foreign Affairs held more extensive hearings on various administration proposals, which included a draft of the International Cultural Exchange and Trade Fair Participation Act. This particular version, unlike Humphrey's S. 3116, did not include the advisory arts committee, an absence that did not seem to trouble the congressmen, however, who expressed more interest in trade fairs than in cultural missions. That changed on the second day of the hearings, when Representative Thompson stirred up the waters with his testimony. Reminding the committee of the importance of cultural exchange in the battle with Russia for allies abroad—"The choice these people make will largely determine our own fate in this closely knit world"—Thompson discussed *his* version of the cultural exchange act, based on the original title I of H.R. 6874, refined the following year, and finally amended slightly to conform to the Senate version.[33] To assure an adequate cultural effort, Thompson had added three sections to the bill: the aforementioned advisory art committee, authorization for an interagency committee to help in carrying out the act, and a list of the major artistic categories in which the cultural exchange program should operate. Such expert cultural guidance as these provisions would offer was crucial, Thompson felt, to meet the Soviet challenge.[34] Nor did he believe in cutting corners in appropriating funds for cultural exchange, preferring that legislative blank check—"such funds as may be necessary"—to the fixed sum recommended by the administration. Five million dollars is not enough when the Russians are spending forty million, Thompson told the committee. "We can't afford to do less than the Russians in this field. We'll lose our shirts if we do."

Although cultural exchange was by far the most popular of all the schemes for government support of the arts—a fact attested to by the passage of S. 3116 and its signing by President Eisenhower on 1 August 1956—the plan was not without its detractors. Some congressmen, recalling the dispute over the Voice of America broadcasts in the late forties, were wary of the kinds of information that might be dispensed abroad in such cultural programs. An even bigger issue, as we shall see, was the rekindling of suspicion about the participation of radical artists in cultural exchange efforts.[35]

In the private sector, there were those, like the ASOL's Helen Thompson, who saw federal cultural exchange programs as setting a dangerous precedent for other, less desirable, government arts programs. "In the opinion of many symphony orchestra associations," Thompson told a House subcommittee in 1956, "plans for expansion of Federal government activity in the fine arts should stem from consideration of that which is sound for the citizenry and the arts of the United States, rather than from consideration of momentarily opportune and politically expedient procedures for dealing with other governments and other peoples." Thompson rejected, then, the notion that the United States must "measure up" to European standards by adopting public arts programs—"keeping up with the Joneses on an international basis"—when the simple truth of private initiative in the arts was America's strongest selling point. Instead of apologizing for not following European practices, Thompson told the subcommittee, "we feel our own people as well as the rest of the world should be told of the widespread arts development already achieved in the United States through the force of individual and group initiative operating in a capitalist society."[36]

For years, actually, the United States *had* been attempting to spread that very message, in a part of the world where it thought it might do the most good—behind the iron curtain. Some cultural exchange with Russia had taken place following World War II, but contact between the two worlds declined from a high point in 1945 to almost no contact after 1948. As Secretary of State John Foster Dulles pointed out in 1955, Soviet practices of news censorship, travel restrictions, and the jamming of western radio broadcasts kept the two countries apart, although the United States had policies of its own, including trade restrictions and the fingerprinting of

Russian visitors, which also contributed to the chill in the air during the cold war years.[37] The international ice began to thaw in the early fifties with the new Soviet policy of cultural diplomacy in Europe, and by 1955 plans for cultural exchange between Russia and the United States began to take shape. Eisenhower discussed the matter that year with Krushchev at the Big Four conference in Geneva, and it was discussed again three months later in a conference of foreign ministers. Not surprisingly, however, the initial cultural exchanges between the two countries were handled on the American end largely by private agencies. Carleton Smith of the National Arts Foundation, for example, flew to Moscow in August to arrange for the American tours of pianist Emil Gilels and violinist David Oistrakh, and later planned the exchange of two hundred paintings and sculpture and fifty "art lovers" from the two countries.[38] The big event, though, was the December appearance of *Porgy and Bess* in Moscow, a display of Americana that similarly lacked the imprimatur of United States government funds.

For its part in the middle fifties, the State Department served largely as an intermediary between VOKS, the Soviet agency that handled cultural relations, and individuals and insitutions in the United States interested in participating in such exchanges. So numerous were the requests from the private sector, in fact, that the State Department set up a separate office to evaluate and process the various proposals.[39] Adding to the department's burden was the sudden flurry of interest displayed by Russia itself. Perhaps sensing the uncertainty on the part of the Eisenhower administration as to the implications of renewed cultural relations, Russia took the offensive in 1956. Soviet Cultural Minister Nikolai Mikhailov caught the United States off guard in March with the announcement of an expanded program of exchange with the United States, Great Britain, France, and Asia, issuing in the process invitations to the Philadelphia Orchestra, soloists from the Metropolitan Opera, Isaac Stern, and Artur Rubinstein. In return for the Americans' visits, Mikhailov promised to send a folk dance ensemble and the Bolshoi Ballet, and spoke optimistically of a series of one-week film festivals in each other's country. Two months later the Soviets made another peaceful gesture, announcing that starting in July it would allow the USIA to distribute 52,000 copies of the Russian-language *Amerika*.[40]

At the same time that this new cultural chess match was being played, however, the old diplomatic arm-wrestling continued. The October 1955 meeting of foreign ministers had failed to produce a final agreement, as the Soviets balked at the American requirement of fingerprinting Russian visitors (dating from the McCarran Act of 1952), while the United States pointed to the countless restrictions placed on foreign visitors to Russia. The cooling trend continued in June when the USSR learned that its entire ninety-member Moiseyev folk dance troupe would have to be fingerprinted for its fall tour, and by the end of the year the cold war, for the moment, at least, was back in full swing. In the face of the invasion of Hungary, the United States suspended all cultural exchange with Russia.[41]

The on-again, off-again relationship between the two world powers continued through 1957, and not until 27 January 1958 was a formal agreement signed by the two countries, permitting cooperation in cultural, educational, technical, and sports fields.[42] But even that agreement, renewed every two years since the original signing, could not prevent events like Sputnik and the Berlin crisis, the U2 incident and the almost continuous rhetorical sniping, from lending an occasional chill to the air. The sniping was especially intense on the American side, where reactionary buckshot was spent on *two* sets of Communists—the Russian variety, and their subversive American counterparts, with the Americans still occasionally disguised, or so the conspiracy theory ran, in the garb of the artist.

"Sport in Art"

"Beauty will not come at the call of the legislature," Emerson once observed. And "even when beauty comes," Brooks Atkinson of the *New York Times* commented a century later, "there is no reason to assume that government will stand behind it."[43] Events in 1956 proved Atkinson's point again and again, as the relationship between government and art endured its worst year since the late forties. Remarkably, the circumstances were very much the same as before, with renewed cries of communism in American art, with a confused government agency withdrawing support from cultural programs, and with Representative Dondero once more on hand, after a four-year silence on the subject, contributing to the hysteria.

The 1956 version of "Advancing American Art" was an exhibition entitled "Sport in Art," sponsored by *Sports Illustrated* and selected by that magazine and the American Federation of Arts (AFA). It was scheduled to tour through several American cities before heading to Melbourne under USIA auspices for the 1956 Olympics. Not the kind of exhibit calculated to stir up much controversy, it did, in fact, attract favorable notices in Boston and Washington, D.C. But the show was scheduled for Texas, too, where a group of disgruntled academic painters and right-wing activists had joined forces to make Dallas safe for democracy.

Even before the exhibit arrived, the Dallas County Patriotic Council (DCPC) had formally protested the appearance of what it called "Communist works of art," petitioning both the Dallas Art Association, whose trustees ran the Dallas Museum of Fine Art, and the Dallas Park Board, whose funds helped maintain the museum.[44] "We're not interested in the nationality or the political bent of the artists," declared the DCPC's Colonel Alvin Owsley. "Nor are we interested in the quality or merit in the productions, nor in the controversy between traditional versus modernistic art. All we're interested in is this: we don't want the exhibition in any public building of works by artists with Communist front records."[45] While the art in question in this instance, depicting a baseball game, two winter scenes, and an elderly fisherman, could hardly be called subversive, the four artists—Ben Shahn, Yasuo Kuniyoshi, Leon Kroll, and William Zorach—had all been linked to left-wing activities. Shahn and Kuniyoshi had been part of the infamous 1946 State Department collection, and all four artists were listed in HUAC's ample files.[46]

The trustees of the Dallas Museum withstood the attacks of the Patriotic Council, however, voting 23 to 0 (with three abstentions) to reject the request to remove the four paintings from the exhibition. "We believe that democracy cannot survive," declared three trustees in a letter to the *New York Times*, "if subjected to book burning, thought control, condemnation without trial, proclamation of guilt by association—the very techniques of the Communist and fascist regimes."[47] The museum's sole criterion for acquiring works of art, the trustees explained, was artistic merit.

The USIA, however, could not afford to act upon such lofty principles, or so it seemed. It was an information agency, after all, the government's public relations firm, in effect, and it was sensitive to the kind of bad publicity—and congressional pressure—that might be generated by events like the Dallas episode. Thus it spent the spring of 1956 trimming its cultural sails, first canceling the "Sport in Art" tour, then calling off an upcoming tour of the Symphony of the Air because of alleged Communist activities among some of its members, and finally halting another AFA-organized program, "100 American Artists of the 20th Century." Of the one hundred artists, the USIA claimed, ten were politically "unacceptable," "social hazards." And when the forty-two trustees of the AFA voted unanimously to withdraw from the show if any artists were barred (citing its 1954 resolution), the USIA canceled the tour. In an effort to avoid such occurrences in the future, moreover, the USIA announced a short time later that it would exclude from its upcoming exhibits "American oil paintings dated after 1917." Works painted before the Russian Revolution, it seemed, were immune to the Communist threat and thus safe for display abroad.[48]

Regardless of what action it took, however, the USIA was certain to be criticized, and in this instance the attack came from all sides. The liberal press, naturally, castigated the agency for canceling the three tours, while conservatives, led by a reactivated Representative Dondero, blasted the agency for setting up the program in the first place. But as before, government art had its defenders in Congress, too, most notably Frank Thompson and Hubert Humphrey, who was "disturbed by the timidity, hesitancy and cowardice exhibited by certain agencies. . . . When some senators stand on the floor and undertake to say that the USIA may be doing something which appears to the left of Grant or McKinley," the senator fumed, "then the USIA stands like it has been stunned and immobilized."[49] Also as before, private agencies rushed in where the government feared to tread. Six months after the cancellations, the Rockefeller-funded International Council of the Museum of Modern Art was formed, giving the museum a new and expanded role in representing the United States abroad.[50]

Yet despite the censorship problems of 1956, arts advocates could point to the passage of the International Cultural Exchange and Trade Fair Participation Act as a step in the right direction. If nothing else, the modest cultural export program helped keep alive discussions of full-scale federal arts support. "It is obvious," Representative Thompson observed in the fall of 1956, "that if we are going to use the arts increasingly in our foreign policy we are soon going to have to do something to encourage the arts to grow here at home or we won't have anything at all to export." But domestic arts support, as Thompson well knew, was another matter entirely. Even the creation of an advisory arts commission, which became the preoccupation of congressional arts advocates for the next several years, proved to be a near impossible task. "Mere lip service and fine phrases about the importance of the arts and other cultural activities and how they 'make our civilization endure and flourish,'" Thompson grimly observed, "will not get cultural legislation through the Congress now or in the future."[51]

5

Who'll Pay the Fiddler?

"Many of us in the Congress," wrote Frank Thompson to Brooks Atkinson of the *New York Times* in 1955, "are convinced that Congress has done little in developing a national policy in the arts in our country largely because the leaders in the cultural field have themselves made little or no effort to formulate sound and constructive proposals at the national level for consideration by Congress." Thompson was not merely passing the buck in this instance. For the "arts lobby" (if the nascent political organization of the arts community can even be called a "lobby") was still a well-kept secret in the middle fifties. Lloyd Goodrich's Committee on Government and Art, limiting its concern to the visual arts, was never conceived of as a broad-based, political-action movement, while other organized voices like ANTA or the National Music Council or Artists Equity all suffered from a similar inability either to cross disciplinary boundaries or to reach the general public. "Where is the Citizens Committee for a National Cultural Policy and where are the artists who are supposed to be deeply concerned with a Federal Arts Program[?]" demanded Thompson.

> Are they hard at work at the grass-roots? No, indeed they are not. Finding, as always, that it is much easier to be critical than constructive they are . . . busy sharpening barbs to hurl at the Congress for its alleged "philistinism." Their rights as citizens, their power in the voting booths, they resolutely refuse to exercise or recognize.[1]

Congress, as it turned out, discovered the power of the arts before artists ever had a chance to discover the power of politics (the election of Ronald Reagan notwithstanding). Still, Thompson's criticism of the arts community for its political apathy was too severe, and his claim that Lillian Gish was "fighting almost a one-person battle to establish a fine arts bureau in the Federal Government" was simply not true.[2] For the actress herself was involved in a uniquely interdisciplinary movement that helped shaped the direction of the federal arts movement, even if it was never able to hasten that movement's course.

The National Council on the Arts and Government (NCAG) got its start in 1954, when Artists Equity called a meeting of representatives of various arts organizations to discuss the possibility of forming a new lobbying group. Led by Clarence Derwent of Actors Equity and later Harold Weston of the Federation of Modern Painters and Sculptors, the NCAG drew on the expertise (and the prominence) of selected representatives of seven major fields: music; drama and dance; literature; architecture; painting, sculpture, and graphic arts; photography and motion pictures; and radio and television.[3] Like the Goodrich committee, it favored a moderate program of federal support, eventually calling for arts subsidy but never making that its sole concern. And like Goodrich's group, the NCAG favored a low-profile approach, focusing its efforts on key congressmen and key legislation, faithfully rounding up witnesses for the yearly arts hearings, but never creating much public stir in the process. "It is not anticipated," explained the NCAG in 1956, "that the Council will ever become more than a small, alert catalyzer for art legislation for the numerous organizations and individuals interested in the arts." Thus although it might not have been the Citizens Committee that Thompson desired, the NCAG left its mark on the federal arts movement in its pioneering interdisciplinary approach, in its close scrutiny of the various arts bills, and in its behind-the-scenes work with congressional staff.[4]

While most of what little attention Congress paid to the arts in the middle fifties concerned cultural diplomacy, the NCAG and the other arts organizations worked for the passage of domestic arts legislation as well, programs ranging from simple tax relief for the arts to a new gallery for the

Smithsonian art collection to the perennial federal advisory commission bills. After the return of Democractic control of both houses in 1955 following the Republican majority of the Eighty-third Congress (only the second time since Franklin D. Roosevelt took office), such legislation increased. Many of the bills, it is true, were the work of Frank Thompson and his staff, but a number of other congressmen, including Senators Alexander Wiley (R-WI) and Herbert Lehman (D-NY) and Representative Emanuel Celler (D-NY) and Stuyvesant Wainwright (R-NY), authored and actively supported various arts proposals.

Most attention focused on the Federal Advisory Commission on the Arts, for that proposed agency symbolized the federal government's limited responsibility for the nation's cultural climate, granting immediate "official recognition" to the arts while holding out, for those who dared to think in such terms, the *possibility* of federal subsidy. The commission, to be established in the Department of Health, Education, and Welfare and composed of twenty-one members appointed by the president, was designed to undertake studies and make recommendations "for encouragement of creative activity in the performance and practice of the arts and of participation in and appreciation of the arts."[5] With both the president's blessings and at least the veneer of bipartisan support, moreover, such an advisory body appeared to be the most logical first step in a government arts program. If nothing else, it promised to remove the burden of cultural planning from both the executive and legislative branches, not only by establishing a separate agency for that task, but by emphasizing the private sector's responsibility for culture in the very charter of that agency. Thus the phrase "while primarily a matter for private and local initiative" became the shibboleth of the congressional arts advocates, assuring skeptics of the limits of federal involvement in the arts while promising supporters that at least *something* would be done.

As it turned out, however, virtually *nothing* was done. Not, at least, until after the death of President Kennedy, whose 1963 executive order establishing an advisory council lapsed without appointments to the body being made. In 1964, finally, an advisory council bill managed to pass the House, and then only as a means of forestalling the more ambitious plans for a federal arts *foundation* that had also passed the Senate that year. The story of the federal advisory council on the arts, long touted as a simple domestic corollary to the nation's international arts activities, is a tortuous one. But its retelling is crucial to an understanding of the arts program that was eventually established, ten years and two presidents after Eisenhower made his initial call for an advisory arts commission in 1955.

"For the Protection and Nurturing of the Arts"

Although the advisory commission legislation never got out of committee in 1955—the House Education and Labor subcommittee was more concerned with Thompson's massive H.R. 6874, title II of which included the commission—it resurfaced in 1956 and made considerable progress. The bill attracted a good deal of attention in the Senate especially, and thanks largely to the efforts of Senators Lehman, Irving Ives (R-NY), James Murray (D-MT), and Paul Douglas (D-IL), it was eventually approved by the Senate on 5 July 1956. Senator Lehman led the way with a statement in March that at once summarized the standard arguments for government arts support while stressing the safeguards of his advisory commission bill, S. 3419. Like the other arts advocates in Congress, Lehman felt constrained to deliver two messages— one designed to rally support for the legislation while the other attempted to disarm the bill's natural enemies, those conservatives of both parties to whom all social programs were anathema. Thus in drumming up support for his bill, Lehman touched on the standard issues of international prestige, increased leisure time, the status of American culture, and economic problems in the arts.[6] He saved his heavy rhetorical artillery, though, for the key issues of democracy and communism, the need, that is, to decentralize the arts at home and to fight the Soviet threat abroad.

"The arts provide the wellspring and pipelines for our Nation's cultural growth," Lehman told his colleagues during his plea for the advisory arts commission, carefully weaving his concern for culture into the sacrosanct area of the American landscape.

> I am a stanch exponent of the protection of the natural resources of our country for the benefit of all our people. Likewise, I believe that our cultural resources should be fostered and developed for the enrichment of all. Are we in America going to continue to be as profligate or as blindly inconsiderate about our cultural resources as we were in the past about our great forests and deep rich soil? The long drought of economic insecurity for the arts in America has spread an aesthetic Dust Bowl across many of our states. For instance, the theater and its people in smaller cities and towns have become as rare as our vanishing prairies. Plans need to be developed by far-sighted statesmen, with the assistance of professional advice, for the protection and nurturing of the arts.

The complement to the argument for the domestic dissemination of the arts was the international theme of combating Communist propaganda abroad, the need to respond in kind to the Soviet's new cultural policies. "The present international situation underscores another reason why Congress should give immediate attention to the arts," Lehman declared, employing the same argument that Humphrey and Thompson would use that year in their successful drive for a permanent cultural exchange program.

> The new look in the policy of the Soviet Union might be said to be a shift in the continuing cold war from the arena of armaments and potential armed aggression to penetration into lands by economic and cultural campaigns accompanied by propaganda against the United States for its laissez faire attitude toward the arts.

Lehman's alternative to the traditional laissez faire approach was the advisory commission, shoring up American culture at home and assuring its continued vitality for the long international campaign ahead, but *not*, however, at the expense of that *other* tradition, "our American desire for freedom and independence." Lehman assured his opponents that arts support in America would continue to be a divided mix of private patronage and public (i.e., state and municipal) support, with the private sector always remaining dominant. "This proposed legislation is consequently not a step toward a department of art with concurrent danger of undesired bureaucratic or governmental control of the artist," Lehman explained. Nor did he propose "any wholesale support of the arts or dole to the artist by the Federal Government."

On the strength of that recapitulation of what had become the official (if not yet majority) line on the proper relationship of government and art, Senators Lehman and Murray conducted the first Senate subcommittee hearing on the arts in nearly twenty years, a one-day stand in New York in April.[7] The hearing uncovered little that was new, however, as twenty-one witnesses dutifully restated their support for the advisory commission, while a minority of three (two representatives of the National Sculpture Society and Margaret French Cresson of the National Academy of Design) rehearsed their arguments against such a body. Of greater interest was the report of the full Committee on Labor and Public Welfare that was subsequently issued on 3 July 1956, offering the unanimous support of that committee to an amended version of S. 3419. ("Commission" was changed to "Council" and the appointment requirements were made more flexible.) In particular, Senate Report No. 2409 was notable for its warning regarding the operation of the proposed council, a statement that became another guiding principle in the eventual establishment of an arts program that would be insulated from the vagaries of partisan politics. "It is the intention of this committee," the report stated, "that the Advisory Council, in carrying out its function, shall not, directly or indirectly, infringe or attempt to infringe in any way, shape, or manner upon freedom of expression in the arts or impose or attempt to impose any form of censorship or governmental control or direction of the arts."[8]

That statement was at once a recognition of the problems that both the WPA and subsequent cultural exchange programs had encountered in Congress, as well as a response to the attacks of conservative arts groups who were fearful of the machinations of a new government agency. As such, the statement (which became something of a watchword for the National Council on the Arts and Government) was a shrewdly crafted two-edged sword, serving both to protect the council from congressional attempts at censorship, as well as to undercut the grim predictions of the conservative artists.

The committee report, of course, had a conservative strain of its own, too, urging as it did that "the proposed council should be solely consultative and advisory in character." Just as the Senate four years earlier had effectively handcuffed the Howell college-art bill, prohibiting any federal financial obligation, Chairman Lister Hill's committee underscored the purely *advisory* nature of the proposed council. "It will have no operating responsibilities," the report declared. "The bill provides for no subsidization of the arts."

In any case, the report gave encouragement to the nation's arts community, and 318 arts advocates responded a few days later, under the auspices of the NCAG, with a statement of support for Lehman's bill.[9] But while that bill had no trouble passing in the Senate, it ran aground in the House, where it failed by a sixteen to seven vote in the Committee on Education and Labor. The major obstacle, as Frank Thompson explained it the following year, was the degree of authority vested in the secretary of HEW, who was authorized to appoint special committees to conduct studies for the advisory council.[10] Judging from subsequent actions in the House, however, where the advisory council legislation bounced around for the next several years, and from the obvious lack of Republican support (only one Republican on the Education and Labor Committee voted for the advisory council bill), it is unlikely that the secretary's power was the only fac-

tor in the bill's defeat. For there were still those in the House—
if not a majority at least a large enough number to scare off
the mass of legislators who were clearly indifferent to the
whole affair—who saw the advisory council legislation as another "foot-in-the-door" measure, a sneak attack by northeastern liberals attempting to feather their own nests.

"Our Culture May Become Lopsided and Misdirected"

Despite the rejection by Congress in 1956, Eisenhower renewed his request for an advisory council in his budget message to Congress the following January, setting off yet another round of congressional hearings on the arts.[11] A
subcommittee of the Senate Committee on Labor and Public
Welfare put in another cameo appearance in New York, where
Senators Murray and Gordon Allott (R-CO) heard the testimony of eighteen arts supporters on 23 May 1957.[12] The
arguments, by this time, were beginning to fray around the
edges, with notions of international prestige and cold war
pressures, of increased leisure time and the need to decentralize the arts, all being traded back and forth like so many
old baseball cards. There was not even a reactionary artist on
hand to condemn the whole idea as a radical plot. But in at
least three areas, the hearing touched on matters that became
increasingly important in the sixties as the drive for a federal
arts program reached its climax.

First was the consideration of the Javits-Clark bill, S. 2081,
calling not for an advisory council but for an arts foundation,
a grant-making agency patterned after the British and newly
formed Canadian arts councils, and designed to assist performing arts organizations.[13] The bill never got off the ground
in the Eighty-fifth Congress, admittedly, but it did mark the
beginning of a serious recognition by some members of Congress of the necessity for government arts subsidy, a controversial matter that was destined to remain in limbo until the
advisory council issue was finally resolved in 1964.

Of more immediate importance was the testimony of Dr. Earl J. McGrath, head of the Institute of Higher Education at Teachers College, Columbia University, and Hyman R. Faine, national executive secretary of the American Guild of Musical Artists (AGMA). McGrath, the former U.S. commissioner of education (1949–53), was one of the first spokesmen for federal arts support from the academic community, that part of the private sector that was of paramount importance in the arts debates of the early sixties, when the humanities legislation suddenly appeared on the horizon. (The humanities legislation was largely responsible, in fact, for the success of the companion arts legislation.) McGrath sounded what became one of the major concerns of the transition years between Eisenhower and Kennedy—the fear of America becoming a mechanized, militarized, materialistic society, one that underestimates the importance of the arts and the humanities. "I fear that if the present overemphasis on science and technology is continued," McGrath warned Murray and Allott, "our culture may become lopsided and misdirected." McGrath was not discounting the importance of scientific enterprise to American life, certainly, as he approved of the billions of dollars of support that the government expended on research. "There are real dangers, however, in this excessive preoccupation with some features of our national life to the neglect of others," he continued.

> There are values in the arts which others more competent than I will doubtless lay before you. . . . If, as a nation, we were to become as concerned about these things of the spirit as we are about the material products of our hands and minds, I am confident that remarkable advances would be made in the quality of both our private and public lives.[14]

Along with this concern for the broader aspects of American culture that was voiced prophetically at the 1957 Senate subcommittee hearing, a much narrower concern—but equally important in the subsequent arts debates—was expressed by AGMA's Hy Faine. Union leaders and assorted arts advocates had grumbled about economic conditions in the arts for years, but the issue never received much public exposure until the early sixties, when Frank Thompson held hearings in New York, San Francisco, and Washington on economic conditions in the performing arts and when, more importantly, Secretary of Labor Arthur Goldberg was called in to settle a labor dispute that threatened the future of the Metropolitan Opera. Faine, however, offered a preview of these events in 1957, citing both the New York City Opera's cancellation of its spring season and the Northwest Grand Opera's cancellation of its entire season after only one production. With less than 10 percent of the AGMA membership earning as much as $5,000 annually from their art, according to Faine, "the facts and the situation are grim indeed." [15]

These concerns were raised again in July when a subcommittee of the House Committee on Education and Labor met for five days of hearings on the advisory council legislation. Fr. Gilbert Hartke of Catholic University, representing the American Educational Theater Association, spoke at length on the need for the arts to temper the increasing technical emphasis in America, while Henry Kaiser, general counsel of the American Federation of Musicians (AFM), presented more evidence on the financial plight of the performing arts. Citing a national survey conducted by the Research Corporation of America (aptly entitled "The National Crisis in Music"), Kaiser spoke of a 40-percent decline in employment for musicians since 1930, a problem caused largely by technological innovations but exacerbated as well by the federal government's cabaret tax. [16] "The musician holds the same relation to the Nation's cultural health as the farmer holds to the Nation's economic health," Kaiser told the subcommittee.

> When the farmer was depressed by economic changes, the Nation, through the Federal Government, gave him help, and still does. But in a period during which the musician has been depressed by technological changes, his economic position has been further impaired by the 20-percent tax on music, dancing and entertainment.

Kaiser's testimony was leading, clearly, into the uncharted waters of arts subsidy, where the AFM's James Petrillo and only a handful of others had ventured in the past. Still generally regarded as "off limits" in Washington, the subject came up several times during the 1957 hearings, but in almost all instances the plan was dismissed as either undesirable or premature. Kaiser, at least, was aware of the opposition to federal patronage, but he insisted on facing the music, so to speak:

> "Subsidy," like "spit," is a horrible word, but I think we have reached that stage of maturity where we ought not to be too concerned with the emotional impact of semantics. It's a hard, solid fact, Uncle Sam has been subsidizing since Uncle Sam acquired nephews. We subsidize all manner of industries. We subsidize the airline industry. We subsidize the farmer. We subsidize the manufacturer. I do not think it has in any meaningful sense altered the quintessential nature of our Republic.

"Who'll Pay the Fiddler?" asked a 1957 article in *High Fidelity* magazine, answering its own query with the suggestion that the federal government should foot part of that bill. But few in 1957 were willing to share that view, to make the leap from what was known in polite circles as a necessary economic "fine tuning" by the government (i.e., massive agricultural subsidies and regulation of the marketplace) to the kind of "cultural engineering" that arts subsidy seemed to imply. And, realistically, it *was* futile to speak about such matters when the creation of a nonfunding agency like the Federal Advisory Council on the Arts was still very much in doubt. For that proposal, despite another open letter of support, signed this time by more than four hundred arts advocates, had its share of enemies, too.[17]

"This Is Not the American Way"

The traditional congressional inertia and the outright opposition to initiating new social welfare programs make it difficult to measure how great an impact the conservative artists had in their campaign against *any* kind of new federal arts program. They were out in full force for the July 1957 hearings, in any case, and Representative Thompson seemed concerned about their efforts. Writing to Lloyd Goodrich of the Committee on Government and Art several months earlier, Thompson had referred to the National Sculpture Society's Wheeler Williams, "who means to stop the Wainwright [advisory commission] bill and its companion measures in the House and Senate by fair means or foul. He seems to be an accomplished artist at innuendo, and he has certainly hurt the bill's chances of passage."[18]

Williams, an academic sculptor best known for the Taft memorial in Washington, had long been active in conservative art circles, dividing his time between the American Artists Professional League (AAPL) and the National Sculpture Society (NSS) and generally proving to be a thorn in the side of those in and out of Congress who sought a federal arts program.[19] At the July hearings Williams was joined in his indictment of the "socialized art bills" by Dorothy Drew, AAPL policy chairman and sometime speech writer for Representative Dondero, and Adlai S. Hardin, president of the NSS. But it was Williams who was the most systematic in his anti-arts support philippic. Beginning with the obligatory exposé of the origins of the government-art conspiracy (namely, the Communist-front activity of the WPA years and the ill-fated Coffee-Pepper arts bureau bill), Williams gradually arrived at the four basic reasons for the conservative artists' opposition to the advisory council plan.

At the top of Williams's list was the fear of the "regimentation" and "socialized control" that would result from the dominance of the so-called art experts on the proposed council. No doubt thinking of the losses that academic artists had suffered in recent years at the hands of the abstract expressionists (aided and abetted by museum curators and art critics), Williams and his associates were not encouraged by the prospects of their adversaries gaining control of an official arts agency. Nor could Williams support the multidisciplinary aspect of the council, "including performing arts and other cultural facets in a hodge podge with the fine arts." Moreover, in view of the success academic painters and sculptors had enjoyed under the existing regime, the "time-honored Commission of Fine Arts" (whose authority, according to Williams, was certain to be violated by the new council), Williams could see little benefit to a new program. And if these three points seemed too specialized or speculative, Williams and the AAPL concluded their indictment with a plea that all Americans could support: "As citizens, we oppose these bills as potentially leading to extravagant boondoggling, despite an over-burdened budget and staggering taxation."

Along with all of the rabid anticommunism ("the Commies pretty well took [the Federal Arts Project] over as their own pork barrel") and antimodernism ("this debauching of all that is noble in art") that informed Williams's statement, it included a more reasonable strain of individualism and common sense, too. He touched on basic American values, after all, values that doubtless had more to do with the opposition in Congress to a domestic arts program than all of Williams's supposed conspiracies combined. (It was a line of reasoning, too, that would have to be overcome by something equally basic—the notion that providing for the general welfare might include the arts and humanities as well as defense and medical research—before an arts program could be established.) "The true artist," Williams declared, "is perforce a rugged individualist and does not want to be kept poodle by the government with dilettante experts as nursemaids. Like all rugged individuals in business for themselves, he knows that few can hope for great success and then only if their work speaks a language that all can understand."

This was nothing more than the message of Emerson and Whitman, in their tradition of public art rooted in private inspiration, but with an ax to grind that they might have found offensive, perhaps, and with a notion of "universal language" that surely would have struck them as simple-minded. Williams's colleague, Adlai S. Hardin, expressed this viewpoint more effectively, without the former's rancor:

> Individual initiative is what our pioneer forefathers had. It is one of the foundation stones on which the whole American

philosophy of free enterprise is built. Individual initiative is at the very opposite end of the pole from government encouragement.

At one pole are initiative, a free system of competition, an equal opportunity for reward for individual capacity, superiority, and achievement. . . .

At the other pole is supervision, direction, conformity, and the danger of subsidizing the support of mediocrity. This is not the American way.[20]

Williams's and Hardin's black-and-white imagery might not have been the deciding blow, but for whatever combination of reasons—including the needless quibbling over questions of format by the bill's supporters themselves—the advisory council legislation failed again in 1957. It did not attract much attention the following year, and although it was the subject of another hearing in 1959, the proposal could never find sufficient support in the House until the sixties, when Democratic administrations with visions of "new frontiers" and "great societies" finally gave the advisory council concept sufficient impetus for passage.[21] In the meantime, as the Eisenhower years drew to a close, Congress was involved with other cultural matters, including a cultural center at home and controversial displays of American art abroad, all of which demonstrated, if nothing else, the need for that elusive Advisory Council on the Arts.

"Sooner or Later, We Have to Grow Up"

"The pages of The Congressional Record are rife with tributes to one or more of the Nine Muses," the *New York Times*'s Milton Bracker observed in a front-page story on government and the arts late in 1958, "although the rhetoric has not been enough to forestall the death of most of the bills introduced."[22] Nevertheless, two major pieces of arts legislation did pass during Eisenhower's second term. Both bills, oddly enough, concerned a disputed plot of land on the capitol mall, although neither project, as it turned out, succeeded in capturing that prime piece of cultural real estate, but were forced instead to find homes elsewhere in Washington.

Back in 1938, when government and the arts were active partners in America, Congress had passed a resolution that created a Smithsonian Gallery of Art Commission and set aside land on the mall, opposite the National Gallery of Art, for a building to house the National Collection of Fine Arts— the growing Smithsonian collection, that is, which for aesthetic or statutory reasons was denied entrance into Andrew Mellon's National Gallery. The resolution even authorized $40,000 for a competition to select a design for the new museum (which Eero and Eliel Saarinen and J. Robert F. Swanson won with a radical model in 1939), but the whole project was allowed to languish during the war and was seemingly forgotten in the fifties.[23] Representative Thompson and others revived the idea in 1956; but with tentative plans underway for the National Cultural Center to occupy that spot on the mall, Thompson, Humphrey, and Senator Clinton Anderson (D-NM) introduced legislation to place the Smithsonian collection, along with a National Portrait Gallery, in the old Patent Office building downtown (used by the Civil Service Commission since 1932 but scheduled to be torn down for a parking lot). That legislation passed in March 1958; while it was not all that the arts community had hoped for, it was at least a positive step on the long road to a domestic arts program, the first such step, in fact, since the ill-fated resolution of 1938.

The National Cultural Center, meanwhile, was having an equally difficult time finding a home and it, too, failed in its bid for the mall site. Early in 1957, the District of Columbia Auditorium Commission, which had been established in 1955 to make plans for such a structure, unanimously recommended to Congress a site known as Foggy Bottom (on the Potomac, near the present location of the Kennedy Center). The government, according to the plan, was to provide the land for the site, while private funds would be used to build the cultural center itself, estimated to cost $36 million.[24] But while the Senate unanimously approved the project, the House voted it down by a better than two-to-one margin, citing both the expense of the land (which some members of the House claimed would run as high as $27 million) and the uncertainty of raising funds for the structure by private subscription.[25]

In response to that defeat, Thompson drafted a bill to put the cultural center on the mall site opposite the National Gallery, thus removing it from the purview of the General Services Administration and placing it under the Smithsonian.[26] Thompson and Senator J. William Fulbright (D-AR) introduced legislation to this effect in 1958, but they encountered a traffic jam on the mall in the form of Senator Anderson's bill to erect a National Air Museum opposite the National Gallery.[27] A subcommittee of the Senate Committee on Public Works held a hearing in April 1958 to settle the matter, but it would be too simple to view the affair as a battle between the forces of culture and technology. Both bills had solid support in the Senate, although it is interesting to note the arts advocates' use of the cold war rhetoric, drawing on the cultural exchange debates, in an effort to build support for a domestic project like the National Cultural Center.

The "Statement of Policy and Purpose" of Fulbright's S. 3335, in fact, got right to the heart of the matter:

> This Act is intended to strengthen the ties which unite the United States with other nations and to assist in the further growth and development of friendly, sympathetic, and peaceful relations between the United States and the other nations of the world by demonstrating the cultural interests and achievements of the people of the United States. This is particularly necessary at this time when the Soviet Union and other totalitarian nations are spending vast sums for the arts in an attempt to lead the peoples of the world to believe that those countries produce civilization's best efforts in the fine arts. It is demonstrably true that wars begin in the minds of men and that it is in the minds of men that the defenses of peace must be constructed.[28]

And in his testimony before the subcommittee, Fulbright cited the "reaction in Moscow to a young pianist from Texas, born in Louisiana and a resident now of Odessa, Texas." That "young pianist," of course, was Van Cliburn, the sensation of the recent Tchaikovsky competition who "had to come to Moscow," the Senator suggested darkly, quoting Dmitri Shostakovitch, "to get proper recognition for his talents as a pianist."[29] Fulbright's remedy, logically enough, was the National Capital Center for the Performing Arts, a cultural shrine where America could honor its own artists, and where it could provide a forum for visiting artists from abroad.

For practical reasons as much as anything else, the air museum got preference for the mall site, while the National Cultural Center was shifted back to Foggy Bottom. And with some surprising support from southern Democrats like James Wright of Texas, Howard Smith of Virginia, and Robert Jones of Alabama, the bill sailed through the House on the day before adjournment, passing by an overwhelming margin of 261 to 55.[30] The bill was a bargain, admittedly; National Capital Planning Commission funds would pay for the single acre of land not already owned by the government, while private funds would be raised to build the physical structure itself. Nevertheless, the signing of S. 3335 by President Eisenhower on 2 September 1958 represented the first clear-cut victory for domestic arts legislation, a victory that saw many of the traditional foes of such legislation aligning themselves with the handful of staunch arts advocates in Congress. For at least one southern Democrat, James Wright, the cultural center debate amounted to something of a conversion experience:

> Let me say this in all sincerity, Mr. Speaker, and I think it is important. I suppose that I have done my share of demagoguing. All of us like to portray ourselves as real, sure enough corn-fed, homegrown log cabin boys. All of us have been just a bit guilty of that. In striking such a pose, it is always kind of easy to ridicule and poke fun at things of a cultural nature. I plead guilty to having done my share of it, but I think, Mr. Speaker, that we have reached a state of maturity in this Na-

tion where that kind of attitude no longer becomes us. Sooner or later we have to grow up and stop poking fun at things intellectual and cultural.

There would be more "poking fun" at culture, of course, and the cultural center itself, as well as a program not merely to house but to *fund* the arts, was still several years off. But Congress *had* grown up a little with the passage of Fulbright's bill, and a genuine arts movement in Congress was beginning to take shape. No longer a political liability or the special interest of northeastern liberals, arts advocacy in Congress began to emerge as another weapon in the politician's arsenal of popular causes. "Some Congressmen," Senator Javits observed the following year, "say that only four years ago they could not have supported an arts program without being laughed at back home. Practically nobody is laughing any more."[31]

"Our Best Foot Forward"

Another measure of the progress that had been made in the area of government involvement in the arts by the end of the Eisenhower years was the handling of the two major overseas exhibitions of the period—those at the Brussels World's Fair in 1958 and at the American National Exhibition in Moscow in 1959. On the one hand, admittedly, these events called attention to the same problems that plagued earlier official cultural efforts. Arts groups complained that not enough was being done by the government; self-appointed critics charged that the art sent did not truly reflect American culture, and, in the case of the Moscow show, the far right waged yet another full-scale attack, complete with a HUAC investigation.

In another sense, though, these storms of the late fifties seemed less threatening than before. The USIA managed to stand its ground this time, with the principle of selection by artistic merit remaining largely intact. The whole public-private structure of government and the arts, in fact, still in its infancy, proved to be sturdier than one might have expected. The two events, in short, unlike the ill-fated State Department collection of 1946 or the USIA fiascos of 1956, offered encouraging, if still inconclusive, support for the theory that art and government could be successfully joined in America.

When sixty-eight members of the Metropolitan Opera sent an open letter to President Eisenhower in January 1958, protesting the small budget for the arts in the American exhibit at the Brussels World's Fair, and when Actors Equity and AGMA repeated the complaint the following month, it was not simply another case of the arts community crying in the wilderness. The president himself asked Congress to restore the $2 million-plus that it had cut from the original $15 million request for Brussels, and for the next several months the halls of Congress echoed with similar pleas for a fitting display of American culture abroad.[32] The major fear was that the United States' exhibit would pale before that of Russia, which had spent about five times the amount America had; but there was also a new awareness of the *quality* of America's cultural effort.

The American art sent to Brussels was an oddly fractured display that featured Indian and folk art on the one hand, contemporary crafts and design and young artists on the other, but overlooked entirely major figures like Homer, Eakins, Benton, and the mature abstract expressionists. It was generally conceded both in and out of Congress that the American display was an uneven affair, neither as bad as some of its detractors, like Senator Styles Bridges (R-NH), claimed, but not nearly so good as it might have been, either.[33] The lesson that was carried into the American National Exhibition at Moscow the following year, clearly, was that the country could not merely rest on its laurels; laissez faire culture was simply not sufficient when it came to displaying the fruits of American civilization on the world stage. Yet in waging its battle for the government's acceptance of such cultural responsibility, the arts community wished to retain at least one facet of the laissez faire tradition—freedom from government control—that had suffered so often in cultural exchange efforts in the past. Tested once again in the Moscow episode, this freedom was again battered severely, but managed in the end to survive.

Plans for the art to be exhibited in Moscow got off to a promising start. USIA director George V. Allen announced that a four-man jury had been selected to choose the paintings and sculpture to be sent abroad: Franklin C. Watkins (painter and instructor at the Pennsylvania Academy of Fine Arts), Lloyd Goodrich (director of the Whitney Museum), Henry R. Hope (chairman of the fine arts department at Indiana University and editor of *College Art Journal*), and Theodore Roszak (sculptor and instructor at Sarah Lawrence College).[34] But it was also clear that this exhibit, the first major cultural contact with the Soviet Union since World War II, was no mere USIA trade fair and talent show, and that the selection panel would be under tremendous pressure, from both the public and private sectors. As the *New York Times*'s Aline B. Saarinen prophesied in an open letter to the jury early in 1959, "There will have been official suggestions and guidelines from the advisory committees of the U.S.I.A. and the State Department; the shadow of Congress' esthetic dogma will have fallen across your meetings; and you will have been subject to pressures from outside officialdom."[35]

By the time the jury's selections were announced (forty-nine paintings and twenty-three sculptures from 1918 to the present), Saarinen's predictions had doubtless come to pass, although there is no evidence that the jury's seventy-two choices were unduly affected by external pressure. But even before the exhibit opened in Moscow in July, that "shadow of Congress' esthetic dogma" had been cast by Representative Francis E. Walter (D-PA), the chairman of HUAC, who denounced the selections for their preponderance of "Communist art." A "routine check" of HUAC files for information on the sixty-seven artists slated for the Moscow exhibit, Walter announced on 3 June, revealed thirty-four with records of Communist involvement, including twenty-two with "significant records of affiliation with the Communist movement in this country."[36]

Aside from these charges, however, it was generally agreed that the jury had put together an excellent survey of the past four decades of American art. "The works indicate clearly," wrote Emily Genauer in the *New York Herald Tribune*, "that however badly the United States may have bumbled the opportunity, in the highly controversial art show at the Brussels World's Fair last year, to tell the rest of the world about our concern for cultural and spiritual values as well as for material things, we will be putting our best foot forward in Moscow this summer."[37]

The most impressive feature of the exhibit, considering its limited size, was its scope. Ranging all the way from Grant Wood (*Parson Weems' Fable*) and Thomas Hart Benton (*Boom Town*) to Jackson Pollock and Willem De Kooning, there were also effective transition pieces, canvases by painters like Charles Sheeler, Georgia O'Keeffe, Max Weber, Marsden Hartley, Lyonel Feininger, and John Marin, which were selected to help the Soviet audience bridge the gap between the realism they knew so well and the abstractions that had been foreign to the Soviet Union since the revolution. Some of the works, like Jack Levine's *Welcome Home*, with its bloated army general, and Peter Blume's *Eternal City*, with its menacing jack-in-the-box head of Mussolini, were obviously included to demonstrate some of the political themes that American artists were free to address.[38]

The potential impact, however, was threatened by Walter's call for an investigation based on the alleged public reaction to his June exposé. "In response to my address," he declared at the opening of the HUAC hearing on 1 July, "from the crossroads of this nation I have received a substantial volume of mail from Mr. and Mrs. America, who, almost without exception, registered strong protest against the makeup of the exhibit and expressed resentment that the work of Communists and Communist sympathizers should be sent to Moscow as examples of American culture."[39]

Fortunately, it was a little late in the day for such a tirade; as the fifties were drawing to a close United States–Soviet relations showed signs of improvement. HUAC was beginning to appear almost as a parody of itself, in fact, doing as much to keep the Communist menace alive in America as the fragmented Communist party itself. Twice before in the late fifties, the committee had dabbled in the arts, in a vain attempt to recapture the glory years of the Hollywood investigations. It sought out Communist musicians associated with the Metropolitan Music School, the Symphony of the Air, and New York's AFM Local 802 in 1957, and managed to embarrass a few more alleged subversives (including producer Joseph Papp) in a similar investigation the following year. But HUAC was fast losing its credibility, and the 1959 probe did not enhance its reputation.[40]

Walter's chief witness against the "Moscow 34" was none other than Wheeler Williams, whose credibility (which had never been too strong in any case) was beginning to suffer, too.[41] Williams testified at length, repeating the same old themes of past public-art failures, of conspiratorial museum directors and critics, and of the Communist plot to destroy America's faith in religion and good art. "They want to destroy all phases of our culture," Williams told the committee, "and if they can destroy our faith in the beauty and wonders of our cultural heritage, including the arts and literature and music and so forth, they can take us over without a hydrogen bomb. They can take us over with popguns." Although Walter had candidly admitted that his committee was "not concerned with the relative merit of the art work as such," the chairman did not discourage Williams's critical analysis of the works sent to Moscow. Singling out the abstract pieces—"here is a design which my wife would not accept for a linoleum for a kitchen floor"—Williams dismissed William Zorach's *Victory* as inadequate "for any student in any class of mine" and Pollock's *Cathedral* as "the worst doodle that you could imagine on a telephone pad. Most of these things are doodles."[42]

Walter had less luck, however, with Ben Shahn and Philip Evergood, the two subpoenaed witnesses whose works were represented in the exhibition but who refused ("not only on the fifth amendment but on the relevant limitations of the

Bill of Rights including the first amendment, the fifth amendment and the ninth and tenth amendments") to discuss the matter with the committee. Staff director Richard Arens spent an hour and a half going over the two artists' voluminous HUAC files, but he failed to extract any dramatic confessions.[43]

Except for the response it elicited from the president and the ensuing discussion in the press, which were ultimately injurious to Walter's cause, the HUAC investigation proved fruitless. It did lead, indirectly, to the addition of some traditional works to the Moscow collection, but this action had more to do with the president's tastes than with Walter's charges. The whole episode, in the final analysis, served rather to extinguish the smoldering twenty-year crusade of the political and aesthetic reactionaries against the alleged left-wing art than to further that dubious cause. It was President Eisenhower who helped close the issue by dismissing the HUAC charges. And if his comments were as hazy as ever, he made one message clear—"I am not going to be the censor."

Eisenhower's initial response to the episode, when questioned at a news conference the day after the HUAC hearing, was to minimize the affair. "The artistic representation is only a minor part of this business," he explained, quite properly putting the seventy-two art works in the larger perspective of the Soviet-American cultural exchange. He exaggerated slightly when he claimed that "no one in the government had a single thing to do with it except Mr. Allen, chief of the United States Information Agency . . . [who] appointed a committee," and he had some difficulty explaining the rationale of that committee in restricting its selections to works produced since 1918.[44] But when pinned down to a specific example of the Moscow show—Jack Levine's *Welcome Home*—Eisenhower managed to declare himself on the side of artistic freedom. General Eisenhower did not *like* Levine's version of the military, certainly, but he resisted yielding either to his own personal preferences or to the HUAC inquisition. That he finished his statement rather lamely, with some cracker-barrel logic about "what America likes," detracted only slightly from the principle of artistic freedom that he had, in effect, declared.

"It looks more like a lampoon than art, as far as I am concerned," the president stated in response to a question about Levine's painting.

> But I am not going, I assure you, I am not going to be the censor myself for the art that has already gone there. Now I think I might have something to say if we have another exhibit, anywhere, to the responsible officials of the methods they produce, or get the juries and possibly there ought to be 1 or 2 people that, like most of us here, say we are not too certain what art is but we know what we like, and what America likes—what America likes is after all some of the things that ought to be shown.[45]

The art world warmly applauded Eisenhower's stand, noting, as the selection committee wrote the president, that withdrawal of the collection "would give the Soviet propagandists an ideal weapon to attack our democratic freedom."[46] The Soviets themselves, as it happened, proved to be the censors at Moscow, at one point removing from the American exhibition some one hundred books which they judged to be too critical of communism. And although the National Gallery's David Finley put together a collection of twenty-five old American standbys (including one of Gilbert Stuart's Washington portraits and a portrait of Lincoln by George Healy, plus other eighteenth- and nineteenth-century works by Copley, Russell, Catlin, Remington, Sargent, et al.) to supplement the modern works originally chosen, the United States came through this crisis rather well, considering the outcome of similar events in the past.[47] At least when those who kept track of such things tallied up the government's cultural balance sheet at the end of the decade, one item that had been a debit since the late forties—cultural exchange—could at last be moved to the other side of the ledger.[48]

"The Pageant of America"

Balance sheets are not normally employed in the task of assessing a society's culture, perhaps, but something nearly as mathematical became fashionable as the decade of the fifties drew to a close and the nation took stock of itself. Much as the turn-of-the-century churches in America had measured their religious fervor by keeping track of attendance each Sunday morning, an odd variety of "culture-counting" took place in the late fifties. In 1958, for example, when the publishers of *American Heritage* decided to introduce *Horizon*, their new cultural venture, they launched the effort with an impressive inventory of America's cultural gains: an increase from $152 million to $592 million between 1933 and 1956 in the amount Americans spent on books; a jump from 54 million to 270 million in the number of juvenile books sold between 1947 and 1957; as well as an increase from 330 million to nearly 900 million in the total number of books sold during that period. Twice as many people played musical instruments in 1957 as in 1938, the *Horizon* publishers informed its readers, announcing as well the startling fact that in 1952 there were three times as many concerts in the United States as in the rest of the world *combined*.[49]

That all of these figures were purely *quantitative*—that nothing was said of the *quality* of the books sold or the *kinds* of concerts being performed—did not seem to matter. When John D. Rockefeller III told a New York audience that support of the arts was a "community responsibility"—a phrase that would become the keynote of the arts advocates in the sixties—he based his claim not on the quality of American culture but on the sheer *amount* of it. There are 5,000 community theaters in the United States, Rockefeller told New York's Hundred Year Association in 1959 ("more theaters than radio or television stations"), over 500 opera-producing groups ("7 times as many as 15 years ago"), and 1,100 symphony orchestras ("twice as many as only 10 years ago"). Why, Americans spend more money on concerts, Rockefeller declared in a statement that captured perfectly the spirit of the culture-counters, than they do on baseball.[50]

Not all of the analyses of American culture at the end of the decade were quantitative, certainly, nor were they all so optimistic as the statistics alone seemed to indicate. For every bombastic statement regarding America's cultural greatness—like Frank Thompson's 1958 declaration that we "stand at this moment on the threshold of a great American renaissance"—there were surely as many expressions of doubt. Thompson himself, in an article that same year entitled "Our Cultural Crisis," voiced a prevalent concern about how America would fare in the inevitable comparisons that would be made between American and Soviet culture. In so doing, he pointed not to growing attendance figures but to the more substantive (if rather grandiloquent) cultural task that lay ahead: "As the city of Athens so long ago became known as the home of all learning, so must America be known not only for her great strength and high levels of production but also for her humane world leadership, her enduring democratic traditions, her rich heritage of the arts of many cultures."[51] Such a concern, similarly, to show "by definite act where our values lie," led Senator Humphrey to introduce yet another bill for a Medal for Distinguished Civilian Achievement. "Americans have often been said to be frivolous or, worse, materialist," he reminded his colleagues in the Senate. "We are anti-intellectual, our critics say. Well, we have never done anything specific to show that we value the results of intellectual or artistic abilities in our national life."[52]

These concerns, clearly, were a large part of the motivation behind the potpourri of arts legislation—the U.S. Arts Foundation, grants to states for arts projects, a National Academy of Culture, a National Showcase of the Arts and Sciences—that appeared at the end of the fifties.[53] Such legislative proposals served, in a sense, as "finishing touches" on American civilization, part of a broader social and cultural program (which included civil rights legislation) designed to complement the nation's industrial and military successes.

"Our generation has seen the United States emerge as

the leading economic, scientific and military force in the world," Senator Javits observed in April 1959.

> Our political institutions, our individual freedoms and our way of life serve as examples, even as an inspiration, to the peoples of the world. We have expended untold toil and countless billions to give our nation this stature and to pre-serve it. Yet in this tremendous progress, one vital element of our national character has been left to struggle with little pub-lic effort and assistance to aid it. The cultural heritage of America—one of the great binding forces holding together and enhancing our varied national life—has been relegated to a lesser role in the pageant of Amerca.[54]

Critics of America's "mass culture" warned, moreover, that in the face of the "tremendous progress" made in eco-nomic and scientific affairs, the "pageant of America" had been allowed to deteriorate into a carnival. Sheer quantity alone was insufficient proof of cultural vitality. Eleven hundred orchestras or five thousand theaters were no match, after all, for the combined assault of Hollywood, Madison Avenue, and even Middletown itself, which had come to represent, by the end of the fifties, not democracy, but mediocrity. Medi-ocrity was one of the concerns, certainly, that prompted Ei-senhower to appoint a Commission on National Goals as his second term came to a close. Organized by the American Assembly at Columbia University and employing the services of some one hundred experts, the commission issued its re-port late in 1960, along with accompanying essays by sixteen scholars and public figures on topics ranging from the indi-vidual to international affairs, from science and education to agriculture and health.

Included was an essay by August Heckscher (former *New York Herald Tribune* editorial writer and director of the Twen-tieth Century Fund), the very title of which—"The Quality of American Culture"—called into question the shallow no-tions of the culture-counters.[55] Indeed, Heckscher (who was advised by Alfred Kazin, Leo Rosten, and Aline Saarinen) addressed himself to the question of *balance* in American life, whether the arts, that is, could ever be brought to the high levels of achievement and emphasis that American science and technology had attained. Although he was not so gloomy as those critics who dismissed American culture as a wasteland, Heckscher did not share the enthusiasm of the cultural statisticians either. "Despite outstanding achievements by individual Americans," he wrote,

> and signs of broad public interest in the arts, there is cause for serious uneasiness. An industrial civilization, brought to the highest point of development, has still to prove that it can nourish and sustain a rich cultural life. In the case of the United States, it is evident that cultural attainments have not kept pace with improvements in other fields.

Not surprisingly, there was a little of the moralist in Heckscher's essay ("the general advance in well-being seems to have brought with it a lessening of moral intensity and a readiness to indulge in secondhand experience"), along with an occasional glimpse of the visionary ("the need is to make possible fruitful interaction between the artist and the mass audience, but at the same time to give the artist the means of keeping a life somewhat apart, under conditions allowing him to develop in his own way at his own pace"). But for the most part Heckscher avoided the easy extremes of condemnation and rhapsody, focusing squarely instead on the crucial issues of leisure time, the mass market, the cultural elite, and arts and education. He was especially insightful in his discussions of cultural standards and of government involvement. In the former area Heckscher went so far as to list four principles— "basic presuppositions which a people must come to accept and respect if its culture is not to fall into mediocrity"—displaying a kind of rigor and economy of thought rarely encountered in such discussions of American culture.

The four principles, quite simply, attested to the *difficulty* of art. It is neither easy to create nor easy to appreciate, Heckscher insisted, nor is it a simple matter of quantity nor of self-expression. In the face of the cultural optimists who told Americans how *much* art was being created, how exciting it was, and how all of us should join in the fun, Heckscher's comments on art were sobering:

Its practice requires training, discipline and the most unflagging dedication.

It requires in the spectator an effort of the spirit and of the mind, sufficient to put himself in harmony with a vision other than his own. . . .

Number and popularity are not related to this kind of art; indeed the preservation of excellence and the setting of ultimate standards may be incompatible with efforts to broaden public appreciation.

Turning his attention to the involvement of the government in the arts, Heckscher acknowledged the failures of the past, the undesirable political influences, the dominance of artistic cliques, with "official art" connoting more often than not bland art. "When government has entered directly into the field of art," Heckscher wrote, "the experience too often has been disheartening," which explained the conclusion reached by many in the art world that "anything is better than the intrusion of government." Yet there were other areas, "no less delicate than art," Heckscher pointed out, in which government involvement had been successful, areas like the judiciary or, to cite more pertinent examples, agencies like the National Institutes of Health or the National Science Foundation. "Certainly in the United States of the next decade," Heckscher insisted, "we should be capable of devoting as much ingenuity to the creation of adequate processes for the nurturing of art as we have for promoting health or science."

Heckscher proposed to add the arts to that list of social welfare concerns that had increasingly become the province of government. As a start, Heckscher recommended a series of "relatively undramatic and indirect means"—a review of the tax laws as they pertained to the arts, the creation of an advisory council, as well as possible "creative innovations," subsidies for the transportation of art, experiments in public television, and even institutional support. But along with such practical considerations, Heckscher was ever mindful of that larger, spiritual concern for American culture as a whole, in particular for the *quality* of that culture as it entered the new decade:

The most significant goal in the field of the arts is that their
enhancement and development should be considered a goal—
that the American people should recognize the objectives in
this area of their common life to be on an equal plane with
those to which in the past they have given their best efforts. It
has been all too natural, during the epochs when a continent
was being subdued or amid the fresh responsibilities of world
power, to think of the arts as something pleasant but peripheral. The time has now come when we must acknowledge them
to be central and conceive their fullest development as essential to the nation's moral well-being.

"Maverick or MacBeth?"

If Heckscher's goals for the arts in America were necessarily
vague, the two candidates for the presidency in 1960—one,
part of the old regime who promised continued prosperity
while the other, an upstart, promised a new commitment to
excellence—failed to come up with anything more specific.
Neither one could manage, even in that last, desperate month
of the campaign, when promises tend to pile up like autumn
leaves, to sound *promising* about the government's involvement in the arts.[56] When asked about cultural exchange Richard Nixon pointed to the accomplishments of the Eisenhower
administration, and on the domestic front cited the passage
of the National Cultural Center legislation. Nor could he resist a little self-congratulatory culture-counting, pointing
proudly to the more than 11,000 orchestras and 700 opera
orgranizations, and to the fact that "every major city now has
its 'good music' radio station." But for the future, Nixon was
reluctant to look past the creation of an advisory arts council.
Federal assistance, he felt, "should be indirect—scholarships,
exchange programs, encouragement rather than subsidy."[57]

And although the Democratic platform called for the
advisory council and made a veiled reference to actual financial assistance ("We shall support legislation needed to provide incentives for those endowed with extraordinary talent . . ."), John F. Kennedy's plans were only slightly more

elaborate than Nixon's.[58] Like the vice president, he opposed a Secretary of Culture, favored the advisory council, and promised to increase cultural exchange. On the subject of federal subsidy, however, Kennedy seemed confused—conveniently so, it must be noted—as he told the liberal Actors Equity that he favored the creation of a federal arts foundation to support the performing arts, while assuring the readers of the *Saturday Review* that he opposed federal grants to orchestras and opera companies, except for purposes of cultural exchange. But if Kennedy's stand on the arts was no stronger than Nixon's, the young Democrat at least had better writers. For Kennedy, the question of American culture was more than one of mere numbers. It involved, as he put it so effectively, our *attitude* toward culture: "It is a question of whether we are more interested in reading books or making book, Maverick or Macbeth, Zorro rather than Zola, Peter Gunn or Peer Gynt. In this day of crisis, 'Wisdom is better than strength . . . a wise man better than a strong man.'"[59]

In the larger fabric of presidential politics, of course, with its broad patterns of foreign relations and domestic affairs, such statements on the arts were just so much minuscule needlepoint. Yet there was something novel to Kennedy's approach, too, something that linked the arts, as Heckscher's essay on the *quality* of American culture had, to those larger concerns of the state, and for the moment, at least, it almost seemed as if the arts really *mattered*. "Creative work is not done to measure," Kennedy wrote *Musical America*. "The climate in which art thrives is a delicate climate. It must foster individual work by sensitive patrons. And it is of real importance that the government not disturb this climate by meddlesome incursions, or limitations on the free play of the mind." Such was the kind of plausible rhetoric that one expected from politicians when they discussed the arts, the reliable assurances that Uncle Sam would neither pay the piper nor call the tune. Yet Kennedy pushed the point further, sweeping the arts up into the regenerative movement that his campaign represented and, like it or not, it made a difference. "If the government must not interfere," Kennedy continued,

it can give a lead. There is a connection, hard to explain logically but easy to feel, between achievement in public life and
progress in the arts. The age of Pericles was also the age of
Phidias. The age of Lorenzo de Medici was also the age of
Leonardo da Vinci. The age of Elizabeth also the age of
Shakespeare. And the New Frontier for which I campaign in
public life, can also be a New Frontier for American Art.

For what I descry is a lift for our country: a surge of economic growth; a burst of activity in rebuilding and cleansing
our cities; a breakthrough of the barriers of racial and religious discrimination; an Age of Discovery in science and space;
and an openness toward what is new that will banish the suspicion and misgiving that have tarnished our prestige abroad.
I forsee, in short, an America that is moving once again.

And in harmony with that creative burst, there is bound to
come the New Frontier in the Arts. For we stand, I believe,
on the verge of a period of sustained cultural brilliance.[60]

Mere campaign rhetoric? Perhaps. Yet even so, it was
clearly the kind of rhetoric that moved people, that got things
done. Three weeks after the election, the new first lady's social secretary announced that under Mrs. Kennedy the White
House would become "a showcase of American art and history." That claim was largely rhetorical, too, as it turned out,
but it was refreshing just the same. In the New Frontier, it
seemed, the arts really *did* matter.[61]

1. George Biddle at work on his murals for the Justice Department, Washington, D.C., 1936. (*Courtesy of the Archives of American Art, Smithsonian Institution.*)

2. Rep. George A. Dondero (R-MI), ca. 1940. "Communist art, aided and abetted by misguided Americans," Dondero charged in 1949, "is stabbing our glorious American art in the back with murderous intent." (*Courtesy of the Library of Congress.*)

3. Yasuo Kuniyoshi's *Circus Girl Resting*, included in the State Department's 1946 "Advancing American Art" exhibition. "If that's art, I'm a Hottentot," declared Harry Truman. (*Courtesy of Auburn University.*)

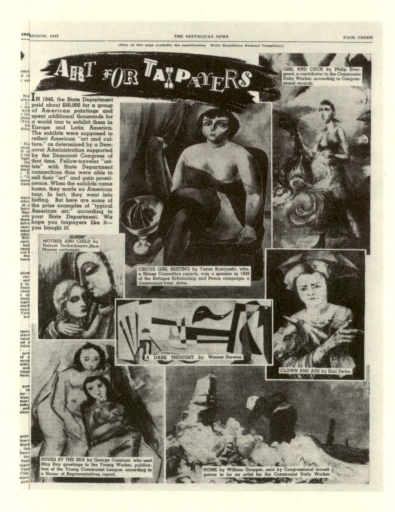

4. The Republican National Committee's response to the State Department's "Advancing American Art" exhibition.

5. Lloyd Goodrich, Associate Director of the Whitney Museum of American Art, Chairman of the Committee on Government and Art, seated before Reginald Marsh's *Human Pool Tables*. (*Photograph by Sidney Waintraub*.)

6. The Commission of Fine Arts, 1953: (left to right) Pietro Belluschi, architect, professor at Massachusetts Institute of Technology; George Biddle, painter; Felix W. de Weldon, sculptor; David Finley (chairman), director, National Gallery of Art; H.P. Caemmerer, secretary of the commission; Edward F. Neild, Sr., architect; Elbert Peet, landscape architect and city planner; Joseph Hudnut, architect and dean of the Graduate School of Design, Harvard University. (*Courtesy of the Commission of Fine Arts*.)

7. Wheeler Williams (left), president of the National Sculpture Society, presenting the NSS Medal of Honor to New York City Public Works Commissioner Frederick H. Zurmuhlen, 1953.

8. Jack Levine's *Welcome Home* (1946), included in the American National Exhibition, Moscow, 1959. "It looks more like a lampoon than art, as far as I'm concerned," stated President Eisenhower. "But I'm not going, I assure you, I am not going to be the censor. . . ." (*Courtesy of the Brooklyn Museum, John B. Woodward Memorial Fund.*)

9. Sen. Jacob Javits (right), who introduced legislation in 1961 for a gold medal honoring Danny Kaye for his work with humanitarian causes and cultural exchange on behalf of UNICEF and the USO. (*Courtesy of Wide World Photos.*)

10. Rep. Frank Thompson (left), with conductor Leopold Stokowski, at the House Education Subcommittee's hearings on the economic conditions of the performing arts, 1961. (*Photograph by Sam Goldstein.*)

11. Harry Truman (at the piano) and pianist Eugene List, performing at the Kennedy White House, 1961. (*Courtesy of the John F. Kennedy Library.*)

12. August Heckscher, President Kennedy's Special Consultant on the Arts, appearing on a CBS television broadcast in 1962. (*Courtesy of August Heckscher.*)

13. Bill-signing ceremony at the White House, National Foundation on the Arts and the Humanities Act, 29 September 1965. (*Courtesy of the National Archives.*)

6

The New Frontier in the Arts

"In the Executive Mansion, where Fred Waring and his Pennsylvanians once played, we now find Isaac Stern, Pablo Casals, Stravinsky and the Oxford Players." Arthur Schlesinger, Jr., addressing the American Federation of Arts in 1962, captured the difference between the old and the new in Washington, contrasting Eisenhower's simple tastes with the grace and sophistication of the Kennedys.[1] Nor had it taken the new president long to establish that essential distinction; his administration sounded a new note in Washington at the very start, when 155 leading figures in the arts and sciences were invited to the inauguration, "in recognition of their importance." Telegrams signed by Kennedy and his wife went out to writers like Hemingway, Faulkner, and Steinbeck, playwrights like Arthur Miller, Thornton Wilder, and Tennessee Williams, artists like Alexander Calder, Stuart Davis, and Edward Hopper, and composers like Hindemith, Stravinsky, and Bernstein. "During our forthcoming Administration," the invitations read, "we hope to seek a productive relationship with our writers, artists, composers, philosophers, scientists and heads of cultural institutions."[2]

It was only a small gesture, perhaps, but it helped set the tone for the Kennedy years, a tone that managed somehow to combine Harvard learning with political savvy, youthful vigor with old-line Democratic tactics, Jack's wit with Jackie's smile. And for all of the fluff of that period, indeed, for all of the dewy-eyed remembrances that inevitably followed, those years put the arts in a new light in America. However much culture served as mere ornamentation in the new administration, the arts served as something more substantial as well—something to strive for, an aspect of life worth seeking out, a part of the larger American environment, finally, that the federal government had an obligation to protect and promote. These were the years, moreover, in which the long-suffering arts forces finally came together (to be joined by a new force of academic humanists more experienced in the political process). Rallied by the sympathetic new administration, the arts community began to mobilize in quest of a new federal arts program; artists unions and cultural institutions, arts service organizations and special-interest groups, museums and symphony orchestras, to say nothing of those solitary artists who resisted affiliation but who recognized a kindred spirit in the White House, all made their presence felt. They were helped—immeasurably—by the new, fashionable status that the arts began to enjoy in American politics. And they were served effectively by that new cadre of university educators who wasted no time in staking their claim for a piece of the New Frontier. This cultural manifest destiny might not have started on that gusty morning in January when Robert Frost helped inaugurate the new president—speaking of that "next Augustan age . . . a golden age of poetry and power," and reaching in an instant the largest audience for poetry in history—but that is as good a time as any to begin an examination of the New Frontier in the arts.

"A Who's Who of Culture"

"I felt afterwards that it was the inauguration which really had begun everything," August Heckscher observed in 1965.

> Everything that was done in this field of the arts—everything President Kennedy did in regard to it—was a trial step. . . . I don't think he ever had any grandiose—he would have hated the word "grandiose"—any large plans from the beginning. So, when [155] scholars and artists and creative individuals were invited to the inauguration, I don't think he had any idea of the stir it would cause in the country. I don't think he had any idea of the reverberations or the expectations that it would create in the mind of the artistic community itself. They

all said, now the President has done this, what is he going to
do next?[3]

What the president did next, with the help of his wife,
assistants like Schlesinger, Heckscher, Pierre Salinger, William Walton, and Secretary of Labor Arthur Goldberg, Secretary of the Interior Stewart L. Udall, and Secretary of Health,
Education, and Welfare Abraham Ribicoff, was to adopt the
arts as one of the symbols of his administration.[4] Although
the president himself was hardly a connoisseur—Heckscher
recalled him as "a little bit like the average husband, sort of
being dragged by his wife to do a lot of cultural things he
really didn't enjoy doing very much"—Kennedy was also aware
of the public-relations value, the prestige, of the arts.[5] He
applied to the home front, in effect, the lesson America had
struggled to learn in the fifties on the international scene,
when it developed its cultural exchange program. If the arts
could win rave reviews abroad, after all, they could be equally
effective at home, setting a positive tone for the new administration. If one judges from the response of the arts community, at least, the White House garnered as many kudos
for its arts effort as the State Department and the USIA had
won abroad in the previous decade.

"The flow of guests from the fields of the arts to the
Executive Mansion," rhapsodized Arthur and Barbara Gelb
in the *New York Times Magazine*,

> has been unprecedented since Mr. Kennedy took office. Not
> only have Metropolitan Opera stars, a troupe of Shake-
> spearean actors and Pablo Casals been issued formal invita-
> tions to perform in the East Room at State dinners, but the
> list of private and official guests invited to the White House
> over the past months forms a Who's Who of culture—every-
> one from Carl Sandburg, Gian Carlo Menotti and Leonard
> Bernstein to Igor Stravinsky, George Balanchine, Elia Kazan
> and Ralph Richardson have been welcome there.

The Gelbs' article, logically enough, was entitled "Culture
Makes a Hit at the White House," but the real point of the

article was the "hit" the Kennedy White House had made with all of its cultural events.[6]

Many of these affairs, surely, were media events, highbrow window dressing designed to generate a little favorable publicity in the face of less attractive scenery on the New Frontier, events like the Bay of Pigs disaster, or the Cuban missile crisis, or the president's nagging inability to work his magic on the Democratic Congress. In other respects, though, most notably in the intervention in the Metropolitan Opera's labor dispute, the appointment of August Heckscher as arts consultant, and in the creation of an advisory arts council by executive order, the strides in government recognition of the arts under Kennedy were substantial. Even in some of those matters which admittedly had more to do with tone than with substance, events like the campaign for a National Cultural Center or the president's 1962 Message to Congress on Education or his Amherst speech the following year, the arts and the arts community emerged in a stronger position to mount the final drive for a domestic arts program, a drive that gained its final impetus, ironically, from the death of the president himself.

"The Vision of a Worthy Goal"

The success of an administration surely depends as much on the staff surrounding the president as it does on the chief executive himself, and in relation to the arts, at least, the Kennedy White House was particularly strong. It included, as noted, men like Schlesinger, Walton, and Salinger (and later August Heckscher), who traveled easily in cultural circles, as well as younger, less visible men like Max Isenbergh and Phil Coombs of the State Department, whose commitment to the arts may have been more businesslike, but who were equally caught up in the spirit of the Kennedy administration, and who sought to insure a place for the arts on the New Frontier. It was Isenbergh, in September 1961, who drafted an early, unofficial cultural policy for the New Frontier, providing a fascinating glimpse of the new federal philosophy that included the arts in its broad sweep.

Isenbergh prepared his paper in anticipation of a dinner, held "to discuss questions of a national cultural policy" on 20 September 1961 and attended by Schlesinger, Salinger, Coombs, and Arthur Goldberg.[7] Although only slightly more than three pages in length (with a two-page list of "Issues Bearing upon National Cultural Policy"), the paper managed to encompass the two major arguments in support of a federal arts effort—that standby of the fifties, international relations, along with the arts community's newest trump card, the national pursuit of excellence. The paper was cast, moreover, in that visionary light so suggestive of the mood of the early sixties, when notions of Camelot captured the national attention. Isenbergh's paper was sufficiently realistic to acknowledge the worldwide pressures of the period, but it was not for a moment deterred by these events. In the fall of 1961, it seemed, anything was possible.

"That other great issues at home and abroad press upon the nation," wrote Isenbergh,

> does not mean that this is the wrong moment to start. On the contrary, in times like these, the decisive national resources are courage and resolution, and nothing can add to these as well as the vision of a worthy goal beyond current crises and the sense of moving toward it despite the sense of stalemate or setback elsewhere.
>
> At the least, therefore, a serious effort to improve the quality of American cultural life would be a boost to national morale. It would inevitably be more. It would confirm that in the endless striving for peace and material well-being, we have not lost sight of why we want them. And if it resulted, as thoughtfully and energetically carried out it surely could, in restoring the pursuit of happiness to the place it had in American thought and faith at the time of the Declaration of Independence, it would do no less than transform the national character and open, for the whole world to see, an exhilarating new chapter in the American Revolution for the nineteen sixties.

In stating these visions of international accord and domestic well-being through the arts, Isenbergh was well aware of the work that lay ahead, of the necessary "assiduous study," as he put it, and of the "sounding of opinion in the Executive Branch" and the eventual development within that branch—foreshadowing Heckscher's appointment early the next year—of "an administrative unit specially qualified to set this new departure in motion." But Isenbergh seemed equally aware of the shifting climate of opinion regarding government and the arts, of the emergence, in particular, of a genuine cultural alliance that had been only a minor, fragmented force in the past. As Isenbergh outlined the elements necessary for the development of a national cultural policy, he offered a quick inventory of this new cultural coalition:

> For a program of cultural advancement, the Executive Branch, which must be the moving force, is strong in the essentials: the President and Mrs. Kennedy, whose personal identification with arts, letters, and learning is universally known and respected, are ideally suited for leadership in this field; cultural leaders, able and willing to contribute ideas, advice, and effort have joined the Administration in good number; public reaction promises to be dominantly favorable; Congressional support seems to be getting stronger; and private citizens, organizations, business enterprises, labor unions, and foundations, as well as academic institutions, learned and professional societies, and religious groups can be counted upon to give their backing.

The vacant position in this emerging federal cultural network, Isenbergh recognized, was an official body to lead the effort. A handful of congressmen had been attempting for several years to create an advisory arts council, of course, initially in HEW and later in the executive office, but in view of the slender prospects for the immediate success of this proposal, Isenbergh suggested "the establishment of a steering committee to lay out strategy, and get the campaign under way."

As it turned out, however, two men, each working independently but sharing the president's blessings, got that campaign underway. The first, Secretary of Labor Arthur Goldberg, emerged suddenly at the close of 1961 as the New

Frontier's unofficial cultural spokesman. He was followed soon after by August Heckscher, the nation's first *official* cultural spokesman, and a precursor of the elaborate federal arts structure that was finally established in 1965.

"An Event of Larger Significance"

In his list of ten national cultural issues that he appended to his paper, Isenbergh proved to be prophetic with the very last item: "What steps should the Federal Government take to counteract economic conditions unfavorable to the arts?" Admittedly, this issue was an old one, having been raised repeatedly, without receiving much public attention, throughout the fifties. But it was also an issue that would serve as one of the primary catalysts of the federal arts movement in the sixties, joining the national pursuit of excellence and replacing international relations as the arts advocates' key argument for a federal arts program. No longer the chronic gripe of the musicians union or the annual lament of cultural fund raisers, the economic plight of the arts in America, and of the performing arts in particular, received widespread attention in the sixties. Perhaps the first hint that something was amiss in the arts was the strike that hit Broadway in the spring of 1960, but it was another labor dispute the following year, involving the Metropolitan Opera and the American Federation of Musicians, that turned the nation's attention to the long-overlooked financial side of the arts.[8]

In retrospect, two decades later, the labor problems of a single New York opera company might not seem of overwhelming importance to the whole of American culture. Yet there were two important differences to this particular dispute, two factors which made the cancellation of the opera's season and its reinstatement just eleven days later front-page news. First, the Metropolitan Opera was truly a national institution, with world-renowned stars and an audience that for over twenty years had tuned in weekly to the Texaco radio broadcasts. Equally important was the role of the federal gov-

ernment in settling the dispute, for President Kennedy asked
Secretary of Labor Goldberg to intervene in an attempt to
end the strike. And, when the musicians' union and the management of the Met agreed on 28 August 1961 to submit to
Goldberg's arbitration, the president expressed the mood of
the arts community across the country—"The Metropolitan
Opera is important to the nation. I am glad we have all found
a way for it to continue"—and quietly signaled a milestone in
the long-simmering government-arts relationship.[9] The government, for all practical purposes, was back in the arts business.

The roots of this return engagement extend far beyond
the Metropolitan episode. They reach back to the WPA projects and were nurtured in the cultural diplomacy of the fifties. But the Metropolitan decision announced by Goldberg
late in 1961 *was* a landmark event, one that firmly established
the New Frontier's commitment to culture and left only the
final details—still a four-year process—to be worked out. Even
before Goldberg announced his settlement, with its visionary
scheme of a sixfold partnership of arts support, the impera-
tive of federal participation seemed clear. Indeed, the day
after the decision to arbitrate was made in August, the *New
York Times* forecast the new role for the government: "Certainly some more stable means of financing is going to be
necessary," the *Times* editorial read, responding to the opera's
$840,000 deficit from the 1960 season. "And everything points
to the fact that, if the United States is going to insist that the
Metropolitan carry on as a cultural institution that the nation
cannot afford to lose, it should provide the opera with a subsidy, with New York State and City sharing the financial responsibility."[10] Five years earlier, when schemes for government subsidy were largely the province of artists unions and
visionary arts advocates, it was all but unthinkable that the
nation's most influential newspaper would support such a plan.
Yet a series of intangibles—the cultural cold war, the spirit of
the New Frontier, and a growing sense of the irrational economy of the arts—had combined to produce the forthright
Times stance. These elements had combined, too, to produce

the Goldberg Metropolitan decision of December 1961, a re-markable document that began with the financial woes of one opera company and concluded with a stirring assessment of the state of the performing arts in America.[11]

"Because Secretary Goldberg embedded his Metropolitan award in a major plea for subsidy for the arts," one observer noted, "the subsidy idea attracted far more attention in the outside world than the award itself."[12] In fact, section three of the decision, "The State of the Performing Arts," had a life of its own quite apart from the arbitration judgment (which granted only a modest increase to the musicians' wages). It was reprinted as a separate document and, addressing as it did the performing arts in general, with its call for a "six-point partnership" of arts support, it emerged as the first official statement of the New Frontier's position on the arts.

It was Daniel Patrick Moynihan, one of Goldberg's young assistants, who wrote the crucial third section, drawing on the secretary's growing files on the Metropolitan and related matters, and weaving together a document edited by Goldberg's executive assistant, Stephen H. Shulman (and, presumably, by the secretary himself).[13] Moynihan had other sources to rely on, too, most notably John D. Rockefeller III and Senator Javits, two interested parties who shared their ideas on arts support with the secretary. Rockefeller, for example, suggested to Goldberg the notion of the arts as a "community responsibility," a theme that the famous benefactor had been using in his speeches on arts support. In a memorandum to Goldberg dated 13 November 1961, just a month before the Met decision was announced, Rockefeller spoke of the "clear call to accept the arts as a new community responsibility, that the arts be placed alongside the community's already-accepted responsibilities for health, welfare and education."[14] Senator Javits, also writing to the secretary in November, was equally specific, and nearly as influential, in his comments on the need for a federal role in arts support.

> This labor dispute, its happy resolution and the danger we ran should teach us that Federal action for the encouragement

and development of the nation's cultural resources must now be taken. It is high time that we, as a people, realize that the visual and performing arts are not a luxury but a necessity in the defense of our free society against the backdrop of the cold war.[15]

But between the two positions—Rockefeller's community responsibility and Javits's cold war—Moynihan and Goldberg hewed more closely to the former, placing economic concerns over international tensions. The split marked, as suggested earlier, the difference between the two decades themselves, between the nervous preoccupation with the Communist threat that characterized the fifties, and the problem-solving, progressive sixties, when threats were more often seen as challenges. "The financial crisis of the Metropolitan Opera," section three began, "which raised the prospect that the 1961–62 season might not take place, may prove to have been an event of larger significance in the history of American culture."

"An event of larger significance . . . " was precisely the kind of language that fired the imagination of the New Frontier, as America moved from the red scares and nagging doubts of the Eisenhower years to the promise of the Kennedy administration. Even the problems of the new decade seemed somehow fortunate: "The problems of the performing arts in America today," read the Metropolitan decision, "are not the problems of decline. They are the problems of growth: a growth so tumultuous, so eventful as to be almost universally described as an explosion."

For Moynihan and Goldberg, then, the problem of the performing arts was economic, involving rising costs and increased competition for limited funds, as more and more arts institutions sought support from fewer and fewer individual benefactors.[16] The solution to this problem was equally straightforward. The support for the arts in America was to be distributed more broadly (just as Rockefeller had suggested), with the federal government assuming a new, leading role:

We must come to accept the arts as a new community responsibility. The arts must assume their place alongside the already
accepted responsibilities for health, education and welfare.
Part of this new responsibility must fall to the Federal Government, for precisely the reasons that the nation has given it a
role in similar undertakings.

The issue of government support had been raised many
times before, but never by a spokesman for the government
itself, and never with such a matter-of-fact appraisal of that
red flag of the fifties, the specter of government control:
"The answer to the danger of political interference, then, is
not to deny that it exists, but rather to be prepared to resist
it." The very diversity of support counseled by the Metropolitan decision was one means of insuring artistic freedom, along
with the principle of matching support—now the hallmark
of federal aid to the arts—recommended by Goldberg. This
diversity was to be insured by the six-point arts-support partnership, composed of the public ("the principal source of
financial support . . . the essence of democratic culture"); the
traditional patrons and benefactors ("a continuing and vital
role"); corporations; labor; local and state governments; and
the federal government. In the last area Moynihan and Goldberg went so far as to suggest that the government become a
"direct consumer of the arts by commissioning sculpture,
painting and awarding musical scholarships," along with supporting capital construction projects for the arts. Recognizing the longstanding impediments to government action in
the arts, however, the Goldberg decision concluded more
moderately, with a call for that "most important immediate
step which the federal government may take"—the establishment of a Federal Advisory Council on the Arts.

Even before the arbitration decision was announced in
December, the Secretary of Labor had received a lot of mail
on the issue, and the response after its publication was unprecedented. Goldberg claimed that he had received more
correspondence on the Metropolitan dispute than in any other
case he had been involved with, and the response was over-

whelmingly favorable. Running nearly three-to-one in favor of his decision, with its call for federal assistance, his supporters included some powerful names in the arts world: the American Federation of Musicians, Actors Equity, the Motion Picture Association of America, the National Music Council, the National Council on the Arts and Government, and John D. Rockefeller III.[17] The opponents, for the most part, were individual citizens, like Mae Gough of Paducah, Kentucky, whose rhetoric called to mind the earlier assaults on federal subsidy plans by the National Sculpture Society and the American Artists Professional League, but who clearly lacked their organizational clout. "Is this Russia," Ms. Gough asked, not bothering to punctuate her query. "Why should Americans who detest Opera and Symphonie be forced to pay taxes to support them. Is America free. If you and the Kennedy bunch like Opera, you support it. You can afford it with all the money in the world behind you. . . ."

It was noteworthy that the woman from Paducah reduced the issue to one of dollars and cents, for that was precisely what was happening from a decidedly different perspective in another quarter, as a House subcommittee began a thorough investigation of the economic conditions of the performing arts. The effort stemmed from a resolution introduced by Representative Robert Giaimo (D-CT) early in 1961, directing the Select Subcommittee on Education "to make an intensive study of the conditions affecting the income and employment of performing artists in America, with a view to determining means by which such conditions may be improved."[18]

The subcommittee, chaired by Frank Thompson and including (at various times) friends like Giaimo and Charles Joelson (D-NJ) and foes like David Martin (R-NB), Roman Pucinski (D-IL), and Donald C. Bruce (R-IN), met in New York, San Francisco, and Washington in late 1961 and early 1962. It compiled over six hundred pages of testimony from nearly one hundred artists, producers, managers, union officials, critics, and public servants, the vast majority of whom related the same story: the arts in America were in trouble.

Such news was hardly a revelation, certainly. Even the Department of Labor's *Occupational Outlook Handbook* for 1961 had recognized the problem. "The difficulty of earning a living as a performer," the *Handbook* declared, "is one of the facts young people should bear in mind in considering an artistic career. . . . It is important for them to consider the possible advantages of making their art a hobby rather than a field of work,"[19] And arts advocates like Senator Javits and countless union officials had been bemoaning the dire economic state of the arts for several years.

But there was something starkly impressive about the litany of economic woes recited by the subcommittee witnesses, esteemed artists like Leopold Stokowski ("The future of the fine arts in the United States is in great danger"), powerful labor leaders like Herman Kenin ("It is the considered opinion of the American Federation of Musicians that serious music cannot survive much longer in the United States without assistance from Government"), and Metropolitan Opera President Anthony Bliss ("Every time the curtain goes up we lose over $3,500"). Perhaps the most eloquent witness on behalf of the arts, though, was a young dancer from the San Francisco Ballet: "Mr. Chairman and gentleman of the committee, my name is Finis Jhung. I am a soloist with the San Francisco Ballet Company. This year I have worked 24 weeks. My expenses exceed my earnings."

Although not so uniform in their versions of the solution to these problems, most of the witnesses favored some form of government action, running the traditional gamut from tax relief to the advisory council to full-scale arts subsidy. Such plans had been heard for more than a decade, however, and at the outset of the hearings Representative Thompson frankly recognized the remote chance of any immediate government action. "I rather do not expect that there will be any quaking dramatic action on the part of Congress," he declared, "because it seems that the Congress is not entirely sympathetic, to say the least, to legislation respecting the arts in almost any form."[20]

Yet, as the New Frontier had promised, and as the Metropolitan decision had signaled, the decade of the sixties marked a new era for the relationship of the arts and the state. Action *was* forthcoming on the part of the government—if not immediately in the various legislative cures that had been prescribed for years, at least in the guise of the nation's first cultural bureaucrat, the president's special consultant on the arts.

"A Quiet Inquiry, without Fanfare"

Early in December 1961, before the Goldberg decision was announced, August Heckscher, director of the Twentieth Century Fund, was asked to join the White House staff to work on cultural matters, and the new arts-and-government partnership began.[21] "I have in mind an inventory of the variety of public activities which impinge on cultural matters—" the president wrote Heckscher,

> from the construction of post offices to the imposition of taxes. Such an inventory would give us an idea of the resources, possibilities and limitations of future policy in the cultural field. Obviously government can at best play only a marginal role in our cultural affairs. But I would like to think that it is making its full contribution to this role.

The key word, surely, was "marginal"—the limited role in the arts that the president forecast for the government. "I have in mind a quiet inquiry, without fanfare." the letter to Heckscher read, "because, until the survey is completed, decisions or announcements would be premature."[22]

Heckscher began the job as the president's special consultant on the arts with somewhat loftier intentions, however. From his experience as the author of the arts statement for Eisenhower's National Goals Commission, as well as from his work with the Twentieth Century Fund (which would soon be initiating the most important economic study of the arts in the sixties), Heckscher had developed some definite ideas about the potential role of government in the arts. "I begin with the personal conviction," he wrote Arthur Schlesinger shortly before the appointment was announced,

> that the time is coming for government at varous levels to take a fresh initiative in the field of art. I do not think it is enough merely to do a little better than we have been doing. . . . Beyond all this is the opportunity for the Federal Government to encourage the States, to supplement their efforts in this field, and to initiate ways of giving support in a new dimension to the institutions of art as well as, in certain cases, a direct encouragement to individual artists.[23]

Once on the job—two days a week at the Executive Office Building across the street from the White House—Heckscher moved "without fanfare," perhaps, but with sufficient conviction to make certain the government's continuing role in the arts. If nothing else, the new special consultant served as a symbol of the federal government's emerging concern for the arts. But in more concrete terms, Heckscher performed a variety of functions in the process of gathering information for his report to the president. With the help of Barbara Donald, his full-time assistant (a former aide to Walter Lippmann who had worked with Heckscher on the Goals Commission Report), Heckscher surveyed the existing government arts activities; he monitored the various stillborn legislative proposals and ultimately coordinated the executive order establishing an advisory arts council; he examined state activities and plans for the arts and collected voluminous files of information on private arts efforts. At the president's own request he looked into foreign practices of arts support. And through his speeches and articles on government and the arts, as well as through meetings and correspondence with the arts community, Heckscher served as a kind of unofficial arts ombudsman—not so much to settle past disputes as to map out future areas of activity.[24] Along with the ever-present legislative questions, Heckscher was particularly concerned with copyright and tax provisions, design matters, arts and education, and historic preservation—actively filling in the details, in short, in that new arts partnership sketched by Goldberg in the Metropolitan decision. "When Kennedy asked me to come down," Heckscher later recalled,

> I think, as he saw it, one of my major functions was to inves-
> tigate the state of government support of the arts and to make
> a report. But I couldn't conceive it in that way alone. I didn't
> think I just ought to spend the time studying and then make
> a report. I thought I ought to spend the time acting and then
> report on the activities.[25]

In any case, Heckscher's report, *The Arts and the National Government*, appeared in May 1963. Smaller than the Commission of Fine Arts' report submitted to Eisenhower a decade earlier, Heckscher's shared with that document a certain businesslike, nuts-and-bolts quality. Neither was an especially visionary document, although Heckscher's, at least, concluded with a strong statement on the future of government involvement in the arts. Yet despite its modest size (running to only twenty-eight pages plus appendixes), the Heckscher report was more inclusive in its sweep.

Beginning with a nod to the culture-counters of the early sixties ("attendance at museums and concerts has increased dramatically"), Heckscher wove the four major arguments for a government arts program into a logical, single-minded position, one designed to attract support from a variety of quarters. First was the quality-of-life factor ("life is more than the acquisition of material goods"), a standard New Frontier fixture that was a part of the era's more general concern with America's historical image: "the United States will be judged—and its place in history ultimately assessed—not alone by its military or economic power, but by the quality of its civilization." The very magnitude of this issue led the New Frontiersman back to less grand, more introspective matters—"The evident desirability of sending the best examples of America's artistic achievements abroad has led to our looking within, to asking whether we have in fact cultivated deeply enough the field of creativity." And coming full circle back to those "material goods" earlier impugned, Heckscher embraced the new cultural materialism of the sixties, the concern with the economics of the arts, spawned by the Metropolitan Opera decision and the House subcommittee hearings, and soon to be given new prominence by Rockefeller Brothers and Twentieth Century Fund studies.

Heckscher went on to cite some of the historical precedents for the proposed government arts effort—the WPA projects, the Fine Arts Commission report, the National Cultural Center—and pointed to the inauguration and subsequent White House events as harbingers of the new era.[26] "Against this background," Heckscher wrote,

> the first Special Consultant on the Arts was named. It was understood that he would be concerned with the progress of the arts primarily as they affect not our international posture, but the well-being, the happiness, and the personal fulfillment of the citizens of our democracy. In this sense the appointment, modest in scope and tentative in form though it was, marked the beginning of a new phase in the history of art and government.

In the survey of existing government arts activities that followed, Heckscher touched upon the acquisiton of art for display in public buildings and the national collections; the raising of federal design standards (commending the president's directive of 23 May 1962 on "Guiding Principles for Federal Architecture"); historic preservation; the presentation and display of art (addressing the performing arts as well as the need for new cultural facilities); education, training, and research in the arts; and government recognition of the artist.

Heckscher also devoted a section to the longstanding concern of the Washington arts advocate with making the nation's capital a showcase for the arts. The capital "should be an example to the rest of the country," Heckscher observed, casting the New Frontier in a seventeenth-century puritan glow, with good taste replacing piety, "a symbol of the finest in our architecture, city planning, and cultural amenities and achievements—a symbol in fact of what the environment of democracy ought to be." Yet for all of these castles in the air, Heckscher provided blueprints, too, practical, no-nonsense discussions of taxation, copyright laws, postal rates, and the like. The arts advocate of the sixties, it seemed, had to work both sides of the street, mixing spiritual values with hard-edged economic schemes, broad cultural symbols with fine-print rules and regulations.

The title of the final section, "Administrative Machinery Relating to the Arts," got to the heart of that split; this "machinery" embraced the political visions of the arts community over the past fifteen years. Heckscher called for a permanent post of special consultant on the arts, for an advisory arts council within the executive office, and, as "the logical crowning step in a national cultural policy," for a national arts foundation. "What is sketched here," Heckscher explained, joining once again the imagination of the arts advocate with the restraint of the political realist,

> represents the beginning of what could become a permanent policy giving form to the relationship between government and the arts. It is a limited policy; for government's role in this area must always be marginal. It is a policy not copied after European models, but keyed to the particular conditions of diversity and decentralization prevailing in the United States.

Thus as the president had requested a year-and-a-half earlier, Heckscher wrote a report, "without fanfare," detailing the "limited," "marginal" role of the government in the arts. And yet is was an extremely effective report, possibly "a historic document," according to one observer, "surprisingly critical of the government's attitude toward the arts," according to another (writing on the front page of the *New York Times*).[27] While not exactly *Common Sense* to the revolutionaries fighting for a government arts program, it at least provided a rallying point for the arts community in the final stages of its long quest for government recognition. The Heckscher report was the first to unify the traditionally fragmented views of the arts community, tying together loose ends and forecasting a plausible federal role. Heckscher recognized that, compared to the private effort, the federal role would indeed be marginal. Yet compared to the indifferent cultural record that the federal government had compiled in the two decades following the close of the New Deal art projects, that new role could be highly significant. "Although the government's role in the arts must always remain peripheral," Heckscher concluded, "with individual creativity and private support being central, that is no reason why the things which the government can properly do in this field should not be done confidently and expertly."

"What Are the Arts?"

Confidence and expertise, unfortunately, were never the hallmarks of Congress' handling of cultural affairs. While individual representatives and senators, and even an occasional subcommittee, performed brilliantly in addressing cultural issues, for the Congress as a whole—and especially for the House—the arts were simply *terra incognita*. The subject, admittedly, did not come up that often, as the vast majority of the arts bills died quietly in committee. When the arts did come up before the full House for substantive action (far less often than the rhapsodic speeches and editorial material inserted into the *Congressional Record* imply), the results were often distressing—a grandstanding George Dondero finding Communists behind every easel, for example, or a befuddled Harold Gross damning the whole thing as a waste of the taxpayers' money. Nor did the progress made in the early years of the Kennedy administration, most notably Goldberg's Metropolitan decision and Heckscher's work as special consultant, serve to elevate the level of the cultural debates in the House. Even the mild-mannered advisory council bill, well along its ten-year odyssey in 1961, suffered another defeat at the hands of the congressional nay-sayers.

It was Representative Thompson's version of the advisory council bill, fittingly enough, that finally came to a House vote in 1961, the first such vote since a similar bill passed the

Senate in 1956. But coming under a suspension of the rules, and thus requiring a two-thirds majority to pass, the September vote was hardly a fair test. Of greater interest was the debate preceding the vote, matching the stock arts advocacy of Thompson, Halpern, Kearns, Elliott, Lindsay, and Giaimo—the importance of American culture and its dissemination, competition with communism, the economic plight of the arts, and the need to organize the various federal arts activities—against some vintage congressional corn pone served up by Representatives Gross, Smith, and Hoffman.

For Gross, who took up where Dondero left off (chasing another kind of "red menace," however), the matter was simply one of dollars and cents. "Mr. Speaker," Gross began, in a recitation that sounds hauntingly familiar twenty years later

> I do not know too much about the arts, but I do know we are more than $290 billion in the red in this country. . . . I am sure . . . spending $100,000 each year for this purpose, for culture, can very well wait until we have a balanced budget in this country and start retiring the federal debt. I just do not see any necessity for this kind of business at this time.[28]

Representative Howard Smith, too, claimed ignorance of the arts, but he used that shortcoming to lampoon the arts in a manner reminiscent of Congress' WPA follies. "I always hesitate to display my ignorance . . . ," Representative Smith declared, in a remark that must have surprised more than a few of his colleagues.

> But, the thing that troubles me is . . . what are the arts? And, here is where I display my ignorance. I do not know. What does it include? What is it about? I suppose fiddle players would be in the arts and the painting of pictures would be in the arts. It was suggested that poker playing was an artful occupation. Is this going to subsidize poker players that get into trouble? . . . What various occupations are included in the arts so we will know what we are getting into and who we will subsidize? This will not end here. This is getting "the nose under the tent."[29]

The bill in question, of course, made no mention of any federal subsidy of the arts, but that made little difference to

Smith, who, as chairman of the Rules Committee, would continue to block arts legislation from reaching the floor of the House.[30] Besides, subsidy or no, more pressing concerns than a new cultural program faced the nation, Representative Hoffman pointed out. Responding (apparently) to the Defense Department's recent call-up of troops to bring the United States, NATO, and Seventh Army forces in Europe to full combat strength, Hoffman employed a bit of creative brinksmanship to deflate the claims of the arts advocates:

> When men are being called, as they are today, to leave their homes and go to war, a war which will strain our ability to provide adequate munitions of war, why should we create a council to provide a balance of representation among the major arts? Or, for that matter, any of the activities named. True, music may cheer the boys as they march off to war or welcome a lessened number as they return, leaving many of those who marched and fought behind.
>
> Why study at the taxpayers' expense, painting, sculpture, motion pictures, and TV or dances, while preparing for a war which we lack the dollars to carry on?

Thompson's bill came to a vote of the full House on 21 September 1961, and although it was in one sense close—166 yeas to 173 nays—it was far from the 226 votes required under a suspension of the rules.[31] The party lines, at least, were clear; 81 percent of the favorable votes were cast from the Democratic side of the aisle, while 92 percent of the nays were cast by Republicans and southern Democrats.

Such votes, however, never really settle issues, and the federal arts debate continued. A televised version featured Russell Lynes and John Kenneth Galbraith on 11 February 1961. Galbraith was an odd choice as a spokesman for the arts advocates, and his philosophical ponderings were no match for the clever logic of the *Harper's* editor, who called government subsidy a step backward to predemocratic times and warned of the "creeping philistinism" that might result from an official arts agency.[32] But the debate was larger than the individual clash on the NBC broadcast (on a series aptly titled "The Nation's Future") and was destined to be won by the more organized side, the side that could turn those 166 yeas or 173 nays into the 218 needed for a simple majority in the House. "This is the only way a member of Congress will vote," Thompson declared a few months after his arts council bill had been defeated. "They are very pragmatic, you know. They are going to vote if the people are interested in it and if they hear from them. Some little veterans' post can get more out of a Congressman now than all of the people who are interested in the arts put together can. It is an amazing thing, but it is true.[33]

In the sixties, at last, the arts community began to develop the organizational clout needed to overcome the conservative core of outright opposition and the large, middling mass of indifference in Congress, a combination that throughout the fifties had frustrated the legislative efforts on behalf of the arts. In a letter to Lynes, a wistful Charles Mark, head of the new antifederalist local arts council movement, noted the new tide of organized, blue-ribbon support for a federal arts program. "On the one side stand those of us who have committed our lives and energies to the mustering of voluntary support," wrote Mark,

> following the outlines laid down by the Community Chest movement. . . . The other side . . . is represented by the National Council on the Arts and Government, headed by Harold Weston. The array of names they display on their letterheads is frightening. All we have to oppose them is an organization without budget or organization. Eight of us have formed the Community Arts Councils, Inc. to represent the voluntary movement.[34]

Even while the arts council bill was bottled up in the Rules Committee once again in 1962—as Representative Smith abruptly called a vote while three of the bill's supporters were absent—the organizational wheels in the arts community had been turning. Dating to the Committee on Government and Art and the NCAG of the fifties, the movement gained new momentum in 1961, when Leonard Bernstein, Ralph Bellamy, Marian Anderson, Van Cliburn, and Lloyd Goodrich met to discuss plans to support Senator Fulbright's bill to consolidate the nation's various cultural and educational exchange programs.[35] The following year, Frank Thompson and John Lindsay (along with Jack Golodner, the former Giaimo aide who, hired by Actors Equity, became the first arts lobbyist in Washington) helped organize a citizens committee, headed by Richard Rodgers and including Leopold Stokowski, Louis Untermeyer, Ralph Bellamy, James Cagney, and Risë Stevens, to help build popular support for the advisory council plan.[36]

Equally important was the gradual unfolding of two other organizational developments—a shift in the American Symphony Orchestra League membership's position regarding federal arts support, and the entrance of the university community into the battle for a federal cultural program. The membership of the ASOL, it will be remembered, included prominent citizens who make up the boards of symphony orchestras across the country and had been one of the staunchest opponents of federal arts legislation during the fifties. Led by its executive secretary, Helen Thompson, the ASOL came out strongly on the side of voluntary, private support of the arts, with 91 percent of its membership opposed to a federal program in 1953. Even as late as the 1961–62 economics-of-the-arts hearings, the ASOL, while tempering its earlier opposition, was unable to declare itself in favor of a federal program, much to Frank Thompson's displeasure ("if you could make up your minds . . . ," he grumbled). But indications of a "tremendous shift in community sentiment toward approval of Federal subsidy for the arts" became apparent at the ASOL convention later in 1962, according to Helen Thompson. There was still a wide disparity in the ASOL viewpoint, and the survey was incomplete, but even the admission of debate was striking in an organization that just a few years earlier was almost unanimous in its opposition to any federal effort.[37] At another Senate subcommittee hearing on arts legislation in August 1962, Ms. Thompson still could not report any unanimity in the ASOL viewpoint, but the stakes themselves had been raised considerably: ASOL representatives were now polling the membership on *cabinet* status for the arts, a proposed Department of Cultural Affairs.[38] Ms. Thompson cited two reasons for the shifting climate of opinion within the orchestral community—economic pressures (especially union demands for lengthened seasons and higher wages), and the "unprecedented interest and support" of the White House in cultural matters (most notably the appointment of August Heckscher, the series of performances at the White House, and the president's support for the National Cultural Center). Thus the stage was set for the influential organization's emergence at the crucial Senate Subcommittee on the Arts and Humanities hearings in 1965 in the growing ranks of the federal arts advocates.

The stage was also being set for the entrance of the academic community into the federal arts debates, long after the arts community had taken up the battle shortly after World War II. In the legislative arena, a new variety of arts bill appeared in 1962, when Representative John Fogarty (D-RI) introduced legislation to create a National Institute for the Arts and Humanities (NIAH) within the Office of Education. The bill was designed to fund research and training in the arts and the humanities, and included a provision for a Federal Advisory Council on the Arts and Humanities, to provide advice on areas of federal support and to identify critical needs to the commissioner of education and the secretary of health, education, and welfare.[39] "There is a pressing need today," Fogarty declared when he introduced his bill on 17 July 1962, "for Federal legislation that will build up nationwide support for the arts and humanities, on a basis comparable to the support that is provided in other areas, such as science and technology. Progress in the arts and humanities is essential." The relationship between culture and technology—and the need in particular to achieve a better balance between the two—had been raised before, of course, but Fogarty was among the first in Congress to seize upon education as the crucial link between the two worlds. "The way to attack the problem," Fogarty pointed out, speaking specifically to the economic plight of the arts but placing his remarks in the larger context of American culture, "is to undergird the development, the preservation and extension of our cultural resources through our educational systems and institutions."

The idea for a cultural equivalent to the National Science Foundation belonged actually to Barnaby Keeney, president of Brown University, who persuaded Fogarty to introduce the NIAH bill. Keeney's participation was especially important, for it led to the creation, early in 1963, of a National Commission on the Humanities, cosponsored by three academic heavyweights—the American Council of Learned Societies, the Council of Graduate Schools of the United States, and the United Chapters of Phi Beta Kappa. Although the commission's key report would not be issued until April 1964, the impact of the university community's involvement in the legislative battle was felt much sooner. Six months after the introduction of his bill, Representative Fogarty proudly displayed in the *Congressional Record* a lengthy list of new-found academic supporters, making it clear that the arts advocates' team had a whole set of fresh forces anxious to enter the fray.[40]

Thus with the arts community gradually falling into line behind the pro-subsidy position, and with the addition of the articulate and powerful academic forces, the prospects for a new federal program looked especially bright as the New Frontier entered its third year. Congress still stood in the way, perhaps, but the White House was already developing a plan to circumvent that very obstacle.

Executive Order 11112

"The majority in political life at all levels still tend to talk of culture as if they were telling an off-color story," August Heckscher told the American Federation of Arts convention in 1963.[41] Heckscher was doubtless overstating the case, but he was not too far off the mark. When it came to anything more ambitious than the advisory council legislation, the reaction in the House could be strikingly similar to Heckscher's description. "It is a rather devastating thing to bring one of these bills up before the House and to hear some of its very senior Members ridicule it . . . ," Frank Thompson told a Senate subcommittee in 1962, commenting on the chances for subsidy legislation in the House. "It is very easy to get laughed out of the hall," he continued. "We find that this is one of the very difficult things about it. I do not think that the climate in the House with respect to subsidies is such that there would be much chance."[42]

But while there was little substantive action in the House following the aborted advisory council bill of 1961, the arts advocates in the Senate were quite active in 1962 and 1963, coming up with three major arts bills and two subcommittee hearings. The first hearing was little more than a dress rehearsal for the fall political campaign, but it gave Senators Humphrey, Clark, and Javits a chance to display their legislative wares. The three bills under consideration at the late August 1962 hearings were Humphrey's S. 741 (Federal Advisory Council on the Arts), Clark's S. 785 (the National Cultural Development Act, authorizing $5 million for grants to the states for arts projects), and Javits's visionary S. 1250 (the United States Arts Foundation, authorizing $5 million initially and $10 million annually thereafter to support non-profit performing and visual arts projects).[43] Realistically, only Humphrey's bill had a chance of passing, a fact underscored by the Department of Health, Education, and Welfare, the Bureau of Budget, and the Commission of Fine Arts, all of whom recommended the passage of the advisory council bill before either of the arts-funding proposals be considered. Even if it had managed to pass in the Senate (as it had in 1956), the bill was doomed ultimately by its Republican and Dixiecrat opponents in the House.

While no legislative victories were forthcoming, the 1962 Senate subcommittee hearings were notable for the prophetic omnibus bill that emerged from the full Labor and Public Welfare Committee the following month. Although bearing the designation of Humphrey's advisory council bill (S. 741), the measure was much more than that.[44] "The bill is

basically my weaving together of Jack Javits' bill to help disseminate the works of the performing and visual arts to the
hinterlands," an enthusiastic Senator Pell wrote the president's wife, "together with Joe Clark's idea of Federal distribution of matching funds to state groups, in order that individual art councils and programs might be established. This
matching fund provision to each state has great political appeal, in that it means that each state derives some benefits
from such a program."[45]

The bill, now known as the National Arts and Cultural
Development Act of 1963, was reintroduced the following
session and enjoyed another round of Senate subcommittee
hearings in late October and early November.[46] By then it
had become woefully apparent, however, that it was easier
for the proverbial camel to pass through the eye of the needle
than for arts legislation to pass through the House, and thus
plans were made to create an advisory council by executive
order. Senator Humphrey had broached the matter to August Heckscher as early as April 1962, and in a memorandum
to Arthur Schlesinger two weeks later, Heckscher described
the gathering of support for the creation of the long-awaited
advisory arts council by executive action:

> Secretary Ribicoff, though supporting the [arts council] bill
> publicly, has told me that he does not think it should be in
> HEW. Secretary Goldberg in his statement at the time of the
> Metropolitan Opera dispute supported the bill as "the most
> important immediate step" which the government could take.
> Mr. Goldberg has said privately, however, that he thinks it
> would be wiser for the President to set up such a Council by
> executive order. Representative Thompson has indicated he
> would be willing to go along with any solution which might be
> acceptable to all concerned. Senator Humphrey in a letter to
> me of April 18 suggests the immediate appointment by the
> President of an Advisory Council on the Arts which he be-
> lieves would be the best way to achieve eventual statutory au-
> thorization which he favors.[47]

In anticipation of the event, August Heckscher began
compiling in the fall of 1962 the names of the potential can-

didates for the thirty private citizens who would serve on the council, and he drafted a resolution for the creation of an advisory council by executive order in November. But the president, ever sensitive to his delicate (and often uneasy) relations with the Hill, was reluctant to appear to have over-stepped Congress with such an order. Thus he would not act until the leading arts advocates of both parties—Frank Thompson and John Lindsay—assured the president that there was no chance for passage of the arts bill in the House. Frank Thompson publicly announced in March 1963 his support of the plan, and the following month a front-page story in the *New York Times* told of the president's intentions to issue an executive order "within two or three weeks." Those weeks turned out to be months, but finally on 12 June 1963, the president issued Executive Order 11112, establishing the President's Advisory Council on the Arts.[48]

"Establishment of an Advisory Council on the Arts," the president's statement read,

> has long seemed a natural step in fulfilling the Government's responsibility to the arts. I acknowledge the support of Members of the Congress in both Houses for this measure. I am hopeful that the Congress will give the Council a statutory base, but, meanwhile, the setting up of the Council by Executive action seems timely and advisable. . . .
>
> The creation of this Council means that for the first time the arts will have some formal Government body which will be specifically concerned with all aspects of the arts and to which the artist and the arts institutions can present their views and bring their problems.

The balance of the president's statement (drafted by Heckscher) reflected the welter of concerns that surrounded the arts-and-government debate—the economic issues that had emerged from Thompson's subcommittee hearings in 1961–62 ("a recent estimate by the Department of Labor presents a gloomy forecast of employment opportunities for the next decade"); the quality of professionalism that Heckscher had stressed in his report ("without the professional performer and the creative artist, the amateur spirit declines and the vast audience is only partially served"); and the need, expressed by John D. Rockefeller and Arthur Goldberg in particular, for cultural affairs to assume their rightful place among the other concerns of government ("we have agencies of the Government which are concerned with the welfare and advancement of science and technology, of education, recreation, and health. We should now begin to give similar attention to the arts"). Among the areas that he wanted the advisory council to investigate, the president cited the following: opportunities for arts training and participation of the young; emerging forms and institutions, including the growing number of state arts councils; the impact of government operations on the arts, including tax and copyright laws, public works, housing, and urban renewal; public recognition of excellence in the arts, including prizes, competitions, festivals, tours, and exhibitions; and the implications of the national cultural scene for cultural exchange projects. And while he made no direct reference to the question of subsidy, the president's closing remarks admitted at least the possibility of some federal action in this regard:

> The cultural life of the United States has at its best been varied, lively, and decentralized. It has been supported—often with great generosity—by private patrons. I hope these characteristics will not change, but it seems well to assess how far the traditional sources of support meet the needs of the present and the near future. In giving form to this reassessment the President's Advisory Council on the Arts will be making a most important contribution to the national life.

The names of the thirty private citizens on the council were to be announced "shortly," but although a list was approved by the president on 18 June 1963, no announcement was made.[49] Changes were subsequently made in that list by Richard Goodwin, head of the International Secretariat of the Peace Corps who was to become Heckscher's successor in the fall of 1963. To accommodate some additional names, the president on 29 October 1963 amended his executive order to expand the council membership to include forty citizens.[50]

Still, no announcement was made, and some of those who lauded the executive order in June began to question the president's sincerity that fall, as the paper council languished without members. Finally, on the morning of 22 November 1963, the president instructed Goodwin to prepare a press release announcing his appointment as special consultant on the arts and head of the advisory council, and to notify the persons selected for that body.[51]

That announcement, which was to have been released on the president's return from Dallas, was never made.

Had the arts not been so centrally tied to the Kennedy administration, they might have easily been lost in the shuffle of events following the assassination. As it turned out, however, far from being forgotten, the proposed government arts effort became one of the enduring symbols of the late president's administration. Indeed, almost immediately, at Lyndon Johnson's request, the National Cultural Center project was renamed the John F. Kennedy Memorial Center for the Performing Arts as a living monument to the late president, and after several years of a pipedream-and-blueprint existence, the center's future was secure.[52] As for the other aspects of a domestic cultural program, it was merely a matter of time and the working out of details before they, too, would be added to the legacy of the New Frontier—and, more properly, to the legacy of two decades of discussion and debate.

The National Foundation on the
Arts and Humanities

Just a week after the assassination of President Kennedy, Arthur Schlesinger, Jr. sent a memorandum to Lyndon Johnson on the matter of a federal cultural policy. He cited the work that August Heckscher had done for the Kennedy administration, and the late president's plans to appoint Richard Goodwin as Heckscher's successor and chairman of the advisory arts council. All of these matters were in limbo until the new president acted, however. "The question is whether you want to go ahead with this effort," Schlesinger reminded the president; "I hope very much that you will." Among the arguments Schlesinger employed to persuade President Johnson—the opportunities to raise design standards and clarify federal policies bearing indirectly on the arts, to work with the emerging state arts agencies and explore new means of public and private support—surely the most attractive to a veteran campaigner like Johnson were the political implications of a federal arts program. "It can strengthen the connections between the Administration and the intellectual and artistic community—," Schlesinger promised, "something not to be dismissed when victory or defeat next fall will probably depend on who carries New York, Pennsylvania, California, Illinois and Michigan." And finishing with one of those rhetorical flourishes that made the arts so useful in smoothing over the rough edges of politics, Schlesinger quoted the President's Goals Commission of 1960: "In the eyes of posterity, the success of the United States as a civilized society will be largely judged by the creative activities of its citizens in art, architecture, literature, music, and the sciences."[1]

If the new president's attitude toward the arts remained uncertain in the early days of his administration—and many were convinced that the "eyes of posterity" would look back

on more barbecues than musical soirees in the Johnson White
House—a handful of senators were determined to keep the
New Frontier's cultural spirit alive. Only a few weeks after
the assassination Senator Claiborne Pell (D-RI) cited the positive influence of the late president and his wife, and spoke
passionately of the importance of the arts to the future of
American civilization; in the process, he fended off Strom
Thurmond's (R-SC) constitutional arguments against a federal arts program and set the tone for the final two years of
arts debates. "Art is no longer the privileged domain of a
relatively few practitioners and connoisseurs," declared Pell
in defense of Hubert Humphrey's "National Arts and Cultural Development Act of 1963," which called for both an
advisory arts council and an arts foundation;

> it no longer exists in a remote and rarified atmosphere. It can
> no longer be considered as incidental or peripheral to our way
> of life. It is central to the life we cherish and to the beliefs we
> hold; for as a nation we are reaching toward maturity, and the
> surest sign of maturity lies in the growing expression of an
> indigenous and creative national culture.

Although unable to resist another cold war bulletin ("the
Russians and the Chinese are making tremendous 'hay' in
terms of impressing upon other peoples the fact that they
sponsor such extraordinarily gifted organizations and artists"), Jacob Javits also stressed the historical importance of a
new federal arts program. "The grandeur and dignity of our
nation are at stake," he declared.[2]

On the strength of such proclamations as these—and in
the absence of ninety-two of their colleagues—eight senators
passed Humphrey's S. 2379 on a voice vote on 20 December
1963, with only Strom Thurmond offering any opposition.[3]
The House still presented a formidable roadblock, of course,
but the Senate, at least, had recorded its support not only for
the advisory arts council, but for a $10 million arts founda-
tion as well. While the House would not hold its hearings on
the bill until the spring of 1964, and would not act on the
matter until late summer, stirrings in the White House indi-
cated that the spirit of the Kennedys might still be alive.

The *New York Times* reported late in 1963 that Johnson was undertaking a study of the late president's cultural policies, in an effort to counteract the feeling that the new administration was indifferent to the arts. August Heckscher, still active occasionally in White House cultural affairs while awaiting the appointment of a successor, urged Johnson to continue Kennedy's cultural plans by appointing a special arts consultant and an advisory arts council.[4] But reluctant merely to follow in Kennedy's footsteps, Johnson appointed a panel in January—Assistant Secretary of State Lucius Battle, violinist Isaac Stern, lawyer and friend Abe Fortas, and White House Press Secretary Pierre Salinger—to devise a plan of action in the arts.[5] Fortas reported back to the president late in January that the committee recommended the "adoption of a new cultural policy for the federal government." The proposed policy, however, with its emphasis on upgrading existing federal programs, the use of the Kennedy Center as a showcase for the best talent in the country, and the mobilization of private-sector support, was hardly new. But the committee did come up with a candidate to succeed Heckscher—Kennedy Center Chairman Roger Stevens—and it produced a new version of the advisory council theme as well.[6] A nine-member Presidential Board on the Arts should be created by executive order, according to the committee, with an advisory panel for each of nine branches of activities (architecture, music, literature, theater, dance, visual arts, television, motion pictures, and international activities). Additionally, a nonprofit corporation should be formed, funded by private sources, with the Presidential Board serving as trustees of the foundation.[7]

In February the *New York Times* reported that the appointment of Stevens and the Presidential Board would be made shortly by executive order, and rhapsodized in a subsequent editorial that "a new and fruitful relationship has been developing between the Federal government and the arts."[8] As usual, however, it was a while before that new relationship bore any real fruit, and when the *Washington Post* proclaimed in a front-page story a few days later that Jackie

Kennedy and not Roger Stevens would be appointed to the post of Special White House Arts Consultant, it appeared that the federal government was no closer to developing a coherent arts policy than it had ever been.[9] August Heckscher reflected the impatient mood of the arts community in a speech in New York in March, declaring that the cultural program begun under Kennedy was in danger of fading into insignificance through delay and confusion on the part of the Johnson administration.[10] Although Johnson did appoint Roger Stevens as his special assistant later that spring, he reneged on his promise of an advisory body ("I shall shortly issue an Executive Order establishing a Presidential board on the arts," the president had announced on 16 April), and it remained for Congress to act on the federal arts policy.[11] That action, too, was slow in developing, as a subcommittee chaired by the indefatigable Frank Thompson conducted yet another hearing on government and the arts.

"The Camel's Nose Under the Tent"

After more than a decade of such affairs, the House subcommittee hearings in the spring of 1964 were fairly predictable.[12] They marked, in fact, both in the witnesses heard and the legislation finally recommended, the close of an era. Twenty-five witnesses (and scores of correspondents) drawn from what might loosely be termed the "arts lobby"—artists, arts administrators, union officials, critics, and sympathetic legislators (led by Senators Pell and Javits and Representative Lindsay)—duly rehearsed the standard arguments in favor of federal arts support. Thompson and his colleagues heard once more of the economic problems of the arts, of the importance of cultural dissemination at home and cultural exchange abroad, of the examples of the British and Canadian—and now the New York State—arts councils, and of the need to find rewarding ways to fill America's increasing amounts of leisure time. Of slightly newer vintage, but standard sixties arts advocacy nevertheless, was the notion of the arts as part of the nation's "general welfare," the notion of a federal responsibility, that is, to foster cultural opportunities just as the government insured domestic tranquillity and provided for the common defense.

"Nearly two centuries have passed since there came out of Philadelphia that declaration 'to promote the general welfare,'" Pittsburgh musicians union president Hal C. Davis reminded the subcommittee.

> We musicians, and our equally underprivileged brethren in the other performing arts, submit to you that our forefathers then were not talking only of the Federal government's obligations to aid alone farmers, sea and air carriers and the countless other necessities of a materialistic existence. They were talking also—we suggest to you—about the Government's obligation to help keep alive and healthy those human resources of cultural bent and talent without whose contribution we cannot reflect to the world around us as a mature civilization.[13]

Davis, then, tied the general welfare argument to America's image abroad, the latter point almost certain to strike a responsive chord in Congress. Others took a narrower, more pragmatic approach, turning from the public welfare to the economic welfare of the arts and stressing the potential catalytic role of the government in the area of arts support, with federal funds stimulating increased private support. "Just as Government support stimulates private money for scientific research . . . ," musician Henry Shaw told the subcommittee, "so it would support and stimulate the arts." In reference to the council and foundation legislation at hand, Representative Thompson noted that "there have been some interesting studies which reveal that there can be expected the generation of $8 more spending for each dollar put into the arts by this priming device."[14]

All of these arguments, the product of fifteen years of debate, had begun to lose some of their luster by 1964. Perennial arts advocate Thompson "was once again optimistic— the constituency in favor of this legislation is growing by leaps and bounds"—but cautious as well. "I hope very much that we won't suffer another defeat," Thompson admitted at the 1964 hearings, "because I think we all know that they are not only humiliating, but they establish in the minds of our colleagues an impenetrable wall." John Lindsay, who from the start had doubts about the propriety of federal subsidy, also displayed pessimism. "I only hope that it can survive the House of Representatives," he said of the House companion of the Senate-passed arts foundation bill. "I do not wish to take another beating on this subject. It would set us back even further than we were set back 4 years ago when the Arts Council bill was beaten."[15]

It is not surprising that the full Committee on Education and Labor voted in June to report only title I of the National Arts and Cultural Development Act of 1963, recommending the creation of an advisory council but rejecting the proposed arts foundation. Still sensitive, moreover, to the old fears of federal control—despite the absence of funds in the legislation for federal arts support—the committee also added to the bill the reassuring note that "the growth and flourishing of the arts depend upon freedom, imagination, and individual initiative."[16] Five Republicans on the committee, however, found neither this declaration nor the stripped-down version of the bill itself acceptable. They offered their arguments, equally ancient as those of the arts advocates but far more colorful, in a minority viewpoint appended to the committee report. Citing the ever-popular national debt and the fact that Congress had already *enacted* arts legislation (the National Cultural/Kennedy Center), the five representatives blasted the arts council bill as an unwarranted federal encroachment into the private sector: "The bill, as reported, is a classic example of a resort to the camel's nose under the tent routine." Painting a rather exaggerated picture of the opposition forces, the conservatives declared that "the pending legislation is the culmination of a sustained effort over the years to promote large-scale intervention by the Federal Government into the area of the arts." That intervention, finally, would be orchestrated by the supposedly harmless advisory council itself:

Inevitably, if not immediately, we can fully expect this Council to come forward with a recommended Federal arts program which will far exceed anything which has thus far been proposed. We can fully expect, if this bill is sanctioned, that the Federal government, in the name of art and culture, will soon be called upon to subsidize everything from belly-dancing to the ballet; from Handel to the Hootenanny; from Brahms to the Beatles; from symphonies to the striptease.[17]

While that particular list of coming attractions was a little off the mark, the five Republicans were not incorrect, after all, in their predictions of an eventual full-blown arts subsidy program. It was not the advisory council, however, that fueled the new program. Indeed, the council had not even met by the time that the foundation legislation was introduced and endorsed by the White House in 1965. Rather, it was the entrance of a new force in the cultural debates, the academic community, adding prestige and the magic word "humanities" to the arts movement, that made the difference. In the space of a year, the movement was transformed from a tent show, creeping along from one Congress to the next with only small increases in attendance each session, to a veritable political bandwagon. Coupled with the humanities, the arts became a respectable force in American politics.

"A Program for All Our People"

The arts advocates and their new scholarly allies turned to the sciences, finally, for a model of federal support. The National Science Foundation, which had begun modestly in 1951 with a budget of $225,000, but which was approaching one-half *billion* dollars by the middle sixties, provided not only the model, but its magnitude dramatized the need for countervailing arts and humanities support. Or so the argument ran in educational circles, the latest force to enter the arts debate. Misgivings about the imbalance between culture and technology, between the arts and sciences, had begun to surface in the late fifties. Nor were those doubts limited to artists and aestheticians. In 1960, for example, the president's Science Advisory Committee declared itself strongly in favor of a balanced curriculum:

> We repudiate emphatically any notion that science research and scientific education are the only kinds of learning that matter in America. The responsibility of this Committee is limited to scientific matters, but obviously a high civilization must not limit its efforts to science alone. Even in the interests of science itself it is essential to give full value and support to the other great branches of man's artistic, literary, and scholarly activity.[18]

The Commission on the Humanities, as noted in the previous chapter, took up the cause early in 1963, and its report issued in the spring of 1964 became the definitive document in support of a federal cultural program.[19] Yet however much the arts advocates welcomed the reinforcements from the academic community, they must have been more than a little surprised by the transformation that had taken place in their program. For suddenly the call was being made for a National Humanities Foundation, and the arts advocates, having run the family business singlehandedly for fifteen years and more, now found themselves the junior partners in a new concern. As veteran arts advocate Harold Weston of the National Council on the Arts and Government put it at the conclusion of the campaign, "When this legislation came to the home stretch in Congress, the arts were hanging onto the coattails of the fast-running sponsors of the humanities."[20]

The arts-subsidy movement, bogged down for so many years over the advisory council issue, was in need of a transfusion of energy and ideas, certainly, and the Commission on the Humanities provided both. In its definition of the humanities—inclusive of the arts and extending far beyond academia—the commission staked a large claim for its constituency, and demanded a correspondingly major role for the government in support of the humanities. For the humanities "not only record our lives," the commission insisted, "our lives are the very substance they are made of. Their subject is every man. We propose, therefore, a program for all our people, a program to meet a need no less serious than that for national defense. We speak, in truth, for what is being defended—our beliefs, our ideals, our highest achievements."[21]

If the logic of the brief report was not always crystal clear, delving as it did into spiritual matters more closely associated with Fourth of July orations than with scholarly essays ("upon the humanities depend the national ethic and morality, the national aesthetic and beauty or the lack of it"), the political appeal of the new, expanded cultural movement was immediately apparent. Here, at last, was a proposal for a federally funded cultural program with more tangible social benefits than the arts program alone could offer. Although no one had argued that the dissemination of culture was not a meritorious objective, it was difficult to say precisely *why* the residents of Fargo, North Dakota, should experience live professional theater or a first-rate symphony orchestra. For many in Congress, moreover, even the admission of the uplifting effects of culture did not explain why funds for such activities should come from Washington instead of Fargo itself. But support for the *humanities*, as the commission pointed out and as Congress was soon convinced, would serve the nation in both its internal operations and its international affairs.

The benefits cited were, to a large extent, the same ones of tone and image, of the *quality* of American life and the country's reputation abroad, that the arts advocates had touted for so long. But the commission stressed as well the *vision* for America that the humanities offered, a vision never spelled out, of course—the humanities were to be as free of federal control as the arts—but rather one whose details were to be filled in as the Great Society or the Republican version of the ideal state unfolded. The federally funded humanists, it seemed, would clarify the rules of the game, promoting good sportsmanship, fair play, and an understanding of the overall design of the contest, while leaving the actual play itself to their fellow citizens. "It is both the dignity and the duty of humanists," the commission solemnly declared, "to offer their fellow-countrymen whatever understanding can be attained by fallible humanity of such enduring values as justice, freedom, virtue, beauty, and truth. Only then do we join ourselves to the heritage of our nation and our human kind." Such values are especially important in America, the report urged, for its citizen-sovereigns must possess wisdom in order to perform their political tasks in an enlightened fashion. Again, the commission was not concerned with details, with the reality of conveying knowledge and wisdom to the masses. At this point, apparently, it was sufficient simply to invoke the presence of the humanities, employing lofty rhetoric and sage advice ("to know the best that has been thought and said in former times can make us wiser than we otherwise might be") in order to build a case for federal support of the humanities.

And if the hazy "general welfare" argument of the arts advocates was transformed by the Humanities Commission into a more politically persuasive program of guidance and wisdom, the international argument was also reworked. No longer simply a case for the adoption of European practices of government arts support and for the importance of cultural exchange in the cold war, the humanists' international argument stressed more substantive matters—the need to communicate with and understand other cultures, and to base our world leadership on something other than military might alone. "Only the elevation of its goals and the excellence of its conduct," declared the commission, sounding for a moment like the founding fathers, "enable one nation to ask others to follow its lead."

Even the leisure-time argument, part of the arts advocates' concern with the larger aspects of American civilization but never one of their strongest points, assumed a philosophical significance in the hands of the Humanities Commission. "'What shall I do with my spare time?' all-too-quickly becomes the question 'Who am I? What shall I make of my life?'" the commission observed, again sounding quaintly old-fashioned, hearkening back to the Puritans in its outlook.

Were it the Bible and Christian conduct and not the humanities and self-expression that were being preached, in fact,
some of the commission's statements might be worthy of Cot-
ton Mather.

> When men and women find nothing within themselves but
> emptiness, they turn to trivial and narcotic amusements, and
> the society of which they are a part becomes socially delin-
> quent and potentially unstable. The humanities are the im-
> memorial answer to man's questioning and to his need for self-
> expression; they are uniquely equipped to fill the "abyss of
> leisure."[22]

Turning to economics, finally, the commission, while it
could not point to starving humanists or debt-ridden English
departments, did raise the issue of the growing imbalance in
academia between the well-funded sciences and the financially malnourished humanities. To remedy this imbalance,
and to help fulfill the promise of the humanities, the commission proposed a National Humanities Foundation to parallel the National Science Foundation. In sharp contrast to
the rhapsodic prose with which the commission had described the powers of the humanities, the description of the
proposed foundation itself was rather prosaic. While designed "to develop and promote a broadly conceived policy
of support for the humanities and the arts," the foundation
appeared to be more concerned with the training of teachers
and the support of scholars than with either policy questions
in general or the arts in particular. Touching on such matters
as publishing and disseminating scholarly works, teacher-im-
provement programs, and the constructing and equipping of
buildings, the commission described the foundation's major
function as ensuring "that suitable means are provided for
educating and developing scholars, artists, and teachers at
every stage of their growth." Nor was it surprising, then, that
the first review of the report, a favorable notice in the *New
York Times*, ignored the arts component altogether and viewed
the effort as one of educational reform.[23]

But if the arts momentarily got lost in the shuffle of the

rallying academic forces, the effect in the long run was beneficial to the arts. For if nothing else, the *Report of the Commission on the Humanities* got the attention of Congress. Within two months Representative William Moorhead (D-PA) introduced the first of what would become the single most popular legislative item in the House in 1965.[24] The president endorsed the proposal in a speech a short time later. "I look with the greatest of favor upon the proposal . . . for a national foundation for the humanities," Johnson declared in September 1964 to a Brown University audience that included Barnaby Keeney, the school's president and Humanities Commission chairman, and Senator Claiborne Pell.[25] Before Congress could turn its attention to the proposed humanities foundation, however, it had to dispense with some other unfinished cultural business—the National Council on the Arts—which had been languishing in the House for more than a decade.

"A Nation in Its Prime"

Although he probably had not given much consideration to the distinction between the new humanities and the old arts legislation, Johnson went on record in favor of the latter, too. In a letter to Speaker of the House John McCormack dated 18 August 1964, the president extended his "wholehearted support" to the arts council legislation. "History has shown that, if we are to achieve the great society for which we are all working," the president observed, "it is essential that the arts grow and flourish."[26]

Two days later, the bill came up for a vote in the House, and for the first time since the National Cultural Center legislation, an arts bill appeared to have more friends than enemies in Congress.[27] Indeed, twenty-five representatives (sixteen Democrats and nine Republicans) rose to speak in favor of the proposed National Council on the Arts, while only seven representatives (all Republicans) took the trouble to fight the measure. The arguments, not surprisingly, were the standard ones, and once again the conservative opponents of the bill proved to be the more imaginative of the two camps. Kentucky Republican M. G. Snyder warned his colleagues, for example, that the advisory council bill was a mere prelude to a subsidy plan that would quickly grow from ten million dollars to one hundred million dollars and, further, strangle the arts in the process. "The curtain comes down on this final act," Snyder cautioned darkly,

> with all local drama clubs, municipal symphonies, private en-
> tertainers, radio and TV stations—either under the direction
> of the newly created Fine Art Department or enjoined from
> functioning for want of a license. All art forms have become
> standardized. Progress is possible only through recognition by
> the bureaucracy. No script, song, play, poem, book, or opera
> is attributed to any one individual. All artistic efforts are the
> work of the establishment.[28]

Proponents of the bill, on the other hand, insisted on the limits of the arts council—the commitment to artistic freedom written into the bill itself—and the absence of sufficient funds to control the arts in any case.[29] But this was a well-worn debate, after all, reflecting an ideological split over the proper role of government that was unlikely to find converts on either side. The theme from the Kennedy years of the quest for excellence in American civilization, subsequently adopted by Johnson's Great Society, was perhaps the most persuasive argument of all. Even if it found more favor with Johnson Democrats than with Goldwater Republicans, it was difficult to argue against this happily all-American, self-congratulatory viewpoint. During the floor debate in August, Representative Torbert MacDonald (D-MA) made certain that the arts were placed in this perspective, that they were not left out, that is, of the grand march of American civilization. "With the passage of this legislation," he optimistically told his colleagues,

> the United States will take a further step along the path which
> saw us, first, a fledgling Nation groping for our bearings, next
> a young, vigorous people, flexing new-found muscles in a dis-

play of industrial strength and now, finally, a nation in its prime, combining raw physical strength and abundant energy with an active interest in developing our national interest.[30]

In the face of such rhetorical splendor, the conservatives could no longer hope to kill the arts council legislation, and their amendments to limit the council—one by prohibiting it from considering subsidy plans and another by delaying its authorization until the federal budget was balanced—were equally ineffective.[31] In the end, the bill swept to a 213 to 135 Democratic-led victory, and it was approved by the Senate the following day and signed by the president on 3 September 1964.[32] Thus, more than fifteen years after Jacob Javits introduced a resolution to create an assembly to investigate plans for a national theater, opera, and ballet, that assembly was created in the form of the National Council on the Arts (NCA), a direct descendant as well of the advisory arts council Eisenhower called for in 1955.

The task of constructing a domestic arts program was still incomplete, of course, and the real test of the new council, as Howard Taubman of the *New York Times* pointed out, would come in its efforts to convince Congress of the need for federal subsidy.[33] But despite some grumbling about "half a loaf," about the arts foundation measure that failed, and despite some doubts about who would be named to the council, the arts community was generally pleased with the progress made in 1964.

Few observers were as perceptive, however, as writer Mark Harris, who managed to penetrate the rhetorical layers that surrounded the NCA legislation like swaddling clothes. Underneath, according to Harris in an essay in the *New York Times Magazine*, was a strain of national self-doubt, a set of misgivings that were in part responsible for Congress' gradual acceptance of cultural legislation. For despite the merits of the prosubsidy position—the economic arguments, the genuine concern for the status of American culture, and the need to disseminate its products at home and abroad—the radical shift in the congressional viewpoint from its almost complete disavowal of any responsibility for cultural affairs following the demise of the WPA, through the indifference and confusion and hostility of the fifties, to the embrace of the arts and the humanities in the sixties, has more complex origins.

That shift must be explained in part, at least, by a collective self-consciousness about life in America—the rise-and-fall-of-Rome syndrome that found Americans simultaneously rushing headlong to greater technological heights and material wealth while looking back nervously over their shoulders all the way. On the one hand, the New Frontier and Great Society marked a new era of genuine interest in improving the quality of American civlization. "You and I have an opportunity," Johnson told the Brown audience in a revealing bit of Great Society rhetoric, "that is not unlike that of the men and women who first formed these New England states. We have the opportunity to plant the seed corn of a new American greatness and to harvest its yield in every section of this great land."[34] At the same time, this concern for quality, for "greatness," was fed by self-doubt. Harris saw in the arts-subsidy movement a desire for reassurance, for a sign, in the absence of some of the stabilizing influences of the past, that America had not lost its way. "Was any nation ever so humbly dedicated to self-improvement?" Harris wondered.

> Was any nation ever so determined to subdue its domestic enemies, whether those enemies were pockets of poverty, or—now—artistic aridity? Almost everybody, even Congressmen, appears to recognize, or anyhow to assert, that as a nation we need a public sustenance to soften and civilize us, to offer us what the church, the Chatauqua or the homogenous community once gave us. We know the tragedy of spending only for warfare to keep the peace.

"Moreover," Harris shrewdly added, "we have heard that it is good foreign policy to appear urbane."[35]

In the sixties, unlike the previous decade, domestic concerns rather than foreign policy quickened the pace of the federal arts movement. As an example of the kind of ameliorative effect that the cultural legislation was supposed to have,

Representative Philip Philbin told his colleagues that the passage of such a measure would "do much to rid American life of some of its most obnoxious, damning characteristics. . . . This is a task we cannot undertake too soon," the Massachusetts Democrat added, "if we would but recall plain lessons of history and the rise and decline of great civilizations of the past."[36] Thus the federal arts struggle continued, whether for art's sake or for Americans' sake or simply for the sake of appearance. The drive for a domestic arts program did not end with the passage of the NCA bill, as measures for federal aid to the arts, joined by the new proposal to include the humanities, received a full hearing in 1965.

"The Pursuit of American Greatness"

"We must also recognize and encourage," President Johnson declared in his 1965 State of the Union address, "those who can be pathfinders for the Nation's imagination and understanding.

"To help promote and honor creative achievements, I will propose a National Foundation on the Arts."[37] With these words, the president removed any doubt that he would maintain the White House's commitment to culture that had blossomed under the Kennedys. Nor were Johnson's inaugural ceremonies later that January any less splendid in regard to the arts than Kennedy's four years earlier; they included a reception for artists and writers hosted by the president's special assistant on the arts, Roger Stevens; a performance by Margot Fonteyn and Rudolf Nureyev at the Inaugural Gala; and a concert by Van Cliburn and Isaac Stern with the National Symphony Orchestra, followed by a reception at the State Department. More significantly, such events seemed almost commonplace by 1965. A greater stir would have been created had the arts *not* played such a prominent role in the inaugural festivities. An even clearer indication of the degree to which culture had become a part of American political life was the veritable stampede of humanities foundation legislation (patterned after Moorhead's 1964 bill) in the House.[38]

Some fifty-seven representatives introduced such legislation on the very first day of the Eighty-ninth session; by the end of January more than eighty such bills had been introduced and the total climbed to one hundred soon after. The humanities bill was an equally popular item in the Senate, where it attracted more than forty cosponsors.[39]

To many congressmen, the humanities legislation, embracing the arts but more notable for its solid, educational thrust, must have seemed an ideal way to begin a new session of Congress under a newly elected president. For the humanities foundation bill, even more than the NCA legislation of the previous year, was rife with positive associations and profound symbolism. Representative Frank Horton (R-NY), for example, citing the "greater national prestige and a more meaningful use of leisure time . . . ," declared that "this measure proposes nothing less than the restoration of man." Not all congressmen indulged in quite that much hyperbole, but all shared with Horton that standard concern for the balance between science and the humanities in America:

> As we continue to clear new hurdles in science and technology and as we race toward the moon, the schism between science and the humanities deepens. The Nation has reached a stage of maturity in which the arts and humanities demand equal status with science and a redressing of the imbalance of the two cultures is required now.[40]

Meanwhile, Representative William Ryan (D-NY), another sponsor of the humanities foundation, made explicit the connection between that legislation and Johnson's Great Society and Kennedy's New Frontier:

> Legislation to encourage the arts and humanities is vital in working toward that improved quality of life that is the essence of the Great Society. . . .
> We can all remember how dear this subject was to President Kennedy. As a monument to him—and as an expression of this body's concern with the future of our national culture, we should quickly enact this bill into law.[41]

Had it not enjoyed a lengthy legislative history, the arts legislation might have become lost in the flurry of enthusiasm for the new humanities measure, which incorporated the arts but gave them comparatively little attention. With veteran arts advocates like Thompson, Javits, and Pell on hand, however, the arts were not forgotten; they shared top billing with the humanities, in fact, in another round of hearings held in February and March 1965.[42] These hearings, as it turned out, including both joint and separate sessions of House and Senate special subcommittees and compiling over 1,100 pages of testimony in the process, were the final ones to be held on the arts and humanities before the foundation bill was passed. As such, the hearings represent both a compendium of the old—the arguments both for and against arts support that had been brewing since the fifties—and a forecast of the new, a means of serving both the arts and humanities, without sacrificing one to the other. Set against the background of the old arguments—civilization versus control, economics versus expense—were new concerns, large questions about the respective jurisdictions of the arts and humanities and the proper governing of the proposed foundation, as well as finer distinctions (the proposed loyalty oath and the question of amateur versus professional support) arising from the legislation itself.

The opening comments of Senator Pell on 23 February established the overall tone of the proceedings, offering the subtle reminder that for all of the expert opinion to be offered by artists and academicians alike, the legislation had as much to do with the American image as it did with American art. Pell began by making that ubiquitous reference to America's scientific achievements, a reminder to the fiscal conservatives that America had long been robbing Peter the poet to pay Paul the physicist. It was time, the Rhode Island Democrat believed, to restore the balance between the two worlds. "If we are to pass on to the future a really meaningful heritage," Pell declared at the opening of the joint House and Senate subcommittee hearings, we must place, I believe, a little more emphasis on our cultural growth; on the creative and performing arts; on the whole scope of humanistic knowledge and understanding. The aim and purpose of life itself is deeply involved in those two broad cultural areas, which are so closely allied to each other.

In a word, I am convinced that the arts and humanities are central not only to our national welfare today, but to the goals we seek for the years ahead. And that is what this legislation, which is now before us, is all about—those cultural areas which widen the understanding of man in relation to his environment as well as to other men; man's ability to appreciate the past, to comprehend the present, to project soaring new thoughts and images, ideas and ideals into the future; man's ability to analyze wisely, to perceive and appreciate, to be fully aware of his particular moment in history in relation to other moments and eons of the past; and, ultimately, man's ability to understand more completely his potentials so that they may be realized.[43]

Without doubting the sincerity of the senators's remarks, one can note that such concerns have a certain rhetorical, ceremonial quality that is far removed from the more practical arguments for cultural exchange and economic relief hammered out in the fifties and early sixties. Even those arguments of the arts advocates which lent themselves to a fair amount of bombast—for the dissemination of American culture; for an educated, cultivated electorate; for America to assume its rightful place alongside the other nations of the world in support of the arts; for the more worthwhile use of leisure time; and for the catalytic role of the government in generating private arts support—even those visions sounded far more practical and realistic than the questions of destiny, the "soaring new thoughts and images, ideas and ideals," around which Pell spun his rhapsody.[44] Such grandiose thoughts, to the extent they were communicated at all beyond the halls of Congress, must have sounded to the indigent poet and the struggling composer about as hollow as words like "sacred," "glorious," and "sacrifice" to Hemingway's soldier in *A Farewell to Arms*. But to the politician, such language was irresistible. "We may make great strides in atomic energy and space exploration, in automation, in biology and chemistry," observed Senator Edward Kennedy (D-MA), never closely associated with the arts legislation but one who knew, like a lot of congressmen, all the "right" causes. "But we will be dull and listless men, amid all these wonders, if we do not also expand the human mind and spirit."[45]

It was the new humanities aspect of the cultural legislation which permitted such flights of fancy as Pell's and Kennedy's. While the arts advocates in Congress recognized the political value of their new allies, some were wary of losing control of the movement. Jacob Javits, the elder statesman among the arts supporters in Congress, hoped that the new quest for humanities support "will not dilute or divert us from the main issue which has always been before us, to wit, the issue of the performing and other similar arts." Javits and Frank Thompson were especially suspicious of the plans, specifically that of the Humanities Commission, for a single foundation embracing both the arts and the humanities. Thompson worried about the arts being "swallowed up" by the humanities, while Javits feared that the single-foundation plan "may harm them both."[46]

The question of whether to establish a single humanities foundation, focusing on teacher-training and research and including the arts, or separate foundations for arts and humanities support, was all but decided on 10 March 1965, when President Johnson submitted a plan to Congress for an independent agency called the National Foundation on the Arts and Humanities, consisting of two separate endowments administered by respective national councils on the arts and the humanities, coordinated by a Federal Council on the Arts and the Humanities. Richard Goodwin, the erstwhile candidate to succeed August Heckscher as the president's special consultant before Roger Stevens got the job, coordinated the administration's effort to arrive at successful cultural legislation, working closely with the Pell and Thompson subcommittees and producing a statement for the president to issue along with the bill.[47] That statement, like most con-

nected with cultural legislation, was fairly rich in philosophical hoopla. It called, wishfully, for "recognition and encouragement for those who extend the frontiers of understanding
in the arts and humanistic studies." It labeled, idealistically,
humanistic studies "a central part of the American national
purpose." And it included, pridefully, artistic achievement
and dissemination "among the hallmarks of a Great Society."

But there were limits, as well, to the range of the president's rhetorical fancy, and his statement displayed a degree
of restraint uncharacteristic of such declarations. The hard
lessons of both the thirties, when Congress burnt its fingers
on the heat of the subsidized creations of the WPA, and of
the fifties, when the heat was generated by the simple-minded
reaction of some congressmen to cultural exchange, were not
lost on the arts advocates of the sixties. Despite their bombast
and their reverie, these advocates recognized the limits of
federal arts support, and counseled administrative restraint
and complete artistic freedom. "We fully recognize," the president's statement read,

> that no government can call artistic excellence into existence.
> It must flow from the quality of the society and the good for-
> tune of the nation. Nor should any government seek to restrict
> the freedom of the artist to pursue his calling in his own way.
> Freedom is an essential condition for the artist, and in pro-
> portion as freedom is diminished so is the prospect of artistic
> achievement.
>
> But government can seek to create conditions under which
> the arts can flourish; through recognition of achievements,
> through helping those who seek to enlarge creative under-
> standing, through increasing the access of our people to the
> works of our artists, and through recognizing the arts as part
> of the pursuit of American greatness. That is the goal of this
> legislation.[48]

The bill itself, introduced in the Senate by Pell and in
the House by Thompson, was woven together by Pell's assistant, Livingston Biddle. Biddle combined Moorhead's humanities foundation and the Javits-Humphrey-Pell arts founda-

tion but did not include the latter's provision of matching grants to state arts agencies. In this latest version, the two foundations would coexist as separate endowments under a single $10 million foundation (equally shared, with up to $10 million each year to match private gifts). The National Council on the Arts, established in 1964 (but which did not hold its first meeting until April 1965), would be transferred from the executive office of the president to the Arts Endowment to advise the chairman (and a similar body would be created to advise the chairman of the Humanities Endowment). The activities of both endowments, finally, would be coordinated by the Federal Council on the Arts and the Humanities, composed of the two endowment's chairmen and various other federal officials.[49] But while this elaborate structure was new, the thrust behind the cultural program, as expressed in the bill's "Declaration of Purpose," remained consistent with the tone of federal arts advocacy of the past several years. The support of the arts and humanities, in short, was linked to the perceived need to shore up private and local initiative in these areas, to balance the nation's emphasis of science and technology, to foster wisdom and vision in the citizenry, and, as always, to win "worldwide respect and admiration for the Nation's high qualities as a leader in the realm of ideas and of the spirit."

Even such a broad mandate had its limits, however, and for the Arts Endowment these limits were prescribed by the *project* support that would be offered. For this was not a general employment scheme such as the WPA had offered; nor did it envisage the state owned-and-operated culture of Europe. Instead, the National Foundation on the Arts and Humanities took a pragmatic, piecemeal approach and had clearly defined areas of support: nonprofit productions with "substantial artistic and cultural significance, giving emphasis to American creativity"; productions of "significant merit" which, without such assistance, would be unavailable to some areas of the country; projects (including individual aid) to encourage and assist artists, and to develop audiences; and "other relevant projects, including surveys and planning in the arts."[50] The Arts Endowment's support, in other words, focused on quality, geographical need, the development of artists and audiences, and planning. It was a limited, level-headed approach, well-insulated from Congress; the chairman, as advised by the NCA, made all decisions. With its 50 percent matching provision, it was largely free from the threat of federal control.[51]

The arts and humanities legislation not only received the president's blessings but also gained support from the appearance the same week of the prestigious Rockefeller Panel Report, *The Performing Arts: Problems and Prospects.*[52] The blue-ribbon panel of patrons, arts administrators, and educators conducted a detailed study of the performing arts, focusing on the various sources of earned and contributed income. With veteran arts advocates like August Heckscher, Helen Thompson, John H. MacFadyen, and John D. Rockefeller III himself on the thirty-member panel, it is not too surprising that it expressed many of the same concerns as the arts advocates in Congress, ranging from national braggadocio to doubts about American culture and the economic future of the arts. The panel also managed to combine, somehow, the most visionary nostroms with a businesslike practicality, coming up in turn with a national cultural blueprint that drew from both extremes. "In the view of the panel," the report noted in a section devoted to future prospects, "a worthy interim objective for the nation would be the development and maintenance of the following high-quality nonprofit professional organizations operating on a year-round basis:

> Fifty permanent theatre companies—a number approximating the metropolitan areas with populations over 500,000, a size large enough to support a year-round resident theatre.
> Fifty symphony orchestras—presenting concerts by the full orchestra as well as providing musicians for smaller orchestral and chamber music groups.
> Six regional opera companies—offering short seasons in several metropolitan areas not yet ready to support year-round

performances—in addition to the four major resident companies and two permanent national touring companies already established.

Six regional choral groups.

Six regional dance companies, in addition to the two major
resident dance groups now in existence.[53]

And a partridge and a pear tree, some disgruntled artists
might have muttered, not sharing the panel's institutional
bias. Nevertheless, for all of its gloss and high-brow predilections, the Rockefeller report did offer a pioneering analysis
of the performing arts in America. And it did come out
strongly in favor of government arts support.[54]

Combined with the companion research on the economics of the performing arts by Princeton economists William
Baumol and William Bowen, and with Alvin Toffler's breezy
yet perceptive *Culture Consumers*, the Rockefeller study provided a stockade full of ammunition for the arts advocates in
the final months of their drive for federal support.[55] With the
naming of the National Council on the Arts in February, and
its initial meeting in Washington in April 1965, the movement was prepared for that last battle (following a curious
day at the White House along the way)—the crucial House
debate on the arts and humanities bill.

"A Magna Carta of the Arts"

"I hope I will be pardoned . . . ," Senator Javits announced at
the opening of the joint House and Senate subcommittee
hearings on 23 February 1965, "for calling attention to the
fact that it is now six months since we authorized the National
Council on the Arts and the National Council on the Arts has
not yet been appointed." As the ranking Republican in the
federal arts movement, and as one of the founding fathers
of that cause, Javits could not resist a little partisan politick-
ing, reminding his Democratic colleagues of the president's
failure to implement the NCA bill. "If it takes six months to
take this elementary small step," he continued, "it seems to

me that with all friendship and respect and understanding that this is not very auspicious in terms of implementing the call which the President issued in his state of the Union message for legislation even further implementing the participation by the Federal Government in this field."[56]

The White House was apparently prepared for such a challenge, however, for when Roger Stevens testified shortly after Javits's opening salvo, the presidential assistant and chairman of the NCA (pending Senate approval) announced that the names of the new council would be released that very afternoon:

Class of 1970

Albert Bush-Brown, President, Rhode Island School of Design, Providence, RI
Paul Engle, poet, writer, teacher, Cedar Rapids, IA
R. Philip Hanes, President, Community Arts Council, Winston-Salem, NC
René d'Harnoncourt, Director, Museum of Modern Art, New York, NY
Oliver Smith, scenic designer, producer, painter, New York, NY
Isaac Stern, musician, New York, NY
George Stevens, Sr., film director, Los Angeles, CA
Minoru Yamasaki, architect, Seattle, WA, and Detroit, MI

Class of 1968

Leonard Bernstein, composer, conductor, New York, NY
Anthony A. Bliss, President, Metropolitan Opera, New York, NY
David Brinkley, newscaster, Washington, DC.[57]
Warner Lawson, musician, educator, Washington, D.C.
William Pereira, architect, Los Angeles, CA
Richard Rodgers, composer, producer, writer, Southport, CT
David Smith, sculptor, Bolton Landing, NY[58]
James Johnson Sweeney, writer, museum director, Houston, TX

Class of 1966

Elizabeth Ashley, actress, Los Angeles, CA
Agnes deMille, choreographer, New York, NY
Ralph Ellison, writer, lecturer, teacher, New York, NY

Fr. Gilbert Hartke, clergyman, theatrical educator, Washington, D.C.

Eleanor Lambert, fashion designer, New York, NY

Gregory Peck, actor, Los Angeles, CA

Otto Wittman, art museum director, Toledo, OH

Stanley Young, author, publisher, Executive Director, ANTA, New York, NY

Ex-officio—S. Dillon Ripley, Secretary, Smithsonian Institution

It was an impressive roster, restoring a measure of hope to those who, like the *Nation*, had been discouraged by the earlier appointment of Roger Stevens ("the symbol of Broadway success," according to the magazine).[59] Still, no one was certain just what this body, the nation's first blue-ribbon arts commission, would actually do.

Despite its broad legislative mandate, to recommend "ways to maintain and increase the cultural resources of the U.S." and to formulate "methods . . . by which creative activity and high standards and increased opportunities in the arts may be encouraged," the precise mission of the NCA, once it finally convened, was never clear.[60] Speaking to the National Book Committee's annual convention in New York on 10 December 1964, Stevens huffed and puffed about the NCA drawing up "a Magna Carta of the arts, which will act as guidelines for Congress and the public in the development of a realistic program of aid and education in the field of the arts."[61] At the same time that Stevens was speaking so grandly, however, Congress was having difficulty deciding whether it actually wanted to pay for the new council's activities. An error in the original legislation, leaving out "per annum" after the $150,000 authorization, threatened to make the NCA bill a dead letter, and the House, led by Robert Griffin (R-MI) and the ever-recalcitrant Harold Gross (R-IA), refused to rectify the matter in March. It was not until after the NCA's initial meeting at the White House in April, when it presented its first resolution, a request that Congress amend the NCA legislation to provide for annual appropriations, that the error was finally corrected.[62]

Frank Thompson and Claiborne Pell were also on hand at the first White House meeting, to urge the Council to endorse the NFAH legislation, which it did, over the strenuous objections of council member R. Philip Hanes. A wealthy veteran of the state and local arts council movement, the conservative Hanes felt that the council had not had sufficient time to study the matter, and that the legislation in its present form granted too much power to the chairman of the Arts Endowment.[63] The rest of the council, on the other hand, agreed with Pell and Thompson that it was important for the council to go on record in support of the proposed arts and humanities foundation, to lend its name to the gathering of forces behind the bill.

Despite the president's call to action at the swearing-in ceremony later that day—"I think it is important to meet, but what is quite important is not just to meet but to get things done"—without funds there was little that the council could do except to pass more resolutions.[64] And that it did, in abundance, with some sixteen resolutions. They ranged from a call to modernize and strengthen copyright protection, to a mandatory one-percent-for-art program in federal construction projects, to the honoring of artists and increasing cultural exchange.[65] It was not immediately clear, however, what all of these parliamentary actions implied, other than providing a graphic example of bureaucratic cultural smorgasbord resulting from years of official neglect of the arts. Such diverse and hopeful resolutions hardly constituted a Magna Carta of the arts, and Stevens himself admitted at the end of the second of the meetings that the NCA would need more time to establish a genuine arts policy.[66]

Along with another flurry of resolutions at its second meeting, at Tarrytown, New York, in June, the Council did manage to come up with a handful of more "concrete proposals," designed to tap both private funds and what public funds might become available.[67] Tentative plans were made for "The Presidential Citation for Excellence in the Arts" (with nominations to be made by the council); for a project to extend the seasons of twenty symphony orchestras for a period of three to four weeks, to highlight young American soloists and American compositions; for the establishment of national and regional companies in theater, opera, and ballet, along with a National Youth Symphony and a Heritage Theatre of Folk Forms; and for pilot grants to repertory theaters and dance companies. The council's *First Annual Report* gives further indication of its major concerns, ranging from arts institutions ("assisting existing arts institutions of quality is of paramount importance"), to individual artists ("the Council is concerned about the lack of opportunities afforded our artists"), to education ("in and about the arts, through formal and informal means"), and communication within the arts.[68] But until the foundation legislation passed, the council deliberations served only as a cultural scattergun. With a mere $50,000 (for administrative expenses) at its disposal, moreover, the council could only fire blanks.

"Praise Poets Even When They're Troublesome"

Even before the council had met for a second time, the NFAH bill had made it halfway through its legislative journey, passing the Senate on a voice vote on 10 June 1965.[69] Although the House debate, always a perilous voyage for the arts, still lay ahead, the nation seemed ready to embark on its second major cultural experiment. It would be guided by an independent agency this time, an agency, unlike its New Deal ancestor, that would be carefully insulated from the partisan politics of Congress. There was still time for one more fiasco, though, one more example of the folly of the government's entrepreneurial role in the arts, a final reminder, that is, of the inherent tension between that kind of compromise and consensus on which a democracy depends, and the independent, uncompromising nature of art.

   "It was called the White House Festival of the Arts," observed *U.S. News and World Report*, describing the lavish cultural display hosted by the Johnsons in June. "It turned out to be a combination of drama and politics in the East Room, music and politics in the State Dining Room, painting and politics in the corridors, sculpture and politics on the South Lawn."[70] Art and politics had been mixed at the federal level before, of course—when Congress turned its firing squad on the Federal Theater Project, for example, or when Representative Dondero blasted subversive art. The results were almost always disastrous. On this particular occasion, however, it was the artists rather than the politicians who brought politics into art, but regardless, the outcome was nearly the same.

The White House affair began in February 1965, when Eric Goldman, the Princeton professor of history on leave to serve as special consultant to the president, sent a memorandum to Johnson suggesting an early spring festival of the arts.[71] It was another attempt, clearly, to recapture some of the Kennedy magic in the White House. It was not so narrowly political as some observers, like Britain's *Economist*, would have it—"This week Mr. Johnson countered the university 'teach-ins,' protesting against his foreign policy, with a cultural 'play-in' demonstrating his respect for the arts."[72] Nor was the event purely one of art for art's sake. The guest list, as Goldman devised it, consisted primarily of "good contacts," people connected with the arts, certainly, but not necessarily artists themselves. The emphasis was on "the people who have been encouraging the arts in their local communities . . . ," Goldman told the president, suggesting a list of potentially valuable allies—"the chairmen of existing state commissions on the arts . . . and heads of representative local symphony associations, art societies, museum boards, etc."[73]

Fat cats, the cynical artist might have said, had that artist not been so busy venting his cynicism against the United States' presence in the Dominican Republic and Vietnam. Goldman put together a day-long festival of American art, with examples of painting and sculpture, music, theater, film, dance, and literature, but he ran aground in that last category, when the poet Robert Lowell at first accepted and then declined an invitation to read his work at the White House. That refusal in itself was not exceptional (Edmund Wilson and E. B. White had also refused), but the grounds for Lowell's action, and his means of explaining those grounds—on the front page of the *New York Times*—were unique. "Every serious artist knows," explained Lowell in his carefully worded open letter to the president, "that he cannot enjoy public celebration without making subtle public commitments."[74] Because of recent United States actions in Vietnam and the Dominican Republic, the poet could not in good conscience join in the public celebration that the White House had planned. The following day, twenty artists and writers (who had not even been invited to the festival) sent a telegram to Johnson supporting Lowell's stand.[75] The arts community was at last getting its revenge, or so it seemed, for the embarrassing attacks it had suffered at the hands of Congress since the days of the Federal Theater Project.

The president, meanwhile, probably unaware of those attacks and certainly not interested in such flimsy justification for these shenanigans in any case, was furious. His first reaction, predictably, was to cancel the whole affair, and since that was impossible, he threatened to undercut the event by refusing to attend and ordering a news blackout of the festival. (He also ordered an FBI check of several of the invitees, but Goldman resisted the order to refuse admission to six artists.) When Johnson learned that John Hersey would be reading from *Hiroshima*, of all things, he attempted through Mrs. Johnson to persuade Goldman to remove the writer from the program. That subtle effort at censorship failed, too, and the festival went ahead as scheduled—another nerve-racking day for federal culture, with the arts finally in the spotlight, but for all of the wrong reasons.[76]

The festival itself, despite the preceding week of backstage maneuvering and the undercurrent of political tension, went surprisingly well. It included an impressive display of American art (including works by none other than Ben Shahn and Jack Levine, veteran federal artists who had the scars to prove it), performances of American music by the Louisville Philharmonic, scenes from *The Glass Menagerie*, *The Subject Was Roses*, *Death of a Salesman*, and *Hard Travelin'*, film clips of the work of Alfred Hitchcock, Elia Kazan, Fred Zinneman,

and George Stevens, Sr., topped off after dinner by performances by the Joffrey Ballet and the Duke Ellington band.[77]
Robert Lowell was not on hand, of course, but he might as
well have been, for the spell he cast over the proceedings. He
was not overlooked, certainly, by those writers who did attend—Mark Van Doren, who offered introductory remarks
for the readings; Saul Bellow, who introduced his own reading with a reference to Lowell; John Hersey, who prefaced
his selection from *Hiroshima* with a grim warning on international violence; and even Phyllis McGinley, who added the
following couplet to one of her pleasantly silly poems, "In
Praise of Divinity":

> And while the pot of culture's bubblesome,
> Praise poets even when they're troublesome.[78]

Literary critics proved to be troublesome, too, as Dwight
Macdonald, one of the invited guests, circulated a petition
(or "statement to the press," as he put it) praising Lowell's
stand and condemning Johnson's foreign policy. In a surprising display of good taste, though—or was it mere timidity?—
only a handful of guests signed the statement.[79]

The president, for his part, acquitted himself as well as
could be expected under the circumstances. He was finally
persuaded to attend by a pleading Jack Valenti ("I prayerfully
suggest you may want to reconsider and be present for your
brief remarks at the Festival . . . ," the aide wrote, probably
sealing the case with his sneering reference to "one erratic,
unstable poet, plus a dozen headline-seekers"). Johnson did
deliver his brief remarks, written by former Kennedy aide
Richard Goodwin.[80] However brief, the speech was a gem,
combining the usual bombast with uncommon good sense
and a wealth of unintended irony.[81] Beginning with a pertinent reference to America's erstwhile dependence on European culture, Johnson dealt only briefly in the usual political
rhapsody ("the farthest horizon of man's possibility") before
turning to the question of what government could do for
the arts.

"First, and most important," Johnson declared, with a

directness that must have startled his listeners, "it can leave the artist alone." Johnson's point, though, was the need for complete artistic freedom; he was not simply counseling that traditional laissez faire attitude that had marked the government's relations with art in the past. For government, Johnson insisted,

> can offer direct encouragement. Most of this help will come, as it always has, from private and local sources. But the Nation has its obligation. And that is why we have proposed a bill to establish a National Foundation for the Arts and Humanities. That historic bill has already been passed in the United States Senate. I would hope that it could soon become law.

"Lastly," the president concluded, "we can work to create an atmosphere for the arts to thrive."

The highly charged atmosphere of the White House Festival, with uncertainty and distrust on both sides of the arts-and-government partnership, was obviously not what the president had in mind. Nor was the president unaware that the political implications of art contribute as much to the tension of that relationship as the blunders of politicians. "Your art is not a political weapon," Johnson told the artists in attendance. "Yet much of what you do is profoundly political." And then, in a powerful statement that managed to encompass Lowell and Hersey and Vietnam and the Dominican Republic all in one ironic sweep, Johnson got to the heart of the politics of art:

> For you seek out the common pleasures and visions, the terrors and cruelties of man's day on this planet. And I would hope that you would dissolve the barriers of hatred and ignorance which are the source of so much of our pain and anger. In this way you work toward peace—not only the peace which is simply the absence of war—but the peace which liberates man to reach for the finest fulfillment of his spirit.

As for the festival itself, it was not immediately apparent whether the event had created more barriers than it dissolved. In one sense, Goldman later admitted, "the White

House Festival of the Arts had been an unmitigated disaster. Almost everything that happened after Lowell's letter and President Johnson's reaction to it had added bricks to a wall between the President" and the intellectual community. "Mercifully," he continued, "much of the story was unknown. But enough had become public to make the wall seem as impassable as the barbed concrete between East and West Berlin." For inveterate Johnson critics like Macdonald and Saul Maloff (the latter called the event a "catastrophe," a vulgar display of "our cultural wares, or booty," a "grievous and ghastly embarrassment"), the festival was powerless to change any opinions.[82] But for other observers, less politically astute, perhaps, or at least with less of an ax to grind, the event signaled a more positive trend in American culture. "Since the Festival was a reversal at the highest possible national level of an American tradition of disdain toward artists as a group," actor Charlton Heston observed, "it's too bad that some of the invited guests missed the whole point." Thomas Hess of *Art News* similarly criticized his colleagues who viewed the festival as nothing more than a political event. "This is a pity," Hess wrote, "—as well as slipshod reporting—because the Festival might be the mark of a turning point in the cultural life of the nation, particularly with regard to federal involvement in the creative arts."[83]

That turning point had actually been reached during the Kennedy years, however, long before the White House Festival. The festival should more accurately be viewed as a signpost along the way to a new federal arts program. Nor was the message of that signpost as clear as Heston and Hess implied. If, on the one hand, it showed the promise of government encouragement of the arts, it demonstrated as well the potential for disaster, the old business of paying the piper and calling the tune—and damaging art in the process.

In any event, the future of that new relation between art and government in America lay not with the White House in June 1965, but with the House of Representatives, where culture had taken so many beatings in the past.

"A Nation's Most Precious Heritage"

"This far-reaching bill, creating Federal czars over the arts and humanities," complained seven Republican members of the House Committee on Education and Labor in reference to the NFAH legislation, "was railroaded through the committee on June 24, 1965, after about 15 minutes of consideration."[84] About fifteen *years* of consideration would have been closer to the truth. For even if there were considerable differences between the Javits and Howell plans of the early fifties and the foundation bill of 1965, it is hard to conceive of the suggestion that the cultural legislation had been "railroaded" through Congress. Even in America, the trains run faster than that.

Yet the metaphor was apt in the sense that the federal arts movement was now unstoppable, having picked up steam with the addition of the humanities forces in 1964. The final debate in the House was largely a matter of form, one last hurdle to be cleared, offering one more glimpse of the arguments for and against the cultural legislation that had been so long in the making. This is not to imply that the success of the bill in 1965 was assured, however, for the House always presented a tortuous path for social legislation, especially when the conservative opposition combined with ancient parliamentary procedures in an effort to thwart liberal programs like Johnson's. Were it not for the president's strong support, in fact, the NFAH bill might have fallen victim to one of those conservative marathon stands. The bill became lodged, as similar bills had so often in the past, in Howard Smith's Rules Committee. Even with the Eighty-ninth Congress' twenty-one-day rule, allowing Congress as a whole to petition bills out of the Committee on Rules after three weeks, there was still room for legislative maneuvering to frustrate the bill's passage. Not until after midnight of a session that began at noon on 13 September was the bill pried loose from the Rules Committee by an overwhelming 260–114 vote, which augured well for the bill's passage in 1965.[85]

Two days later the bill came up for floor debate in the House, an equally lopsided showing; forty-five representatives spoke in support of the bill against only ten in opposition, leading to the defeat of a motion to send the bill back to committee by a 128 to 251 vote. For nearly four hours the standard arguments were traded back and forth. Only Claude Pepper and Harold Gross broke out of the mold: Pepper reached back to the WPA, and Gross into the deepest recesses of his conservative midwestern imagination.[86] This was the second time around for Pepper, having left the Senate in 1951 and not returning to the House until 1963, it all must have sounded slightly familiar to the Florida Democrat. He had been a cosponsor of the legislation to establish a Bureau of Fine Arts in the late thirties, a futile attempt to make the WPA art projects part of a permanent program. Citing the "tremendous impact of the WPA arts programs on the country and the artist" (no longer an extraordinary viewpoint in Congress), Pepper neatly summarized the transformation that had taken place in the mood of Congress since the thirties. "We are still debating the merits of Federal support," Pepper instructed his colleagues, with a voice of experience that not even Javits in the Senate could match. "The difference now is that it is not so much a question of humanitarian relief for the destitute artist as it is a question of relief for our whole society, relief to meet fundamental needs of our people."[87]

For Gross, an opponent of such legislation for years, the appeal was not to history but to humor. He offered the parting shots of the conservative forces, which had managed to delay the passage of arts legislation since 1949, but which were now clearly outnumbered. In mock seriousness, Gross regretted that he was unaware that the bill was coming up at this time, "or else I would have tried to appear in my tuxedo and my dancing shoes to be properly equipped for this further going away party for the Treasury of the United States." In a clever attempt at parody, the technique which had been used with such devastating effectiveness against the arts in the past, Gross introduced an amendment to clarify the definition of "dance" in the list of art forms to be supported by the Arts Endowment: "including but not limited to the irregular and/or rhythmic contractions and coordinated relaxation of the serrati, obliques, and abdominis recti group of muscles—accompanied by rotatory undulations, tilts, and turns timed with and attuned to the titillating and blended tones of synchronous woodwinds."[88] That amendment failing, Gross later attempted to secure support for basketball, football, golf, tennis, squash, pinochle, and poker under the provisions of the bill, before finally resigning himself to defeat. "Incidentally," he added, his commentary taking on an increasingly bitter tone, "there is another art that is not recognized in this bill, and I believe it ought to be recognized. It is the art of picking the pockets of the taxpayers to get $20 million to pay for this business, when the federal treasury is $325 billion in debt."

In the end, the only real debate was between the sponsors of the bill themselves, over the balance of power between the chairman of the endowments and the advisory councils; Frank Thompson's faction, placing ultimate authority in the chairmen, prevailed. The bill itself prevailed, too, on a voice vote as it turned out; the overwhelming defeat of Representative Robert Griffin's motion to recommit was a clear indication of the mind of Congress. The House bill was quickly passed in the Senate the following day, and the long-awaited cultural program was ready for a final send-off on 29 September 1965, a signing ceremony in the Rose Garden of the White House, with some three hundred legislators, scholars, and leaders in the arts on hand.[89]

Given the stormy relations between government and the arts in the past, and the controversies that the Arts Endowment would be destined to endure in the future, it would not have been quite right had everything gone smoothly following the passage of the NFAH bill. It was fitting, then, that Representative Gross should send a telegram to the president requesting a veto of the bill—"Let's . . . balance the budget before subsidizing the longhairs and the little twinkletoes"— and that one of those "longhairs" (playwright Arthur Miller) should publicly refuse an invitation to the signing ceremony, in protest of the bombing of North Vietnam.[90] Given the nature of the arts themselves, moreover, it was fitting that the president should startle those present in the Rose Garden with an ambitious cultural blueprint for the activities of the new Arts Endowment.[91]

"In the long history of man," the president began, pre-dictably enough, with that spread-eagle prose reserved for bill-signing ceremonies,

> countless empires and nations have come and gone. Those which created no lasting works of art are reduced today to short footnotes in history's catalog.
>
> Art is a nation's most precious heritage. For it is in our works of art that we reveal to ourselves, and to others, the inner vision which guides us as a Nation. And where there is no vision, the people perish.
>
> We in America have not always been kind to the artists and the scholars who are the creators and the keepers of our vi-sion. Somehow, the scientists always seem to get the pent-house, while the arts and the humanities get the basement.

The president followed that refreshing bit of candor about America's priorities with the obligatory congressional credits, conspicuously omitting the Republican Javits from his list of legislative heroes. Instead of ending his speech with another rhetorical flourish, however, lauding once more the new cul-tural legislation, the president insisted on telling the as-sembled guests "what we are going to *do* with it." "Working together with the States and the local governments," Johnson observed, "and with many private organizations in the arts:

> We will create a National Theater to bring ancient and mod-ern classics of the theater to audiences all over America.
>
> We will support a National Opera Company and a National Ballet Company.
>
> We will create an American Film Institute, bringing to-gether leading artists of the film industry, outstanding edu-cators, and young men and women who wish to pursue the 20th century art form as their life's work.
>
> We will commission new works of music by American com-posers.
>
> We will support our symphony orchestras.

We will bring more great artists to our schools and universities by creating grants for their time in residence.

These plans (which were worked out by Johnson aide Will
Sparks and Stevens assistant Frank Crowther the previous
evening, when it was felt that the president would want some
specific proposals to offer), "are only a small part of the programs that we are ready to begin," the president continued.
"They will have an unprecedented effect on the arts and the
humanities of our great Nation."[92]

Except for the National Theater, Opera, and Ballet plans,
discarded in favor of more decentralized support to existing
and newly organized nonprofit professional companies, the
plans mentioned by Johnson, along with numerous others,
were eventually carried out by the Arts Endowment. And
their effect *was* "unprecedented," surely, if only because the
nation had never before attempted such an experiment in
public arts support. An analysis of that effect, of the growth
and development of the arts and humanities endowments, is
a separate story, a task quite distinct from an investigation of
the origins of federal support.

Yet the two stories should never be divorced entirely, for
the events of the "prehistoric" years of the National Endowment for the Arts—the early dreams of the arts advocates
following the demise of the WPA; the pioneering arts legislation of the early fifties; the timid report of the Fine Arts
Commission and the increasingly ambitious studies of the
President's Goals Commission, Kennedy's Secretary of Labor
and special consultant on the arts, the Humanities Commission, and the Rockefeller Panel; even the failures of the State
Department and the USIA, and the often meddling, confused Congress—all left their mark, one way or another, on
the new program that began in 1965. In the relations between government and art, at least, the past has always maintained a certain hold on the present. Thus it is especially
important as the debate regarding the relationship of government and art continues—and it is not clear, in fact, just
where we are headed—to recall where we have been.

Epilogue

Looking Backward

"Twice in recent decades," wrote August Heckscher in 1962,

> the Federal government has shown itself interested in promoting the cultural and artistic life of the United States. On both occasions it was for narrow reasons. . . . The first occasion was during the Great Depression, when the aim was to succor impoverished artists. The second has been in the course of the Cold War, when the aim, quite simply, was to beat the Russians. But the real reason for the fostering of art is, I suggest, that art is important to the life of the people, and that without it the political community falls short of its ideal potentialities.[1]

The arts program that was established in 1965 drew on all three of these motives. It was not a relief program modeled after the WPA, certainly, but the economic arguments of the arts advocates, bolstered by the investigations conducted in the early sixties, were a major factor in mobilizing the arts community. These arguments permitted the alliance of management and labor—of boards of trustees and artists unions—that made for a remarkably unified, if comparatively small, political force. One of the messages of Goldberg's Metropolitan Opera decision, after all, was that *both* sides were justified in their demands: the orchestral "workers" were underpaid, while the opera management lost money every time it raised the curtain. Thus the need to appeal for assistance to an outside party—the government—became manifest.

So, too, was the cold war a factor in the development of the arts and humanities foundation. If no one was tactless enough to keep score in the national effort to "beat the Russians" (although Jacob Javits came close at times), the whole notion of America's reputation abroad weighed heavily on the minds of the proponents of the cultural legislation. Tied to the cultural exchange efforts of the forties and fifties, in which postwar America served its federal arts apprenticeship, the international prestige factor was the one argument that cut across ideological lines; it could attract the conservative support that economic relief and social welfare concerns, running afoul of old political prejudices, could not. For there was something particularly galling, to northern liberal and southern conservative alike, about the oft-repeated notion that America was the only civilized nation without some kind of government arts program. It did not sway all parties in the debate, but along with Heckscher's "real reason" for arts support, it enjoyed the broadest appeal.

The reason on which Heckscher based his claim for federal support—"that art is important to the life of the people"— or, as Claiborne Pell was wont to declare, that art is important to the future of American civilization, became the single most persuasive argument of the federal arts advocates. Especially after these advocates were joined by the humanists, Congress became increasingly preoccupied with the future of "American culture," with the "maturity" of the nation, with the "legacy" that it would pass on to future generations. Following the alternating social complacency and anti-Communist campaign of the fifties and in the midst of the civil rights activities and antiwar protests (to say nothing of the political corruption of the seventies), this concern for American civilization sounds rather quaint today. Especially in these times of fiscal restraint in Congress (aptly described by one observer as a pull-up-the-ladder-Jack-I'm-aboard mentality), we are likely to smile at the expansive mood of the New Frontier and the Great Society, proclaiming that the body politic was capable of great feats. Nor were these feats to be confined to acts of physical strength and technological mastery. The early sixties were a time for speaking of the soul of America as well as of the body politic, a concern for the spirit and the mind of the nation that seemed to cry out for the arts and humanities (which appealed, in turn, for federal assistance, a *quid pro quo* that eluded the Harold Grosses of Congress, who saw only the needless expense of the cultural program). Without such support, Heckscher pointed out, "the political community falls short of its ideal potentialities."

It is always sobering, however, in the course of such oratorical preening, to turn from the ideal to the actual, from plans for "beautifying" America to its pollution-choked cities, from plans to integrate America to communities divided by hate, from plans to uplift America to the Nielsen ratings and the best-seller lists. The truth about the arts in America was not so grim, perhaps, but it soon became apparent to those who prescribed the cultural tonic for the nation—a federal arts program—that the matter was not so simple as revenue-sharing plans or grants to higher education. The arts, in the federal context, are complex, difficult, beyond the reach of mere financial aid alone. They are a part of American life, unlike environmental matters or race relations or education—and very much like religion—that has always been separate from the state. The arts may have served as ornamentation, for the capitol or the White House, or in traveling displays abroad, but except for the brief federal fling in the thirties, they had never been directly tied to the affairs of state.

The New Deal arts projects, clearly, were anomalous, contingency plans developed during a national crisis, and the legislative attempts in 1937 and 1938 to place the projects under a permanent Bureau of Fine Arts were doomed from the start. Nor was it simply a matter of a conservative backlash against the New Deal, nor even the charges of subversion in the theater and writers' projects, that undermined the effort to gather support for the proposed Bureau of Fine Arts. Rather, it was the absence of a precedent (beyond the emergency measures themselves) for direct federal involvement in the arts. Never having operated a theater before, nor hired vast numbers of artists and writers and musicians, most congressmen were convinced that such patronage should not occur again. And there were few around to tell them otherwise. Aside from a handful of well-intentioned but politically naive members of Congress, joined by a scattering from the fractured arts community, there was no arts lobby or collective interdisciplinary voice to convince Congress that *it* should establish the precedent for a permanent federal arts subsidy.

Looking back to the forties, then, after the last vestiges of the arts projects had been trampled under the national defense effort, one can discern three interlocking patterns in the federal arts picture, three key elements that required nearly a quarter century to develop—a plan, a rationale, and a movement. The delay in these developments was the product of a number of factors, chief among them the simple fact that the arts have never enjoyed a high priority in America. (No politician ever said "Speak softly and carry a big paintbrush," after all, and Mr. Reagan's acting ability, while perhaps indispensable to his campaign, was not part of the Republican platform.) Although too much has been made of the Puritan legacy of disdain for the arts, it is nevertheless true that the arts in America have most often been left to fend for themselves, with little official encouragement. Developments in the realm of art and government depended moreover, on a whole range of factors inherent in the political process—timing, practicality, association, leadership; and public art in America became mired in a variety of nonaesthetic issues, most notably cold war politics at home and abroad, that slowed the federal arts movement considerably. Suffice it to say that the ultimate answers to the questions raised in the failure of the Bureau of Fine Arts legislation in 1938 were slow to develop simply because such events, neither crucial to the future of the country nor directly tied to its past, always take time.

The development of the new federal plan was based initially, not on rational policy development, but on threats and failures—the failures of the WPA and cultural exchange, and the threat of government control of the arts. The rationale, too, proceeded in a helter-skelter fashion, subject to the mood of Congress and the country, and passing through its various phases—the international prestige argument, the cold-war argument, the leisure-time argument, the cultural-dissemination argument, the economic argument, and, finally, the "American-civilization" argument—in a cumulative, snowballing fashion, gathering support along the way, but always at the risk of offending (or at least trying the patience of) the earliest supporters. The arts movement itself, finally, was even more difficult to pin down than either the rationale for government support or the specific subsidy plan that was finally adopted. That movement was inevitably an assemblage of shifting, temporary alliances, a waxing and waning collection of unfamiliar partners who not only shared in the slow, frustrating plan- and rationale-building process, but who were concerned with defending their position as well. For the federal arts movement, it must be remembered, was confronted throughout its uneven career by strong opposition forces. The opposition was an equally diverse, disorganized alliance, actually, but it enjoyed the immense advantage of having tradition on its side and facing the comparatively easy task of saying "no" to whatever rationale and plan came forward as that year's model for federal arts support. Basing its claims on respected political values—frugality, state's rights, private initiative, combined with an acceptance of the status quo and a recognition of higher priorities than the arts—the antisubsidy faction had the upper hand, at least in the early years of the debates.

The plan, the rationale, and the movement intermingle, then, as three aspects of the federal arts program that was established in 1965. Yet these three components are oddly distinct, each freighted with its own particular burden and each demanding a separate analysis. The plan, for example, with its task of distinguishing clearly between the old and the new, between the broad strokes of WPA work relief and the detailed etchings of the new competitive arts program, must be viewed in an appropriate historical context. The rationale, too, requires special attention, the services of an interpreter, in effect, to translate the diplomatic implications and domestic policy issues arising out of the federal arts effort. And the movement, finally, is unique, too. For it included not only the philosophers and architects who developed the rationale and constructed the plan, the artists and audiences to be served by the program, but inevitably, because this was a *federal* program, the politicians.

In retrospect, devising the plan for a new federal arts program was the easy part of the process, proceeding largely on the basis of what should *not* happen. The new program should *not* be like the old one, like the New Deal projects, with the government directly involved in the arts. Such programs, putting federal funds squarely on the line for art, received little of the credit when the art was judged to be good (as much of the federal art of the thirties was), since Congress was ill-equipped to evaluate such judgments; and when the art was bad, or controversial—and Congress specialized in the latter—the federal programs took all of the blame. The transition from individualized cultural laissez faire to the collective expression of the WPA was simply too abrupt for the nation to make easily. Were it not for the general flux of the times, when social engineering was permitted, the New Deal art projects would never have taken place. By the time the smoke of World War II had cleared, certainly, a majority of Congress were convinced that such programs should never be attempted again.

It is not surprising, then, that it was the collection of art that the State Department *purchased* in 1946, rather than the one that it borrowed that same year, that created the uproar in Congress. Nor is it surprising that the earliest examples of postwar arts legislation, appearing ten years after the Bureau of Fine Arts bills, were all modest proposals that carefully avoided the direct-subsidy issue. Beginning with Jacob Javits's 1949 resolution for an assembly of private citizens to *consider* plans for a national theater, opera, and ballet, the early fifties saw a spate of similarly tentative measures, calling for admissions-tax exemptions, a new arts commission, an academy of fine arts, a capital arts center, or for plans to bring college performing arts groups to Washington (at no expense to the taxpayer, to be sure). The archetypal fifties federal arts bill was the plan for a federal advisory council on the arts, politically attractive simply because it was so *unlike* the WPA. It would neither create art itself nor sponsor the creation of art by others; it would merely *talk* about art. These deliberations would be conducted, moreover, by private citizens, experts in their respective fields who (unlike the New Dealers) could be trusted to recommend a rational federal arts policy. Thus while the advisory council scheme admitted the *possibility* of actual federal support for the arts at an unspecified future date (when Texas freezes over, according to some southern Congressmen), it assured the opponents of such aid that no federal action would be hasty. As if to drive home that point, Congress mulled over the advisory council bill for ten years before passing it; even then the legislation was a compromise—the acceptable half of an ambitious arts package that had included a national arts foundation.

The foundation plan grew out of Representative Charles Howell's prophetic (and hopelessly premature) "American National Arts Act" of 1954, a bill that blossomed the following year into Frank Thompson's "American National Arts, Sports, and Recreation Act," equally premature but including the important new provision for grants to the states for cultural programs. Subsequently refined to involve equal matching grants to each state having an official arts agency (with nonmatching grants to assist states to establish such agencies), the arts foundation plan at once became more politically attractive—all states now had something to gain from the bill—and more expansive. It promised to create, in effect, its own constituency, by helping to develop a network of public arts support at the federal and state levels. In this sense, at least, the foundation plan mirrored the WPA projects, which, while administered in Washington, were carried out at the state and local levels. The foundation was distinct in all other respects from the earlier direct sponsorship and employment of artists; the new agency was designed merely to assist nonprofit projects (at a maximum of 50 percent of the total project cost), projects of "significant merit." That qualitative judgment—as distinct from the quantitative criteria of the WPA— was to be made, not by government officials, but by private citizens (the presidentially appointed members of the long-awaited National Council on the Arts) acting in a public capacity, periodically convening to determine how the federal funds should be disbursed. In operation, the foundation-council scheme proved ultimately to be insufficient to handle the number and range of the applications for assistance, and thus a system of advisory panels (again private citizens acting in a public capacity) was devised. This system of peer review, insulated from Congress by the Arts Endowment staff and the National Council alike, has become one of the hallmarks of federal support and a model for arts subsidy at the state level.

Although there were other details to be worked out (including the relationship between the chairman, the council, and the foundation, for example, as well as the relationship between the two endowments themselves), the essence of the plan—matching funds, including state block grants, awarded through a process of peer review—was fully developed by the early sixties. The experience of the British Arts Council and the New York State Council on the Arts was influential, but no more so than the trial-and-error events of the past, namely, the WPA and the cultural exchange projects, which were thoroughly explored over the course of the several congressional arts hearings that began in 1952. The foundation plan had to wait in line, so to speak, behind its predecessor, the advisory arts council, and in the process other plans (such as that for a secretary of culture in the cabinet) were put forth and rejected. It was not the development of the foundation plan itself that caused the delay; rather, it was the reluctance of Congress to embark on any new federal arts ventures, a reluctance that was only gradually overcome as the rationale for federal subsidy expanded to attract all but the most conservative lawmakers. Even after fifteen years the arts alone could not hope to accomplish this task. Only with the addition of the humanities, and the attendant strengthening of the federal arts rationale, could the arts foundation plan be put into effect.

If the WPA arts plan was inappropriate for the post-Depression nation, the WPA rationale—emergency work-relief—was even more obsolete. Unlike the development of the plan for federal arts support, which occurred in a fairly orderly, if long-winded, process, the development of the federal arts rationale was a complicated affair. A tortuous path might be traced, for example, from the WPA to the arts and humanities foundation, with detours abroad for cultural exchange and with periodic congressional roadblocks; but no single route is sufficient to describe the multiplicity of reasons that attracted supporters to the federal arts cause. At best, one can only cite the major arguments to attempt to convey a sense of the juggling act that saw a variety of motives circulating above the evolving arts plan.

The earliest stirrings in the realm of government and art in the forties were perhaps motivated largely out of the sense of vacuum that existed following the dismantling of the New Deal projects. Having witnessed the promise of the government's role as stimulator and disseminator of culture, and convinced that the negative aspects could be eliminated by removing the relief factor that tainted the WPA's reputation, federal arts veterans like George Biddle cast about for a streamlined, postwar version of the WPA arts projects. Others, like Actors Equity and the American Federation of Musicians, less concerned with memories of the New Deal than with the current adversities in the performing arts, sought government aid as a practical solution to economic problems, much as the agricultural sector looked to the federal government for price supports. At the level of government itself, finally, the early postwar efforts at cultural exchange, tentative projects that as often as not backfired, served at least to raise the issue of public arts support.

It was not until Representative Javits introduced his joint resolution for the arts assembly in 1949 that a more positive dialogue began in Congress. The concern, for Javits, was twofold: America's reputation abroad, where government subsidy had a lengthy tradition, and the absence of cultural opportunities at home ("especially outside the great centers of population"). Along with the burgeoning interest in cultural exchange during the cold war, these two arguments were joined by two related concerns in the early fifties, the status of American culture in general and the economic future of the arts in particular, and formed the basis for the next ten years of debate. The process was largely one of refinement and shifting emphases, as the cold-war argument gave way to a heightened sensitivity to the imbalance between science and culture in America; as the concern for economic conditions in the arts became more sharply focused; and as that almost instinctive belief in a democratic culture grew into a preoccupation with "American civilization," and the humanities were packaged with the arts and promoted as a two-stage treatment for the nation's ills.

Also important to the process of building a rationale for federal arts support (and to the development of a plan and a movement as well), were the opponents of such aid, that confederation of reactionary legislators and conservative arts organizations who resisted federal expansion in general, along with those intellectuals and artists who objected, in particular, to state encroachment into the cultural realm. These combined forces frustrated the federal arts movement for years. At the same time, though, the antifederalists prodded the prosubsidy faction into sharpening their arguments and reaching beyond the narrow interests of the arts community in an effort to make connections with the more general concerns of American society. Not until the entrance of the academic community in 1964 could this process be completed, but such events as Eisenhower's Goals Commission report and the adoption of the arts as a mark of national distinction by the Kennedy and Johnson administrations were milestones in the development of a federal arts rationale sufficiently broad to assure its success in Congress.

It is equally important to discuss the movement that both shaped and rallied around the federal arts plan and the rationale behind that plan. The story of the origin and emergence of the new federal arts program of the sixties, in fact, is largely the story of the coalescence of the many diverse segments of what has been termed the "arts community"— the artists, critics, arts administrators, artists unions and associations, service organizations, boards of trustees, patrons, and those Americans in and out of Congress, finally, whose commitment to American culture extended beyond that of the passive spectator or consumer. Initially, these several factions were fragmented, even opposed in their view of the government as potential arts supporter. If a handful of WPA veterans and the actors and musicians unions called for federal support as early as the forties, symphony orchestra boards and conservative art organizations like the National Sculpture Society were adamantly opposed to such plans in the fifties. Perhaps most notable was the impact of Congress on the movement. For while Congress mortally wounded federal art in the thirties with its attacks on the New Deal projects, the subsequent verbal assaults on "subversive art" by a handful of congressmen served rather to stimulate the arts, fostering the organization of the arts community in its own defense, a process that in turn served the federal arts movement as well. It is doubtful, despite all of the useful services rendered by organizations like the Committee on Government and Art and the National Council on the Arts and Government, as well as the efforts of the artists' unions, that the interdisciplinary organization of artists would have taken place as swiftly as it did in the fifties without the attacks of reactionary congressmen like George Dondero. So, too, did the ax-wielding rhetoric of Harold Gross, attacking every plan for federal arts support that came along, serve to convince the arts community of the need to adopt more sophisticated lobbying techniques than impassioned letters to the editor of *Art News*.

Positive actions by the federal government also contributed to the organization of the arts community, of course. For example, cultural exchange, if not always a happy marriage of art and state, did provide some favorable publicity along with all of the congressional fireworks, and by the end of the fifties, the arts community could point with pride to its contribution to international good will. Similarly, the legislation for the advisory arts council and the National Cultural Center, however tardy their arrival, provided focal points for the arts community, as did the almost yearly subcommittee hearings on the arts.

These events merely set the stage, however, for the entrance of the Kennedy administration, which from the outset attempted to exude good taste and which embraced culture, more importantly, as one of the responsibilities of the state. The Secretary of Labor's decision in the Metropolitan Opera strike, with its call for a six-point partnership of arts support, followed by August Heckscher's report, added to the anticipation of action at the federal level and contributed to the most fertile period of organizational development in the arts community, with state and local arts councils and new regional and national associations dotting the cultural map across the land.

With the entrance of the humanities forces during the Johnson years, finally, adding an important new thrust to the federal arts rationale by joining scholarship to the arts, Congress and the nation were at last ready to accept another federal cultural experiment. The arts movement finally prevailed, twenty-two years after the demise of the New Deal projects, with the signing of the National Foundation on the Arts and Humanities Act on 29 September 1965.

Any fears remaining about the new agency placing a steel grip on the arts in America were all but eliminated the following month when the Arts Endowment's 1966 budget was announced: $2.5 million in program funds (plus up to $2 million in funds available for the matching of private donations, of which only $34,308 was used the first year). The total figure ($2,568,616, including the matched donations) was not even a third of what the Ford Foundation had spent on ballet alone the previous year, and it was a mere drop in the punch bowl compared to the $85 million symphony orchestra program announced by the Ford Foundation in October.[2] The Arts Endowment, moreover, was expected to cover all of the arts, all over the country, as hundreds of requests for funding that came into the endowment every week in the fall of 1965 attested.[3]

Even before these appeals began to arrive, even before the foundation was a reality, in fact, Roger Stevens and the National Council and its staff had begun to explore possible funding areas; they were guided by the council's expressed commitment to excellence and availability, individual and institutional support, innovation and preservation, artistic training and audience development. Either unfocused or admirably broad-minded, according to one's point of view (or according to the results of one's request for funding), the emerging NCA/NEA philosophy produced a rainbow of financial commitments at the council's November 1965 meeting, helping to establish what would become the pattern of endowment support over the years. There was a little of the old—funds for cultural exchange—as well as a preview of the new—support for a feasibility study for an American Film Institute. There was even a little of Uncle-Sam-to-the-rescue, as a $100,000 grant went to the hard-pressed American Ballet Theater (ABT) to insure its continued existence. But more importantly the grants reflected what would become the basic themes of federal arts support: a *touring* grant to ABT, to make its art available across the land; grants to the *individual artist*, for composer and chroreographer fellowships, for sabbatical leaves for artists who teach, and for the provision of low-cost studio/housing for artists; grants for *innovation*, for the production of new plays by resident professional and university theater companies; grants for *technical assistance*, aiding the administrative efforts of national arts organizations; and grants for *arts education*, setting up the Laboratory Theater Project to bring theater to students in Providence, Los Angeles, and New Orleans.[4]

With the implementation of the state block grants the following year, the basic patterns of federal support for the arts were established. There would be new developments and innovations, of course—a program called "Expansion Arts," focusing on minority and neighborhood arts events, for example, and another called "Inter-Arts," for interdisciplinary arts activities. As the endowment coffers grew, nearly doubling in size each year under Richard Nixon and reaching a peak of over $150 million under Jimmy Carter, variations on the old themes became possible, including full-scale museum and media arts programs, along with support for orchestras, jazz, folk arts, opera-musical theater, and design.

There were questions to be answered, too, if not the obvious ones about censorship and control, which proved to be groundless concerns, then about more subtle matters. Given the scarce economy of the arts and arts support, for example, what should the proper balance be between reward for excellence and support based on financial or geographic need—between the institutional wealth of New York and the scarcity of art in Wyoming? Similarly, what should the federal role be in the inevitable traditionalist-modernist debate—support for the tried-and-true or seed money for experimentation? What are the implications, moreover, of federal support of the individual artist, at once the most fundamental and least predictable part of the cultural process? And would the federal program, finally, foster diversity or standardization, vitality or dependence, catalytic support or bureaucratic red tape?

As 1965 drew to a close, however, these developments and the questions they raised lay in the future of the Arts Endowment. For the moment, it was sufficient simply to look back on that long struggle to achieve the program. Nor is it any less important today to reflect on those years of planning and debate, if only to be better prepared for the future, as federal support of the arts seems destined to remain a source of controversy and discussion.

Notes

Prologue

1. This is not to imply that the WPA and the NEA have been the only examples of federal arts activity in America, but they are the only major programs of arts support. Other federal arts activities, like the decoration of the capitol, the procurement, maintenance, and display of the national art collections, and the activities of the Commission of Fine Arts, have been treated in the past by Grace Overmyer, *Government and the Arts* (New York, 1939), and Ralph Purcell, *The Arts and the National Government: A Study of the American Experience* (Washington, D.C., 1956).

2. The shock of a proposed 50 percent cut in the Arts Endowment's fiscal year 1982 budget, amid rumors that OMB Director David Stockman had plans for phasing out the endowments altogether, produced a lot of doomsday prophecies in the arts world. The task force on the arts and the humanities that Ronald Reagan appointed in the spring of 1981, similarly, charged with examining the future of the endowments, was viewed with fear and suspicion by many; its final report to the president, however, proved to be innocuous. Presidential Task Force on the Arts and the Humanities, *Report to the President* (Washington, D.C., 1981).

3. Michael Straight, *Twigs for an Eagle's Nest, Government and the Arts: 1965–78* (New York, 1978), p. 13.

4. Artists had organized before in an effort to influence Congress, but never with any lasting effect. In 1859, 127 American artists, protesting the employment of so many foreign artists in the decoration of federal buildings, persuaded Congress to establish a National Art Commission to select artists and designs for the embellishment of national buildings, but this body lasted less than two years. Purcell, *The Arts and the National Government*, p. 20. A short-lived artists' lobby also formed around the ill-fated Bureau of Fine Arts legislation of the late thirties. The Federal Arts Committee, chaired by Burgess Meredith and including subcommittees headed by Leopold Stokowski, Lillian Gish, Ruth St. Denis, Donald Ogden Stewart, and Max Weber, favored the creation of a new arts bureau, incorporating the WPA arts projects, as did the Friends of the Federal Arts Projects. At the same time, the Fine Arts Federation of New York and the National Committee for the Protection of the Arts opposed such a measure.

Chapter One

1. "Unemployed Arts," *Fortune*, May 1937, p. 111.

2. *Congressional Record*, 75th Cong., 3d Sess. (1938), pp. 9491–92.

3. Quoted in Jerre Mangione, *The Dream and the Deal: The Federal Writers' Project, 1935–1943* (Boston, 1972), p. 308.

4. Ibid., pp. 321–22.

5. Richard McKinzie, *The New Deal for Artists* (Princeton, 1967), pp. 166–69.

6. See Monty Noam Penkower, *The Federal Writers' Project* (Urbana, IL, 1977), pp. 228–37.

7. Quoted in U.S. Congress, House, *Hearings before the Subcommittee of the Committee on Appropriations on the Military Establishment Bill for 1944*, 78th Cong., 1st Sess. (1943), p. 326. (Hereafter cited as *Military Hearings-*1943).

8. The Art Advisory Committee originally consisted of artists George Biddle (chairman) and Henry Varnum Poor, David Finley (director, National Gallery of Art), Edward Rowan (director, Treasury Department's Section of Fine Arts), Reeves Lewenthal (president, Associated American Artists), and John Steinbeck. Biddle, Poor, and Steinbeck subsequently resigned, with the two former New Deal muralists becoming painters on the project. Biddle wrote the letter to Kroll from the Advisory Committee, 17 Mar. 1943. Leon Kroll Papers, Archives of American Art, Smithsonian Institution.

9. *Military Hearings-*1943, pp. 324–25. The article, which ran in the *Washington Evening Star* on 1 June 1943, included a photo of Biddle's Justice Dept. Mural. For Francis Biddle's battles with the House Un-American Activities Committee, of which Starnes was a member, see Walter Goodman, *The Committee* (New York, 1964), pp. 135–37.

10. *Congressional Record*, 78th Cong., 1st Sess. (1943), p. 6174. The House-Senate disagreement was settled in a conference committee, with the Senate agreeing to terminate the art project as of 31 Aug. 1943. House Report No. 620, 78th Cong., 1st Sess. (1954). See also George Biddle, *Artist at War* (New York, 1944), pp. 1–2, 56–58. At the same time that it killed the War Art unit, Congress also ended the Section of Fine Arts and the Graphics Division of the Office of War Information.

11. Pepino Mangravite, "Congress Vetoes Culture," *Magazine of Art* 36 (Nov. 1943), 264–65.

12. Born into the famous Philadelphia Biddle family in 1885, George Biddle graduated from Harvard College and Harvard Law School before taking up painting as his career. Biddle wrote President Roosevelt in 1933 with a proposal for a government-sponsored mural project, and three years later executed murals at the Justice Dept. building under federal auspices. (His other murals include those at the National Library in Rio de Janeiro and at the Supreme Court building in Mexico City.) See McKinzie, *New*

Deal, pp. 5–10, and William F. McDonald, *Federal Relief Administration and the Arts* (Columbus, OH, 1969), pp. 357–61.

13. "The Government and the Arts: A Proposal by George Biddle, with Comment and Criticism by Others," *Harper's*, Oct. 1943, pp. 427–34.

14. The two "Art Weeks" of 1940 and 1941 had only limited success. See McKinzie, *New Deal*, pp. 121–23.

15. "The Government and the Arts," p. 432.

16. Ibid., p. 434.

17. Ibid., p. 433. If he never changed his mind about the number of "original creators" in the U.S., Moe at least changed his opinion of government subsidy. He became the first chairman of the National Endowment for the Humanities.

18. For a plan for federal aid to theater, see Robert Porterfield and Robert Breen, "Toward a National Theatre," *Theatre Arts* 29 (Oct. 1945), 599–602. In music, Serge Koussevitzky, conductor of the Boston Symphony Orchestra, called for a postwar program in which each state would sponsor a symphony orchestra as "spiritual food for its residents." *New York Times*, 2 Aug. 1945, p. 15; 13 Oct. 1945, p. 10; and 30 Sept. 1947, p. 25.

The two legislative proposals were introduced by Rep. James Mc-Granery (D-PA) in an attempt to create a Bureau of Fine Arts in the Office of Education "to conduct surveys relating to education in the fine arts and to collect and disseminate information for the development of cultural activities among the people." Both bills (H.R. 600, 1941, and H.R. 900, 1943) died in committee.

19. American Artists Professional League, "Another Bureau of Fine Arts," *Art Digest* 20 (1 Dec. 1945), 32–33. For a typical AAPL attack on the WPA Art Project, see Albert T. Reid, "WPA—RIP!" *Art Digest* 18 (15 Mar. 1944), 28.

20. Quoted in *Art News* 45 (Oct. 1946), 19.

21. Rep. Fred Busbey (R-IL) later disputed the claim that foreign governments had actually requested modern art, charging that the State Dept. itself had solitcited those requests. See note 33 below.

22. "Showing the World," *Newsweek*, 14 Oct. 1946, p. 116; *New York Times*, 3 Oct. 1946, p. 25. For a list of the 79 paintings and 47 artists, see "American Art Abroad: The State Dept. Collection," *Art News* 45 (Oct. 1946), 20–31.

23. See, for example, reviews by Edward A. Jewell, *New York Times*, 6 Oct. 1946, sec. 2, p. 8; Jo Gibbs, *Art Digest* 21 (1 Oct. 1946), 13; and Ralph M. Pearson, *Art Digest* 21 (15 Oct. 1946), p. 29.

24. *New York Times*, 13 April 1947, sec. 2, p. 10. Davidson had, in fact, secured some genuine bargains, with several dealers and artists agreeing to cooperate with the novel venture by offering works at below-market prices. Georgia O'Keeffe, for example, whose paintings had brought up to $10,000 at the time, offered two works for $1000 each.

25. John D. Morse, "Americans Abroad," *Magazine of Art* 40 (Jan. 1947), 21.

26. The AAPL letter to Byrnes, dated 6 Nov. 1946, is reprinted in *Art Digest* 21 (15 Nov. 1946), 32.

27. Ralph M. Pearson, "Hearst, the A.A.P.L., and Life," *Art Digest* 21 (15 Dec. 1946), 25; *Art News* 45 (Dec. 1946), 13. Even more responsible newspapers than Hearst's yielded occasionally to the temptation to make sport of the State Dept.'s art. Describing Kuniyoshi's *Circus Girl Resting* in a front-page story, the *Washington Post* said the work resembled "something between Primo Carnero taking an enforced siesta and the product of an early Easter Islander after a bad night" (6 May 1947). It was doubtless the most infamous of all the works in the collection, and even circus girls protested the "unflattering" portrait. Harry Truman commented that the artist "must have stood off from the canvas and thrown paint at it. If that is art, I'm a Hottentot." Quoted in *Art Digest* 21 (15 Mar. 1947), 7.

28. U.S. Congress, House, *Hearings before the Subcommittee of the Committee on Appropriations on the Department of State Appropriations Bill for 1948*, 80th Cong., 1st Sess. (1947), p. 28. (Hereafter cited as *State Dept. Hearings-1947.*)

29. *New York Times*, 18 May 1947, p. 53. No record exists of such a panel of experts ever being appointed or meeting.

30. *State Dept. Hearings*-1947, pp. 415–16.

31. *Look*, 18 Feb. 1947, pp. 80–81. Ironically, seven of the top eleven artists in the magazine's art poll the following year were represented in the State Dept. collection.

32. House Report No. 33, 80th Cong., 1st Sess. (1947), pp. 6–7. Congress, of course, had a number of complaints about the affairs of the State Dept., and the attack on the art program was a comparatively small skirmish. Of greater concern in the department's information and cultural relations program, for example, was the Voice of America, which the House Appropriations Committee also refused to fund.

33. A useful overview of art and politics of the period is Jane De Hart Mathews, "Art and Politics in Cold War America," *American Historical Review* 81(Oct. 1976), 762–77, which cites three stages in the anti-Communist, antimodernist attack: opposition to "left-wing" social commentary in predominantly representational art, objections to the political affiliations of the artists, and objections to "modern art" as a Communist conspiracy. In practice, however, the three stages were neither so sharply defined nor strictly sequential.

34. *Congressional Record*, 80th Cong., 1st Sess. (1947), pp. 5220–21.

35. Busbey claimed that while most of the State Dept. art purchases were made in the spring of 1946, most of the requests from foreign governments did not arrive until the following October. The culprit here, too, was Davidson, who had collaborated, according to Busbey, with Hannah Goldman of the Press and Publication Division, OIC, to "drum up requests

from abroad" in the "Weekly Round-Up Artcast" sent out on 20 Sept. 1946. Ralph Pearson, in two *Art Digest* articles, defended the State Dept.'s claim of numerous requests for contemporary American art prior to the purchases. See "They Asked for It," *Art Digest* 21 (15 Sept. 1947), 32; and "State Dept. Requests," *Art Digest* 22 (1 Oct. 1947), 29.

36. Other comments in Congress included Georgia Democrat Edward Cox's reference to "crazy" pictures, Mississippi Democrat John Rankin's suggestion that they were "Communist caricatures," and Kentucky Democrat Frank Chelf's classic statement: "If any pictures are sent abroad, we should see to it that they represent American home or family life. Not some silly thing that resembles the north end of a south-bound freight train which inadvertently is headed west."

37. *Republican News*, Aug. 1947, p. 3.

38. Quoted in "The Comrade Is Decadent," *Time*, 25 Aug. 1947, p. 68. "In Moscow . . . ," according to John Berger, Picasso's "reputation as a great man was used for propaganda purposes—whilst his art was dismissed as decadent. His paintings were never shown. No book was published on his work—not even one setting out to prove the alleged decadence." John Berger, *The Success and Failure of Picasso* (Baltimore, 1965), p. 175.

39. Although never a member of HUAC, Dondero (who served in Congress from 1932 to 1957) shared that committee's preoccupation with the Communist threat, making numerous speeches in Congress on the subject. His relationship with art, however, is less clear. An admitted novice in cultural matters, Dondero apparently relied on Dorothy Drew of the AAPL to prepare his diatribes. In 1960 he called her the "sole work horse in exposing communism in American art," and later claimed that she was "solely responsible for assisting a committee of legitimate artists in preparing material for eight speeches." See the letter Dondero wrote to Drew, 19 Jan. 1960, as well as his letter to Hon. Clarence J. Brown, 28 May 1963, George A. Dondero Papers, Archives of American Art, Smithsonian Institution.

40. Among the responses was the Stop Censorship Movement, a group formed "to combat the rising menace of censorship threatening to engulf and stifle freedom of expression in every field of creative art in America." *New York Times*, 15 Mar. 1948, p. 26.

41. *Congressional Record*, 81st Cong., 1st Sess. (1949), pp. 2317–18. For a critical response to Dondero's accusations, see Peyton Boswell, "Assasination by Implication," *Art Digest* 23 (15 Mar. 1949), 7.

42. Dondero cited seventeen artists whose works were included in the St. Albans exhibit, fifteen of whom were "of known radical affiliation," and nine of whom "were included in the ill-fated State Department art show." The fifteen alleged radicals were Xavier Gonzales, Yasuo Kuniyoshi, Jean Liberté, Ben Shahn, Jack Levine, Abraham Rattner, Reginald Marsh, I. Rice Pereira, Louis Bosa, George L. K. Morris, Joseph Hirsch, Max Weber, Rufine Tamayo, Alexander Brook, and Arthur Osver.

43. The two artists who participated directly in the St. Albans program were Irene Rice Pereira and Sol Wilson, neither of whom gave any evidence of being involved in any propagandizing at the hospital. Boswell, "Assasination," p. 7.

44. *Congressional Record*, 81st Cong., 1st Sess. (1949), pp. 3234–35.

45. For Artists Equity's response to Dondero's attack, see the letter from Hudson Walker, executive director of Equity, along with a statement from the organization, both placed in the *Congressional Record* by Charles A. Plumley (R-VT). Ibid., pp. A3804–06.

46. Mathews, "Art and Politics," p. 70. For an example of the modernists' side of the debate, see the "Museums' Manifesto," a joint statement issued by the Museum of Modern Art, the Whitney Museum of American Art, and the Institute of Contemporary Art in Boston, defending modern art and rejecting the current pleas for a return to "American" art, and citing as well the dangerous parallels to Nazi and Soviet repression of art in the recent attacks on modernism. The manifesto is reprinted in Peyton Boswell, "Modern Manifesto," *Art Digest* 24 (1 Apr. 1950), 5.

47. Alfred M. Frankfurter, "Abstract Red Herring," *Art News* 48 (Summer 1948), 15. The article makes explicit as well Dondero's connections to conservative arts organizations.

48. James Thrall Soby, "A Going into the Mulberry Trees," *Saturday Review*, 2 July 1949, pp. 30–31.

49. *Congressional Record*, 81st Cong., 1st Sess. (1949), p. 11750.

50. Ibid., pp. 12099–12100. Javits also introduced into the *Record* several letters of protest, including one from Hobart Nichols, president emeritus of the conservative National Academy of Design.

51. Both Javits and Sen. James Patterson (R-CT) called for an investigation of the library's award. Ibid., pp. 9924, A4617; *New York Times*, 8 Aug. 1949, p. 13. The Joint Library Committee decided not to investigate the Pound matter, but canceled all such awards thereafter, including the Elizabeth Sprague Coolidge Medal for eminent services to chamber music, and three awards made in connection with the annual national exhibition of prints. *New York Times*, 20 Aug. 1949, p. 13. Yale University subsequently awarded the Bollingen Prize.

52. The conservative National Sculpture Society was the lone organization to refuse the invitation to join the committee. Lloyd Goodrich, "Art and Government," *College Art Journal* 8 (Fall 1948), 41–42. Original members of the CGA included representatives from the American Federation of Arts, American Association of Museums, College Art Association, Association of Art Museum Directors, Artists Equity, and the National Academy of Design. Six other organizations joined soon after: American Institute of Architects, American Institute of Decorators, National Association of Women Artists, National Institute of Arts and Letters, National Society of Mural Painters, and Sculptors Guild.

53. Minutes of the first meeting of the Committee on Government

and Art, 14 Feb. 1950, Whitney Museum of American Art. Copy in Leon Kroll Papers, Archives of American Art, Smithsonian Institution.

54. Quoted in Commission of Fine Arts, *Art and Government* (Washington, D.C., 1953), pp. 122–23.

55. *New York Times*, 9 Dec. 1948, p. 35.

56. There is some mystery surrounding "Carleton Smith," who was often confused with Carleton Sprague Smith, chief of the Music Division of the New York Public Library who served as a cultural officer in Brazil during WW II. According to this Carleton Smith, the NAF director's real name was Robert Smith, whose organization had a modest budget of around $1,200 a year and was more of a self-promotional enterprise than anything else. The State Dept. sent out a warning about the activities of the so-called National Arts Foundation, Smith recalls; and his namesake, much to his relief, has dropped out of sight. Interview with Carleton Sprague Smith, 25 Sept. 1980.

In any event, the NAF was instrumental in setting up the initial U.S.-Soviet cultural exchange in the mid-fifties. These developments and the Rockefeller and CIA involvement in cultural relations are discussed in later chapters.

57. Described as "not a state handout for artists but a fair partnership of interests," the proposed New York program involved the creation of a state art commission to purchase and/or commission works of art for touring or installation in public buildings. See James Thrall Soby, "An Art Program for New York State," *Magazine of Art* 40 (Jan. 1947), 29–30.

58. *National Music Council Bulletin* 9 (Jan. 1949), 8–10; Henry Marx, "We Note That . . . ," *Music News* 41 (Sept. 1949), 5.

59. "Government Subsidy: A Dangerous Expedient," *Musical America* 69 (Sept. 1949), 14.

60. J. P. Shanley, "Toward Subsidy: Drive to Gain Governmental Support for National Theatre Is Planned," *New York Times*, 14 Nov. 1948, sec. 2, p. 3; Henry Marx, "Theatrical People Are More Alert than Musicians," *Music News* 41 (Jan. 1949), 77; *New York Times*, 18 Dec. 1948, p. 14; William Beyer, "State of the Theatre: Renaissance in Embryo," *School and Society* 69 (26 Mar. 1949), 228–31.

Chapter Two

1. U.S. Congress, Senate, *Bureau of Fine Arts. Hearings before a Subcommittee on Education and Labor on S. 3296, a Bill to Provide for a Permanent Bureau of Fine Arts*, 75th Cong., 3d Sess. (1938, p. 185).

2. *Congressional Record*, 75th Cong., 3d Sess. (1938), p. 9497.

3. *Congressional Record*, 81st Cong., 1st Sess. (1949), p. 514. For a copy of Javits's introductory remarks and H.J.R. 104 itself, see "The Javits Resolution," *Music News* 41 (Mar. 1949), 4.

4. In Feb. 1949, Rep. Celler (D-NY) introduced H.R. 3038, which would have reconstructed and remodeled the old Belasco Theatre (at that time a Treasury Dept. warehouse), to be leased to a private producer. See the *Congressional Record*, 81st Cong., 1st Sess. (1949), pp. A1710–11.

5. Ibid., p. A4072; Jacob Javits, "Address on a Bill to Establish a National Theatre, Opera and Ballet," *National Music Council Bulletin* 10 (Jan. 1950), 6–7.

6. Rep. Barratt O'Hara's comments were part of his tribute to the National Ballet, a wholly private operation in Washington. *Congressional Record*, 81st Cong., 2d Sess. (1950), p. A5392.

7. George Biddle, "A United States Bureau of Fine Arts," *Art Digest* 24 (1 Aug. 1950), 5.

8. "A Symposium: Government and Art," *Magazine of Art* 43 (Nov. 1950), 242–59. Other symposium participants included architect Douglas Haskell, who also opposed federal arts support, and Lloyd Goodrich and James T. Soby, who favored it.

9. *New York Times*, 4 Jan. 1951, p. 33.

10. Article 33, Section 17, of the AFM constitution. The Lea Act stemmed from an episode in which the AFM had barred a Michigan radio station from broadcasting amateur muscial performances from the Interlachen Music Camp. The legislation made it unlawful to threaten or compel a broadcaster to employ or pay fees for more persons than it needed or to pay for services not performed, or to refrain from broadcasting noncommercial educational programs. Thus the law eliminated traditional AFM labor practices and served warning to other unions as well. See Robert D. Leiter, *The Musicians and Petrillo*, (New York, 1953), pp. 149–63.

11. Henry Marx, "Subsidies for Musical Organizations Are Part of Cultural Mobilization," *Music News* 42 (Nov. 1950), 3. See also the *New York Times*, 11 Sept. 1950, p. 7.

12. The AFM booklet, "Diminuendo," tracing the economic plight of professional musicians, is reprinted in U.S. Congress, House, *Federal Grants for Fine Arts Programs and Projects. Hearings before a Special Subcommittee of the Committee on Education and Labor, on H.R. 452, 5136, 5330, 5397, 7106, 7185, 7192, 7383, 7433, 7533, 7953, 8047, and 9111*, 83d Cong., 2d Sess. (1954), pp. 169–82. (Cited hereafter as *Arts Hearings-1954*.)

13. *New York Times*, 10 Nov. 1950, p. 26; 5 June 1951, p. 29. The revenue bill of 1951 did grant admissions-tax exemption to nonprofit symphony orchestras and educational institutions.

14. Paul S. Carpenter, *Music: An Art and a Business* (Norman, OK, 1950), p. 197.

15. *New York Times*, 27 Dec. 1950, p. 31; *National Music Council Bulletin* 11 (14 Jan. 1951), 7.

16. Among the features of the British Council most often praised were its independence from Parliament, its emphasis on decentralization,

and its use of regional committees and advisory panels of experts. All would become facets of the eventual National Endowment for the Arts.

17. S. 4165, introduced by Matthew Neely (D-WV), Emanuel Celler's H.R. 9717, and Glen Beale's (R-MD) H.R. 9723 were all designed to bring theater productions of land-grant colleges to Washington.

18. At least nineteen bills modeled after the original Neely-Celler proposal of 1950 were introduced over the next three years. The Secretary of Agriculture was replaced in various versions by the Commissioner of Education, the Federal Security Administrator, or the National Capital Sesquicentennial Commission, while the "theatre productions of land-grant colleges" was gradually expanded to include the "fine art productions of State and land-grant and other accredited non-profit colleges and universities." For a list of these and other arts bills of the period, see *Arts Hearings-1954*, pp. 1–7.

19. Celler's H.R. 2890 was introduced on 26 Feb. 1951, followed thereafter by similar measures sponsored by Reps. Arthur Klein (D-NY) and Roy Wier (D-MN). "In my proposed bill . . . ," Celler emphasized, "there is no thought of domination, not one iota of suggested control over the institutions or the practitioners of the fine arts." Celler's remarks to the NMC are reprinted in the *Congressional Record*, 82d Cong., 1st Sess. (1951), p. A3249.

20. *New York Times*, 17 May 1951, p. 39. Truman had also paid lip service to the importance of the arts in a message praising the work of ANTA—"One of the hallmarks of the maturity of any nation is the extent to which it has developed its own philosophies, artistic standards and cultural patterns, as well as the care and attention it devotes to these enduring aspects of its civilization"—but he never mentioned the use of public funds to achieve these goals. *New York Times*, 25 Apr. 1951, p. 34.

21. For Javits's comments on his bill, H.R. 8216, see Jacob Javits, "For an Academy of Music, Drama and Ballet," *Music News* 144 (Sept. 1952), 13. The government had, in fact, created a National Conservatory of Music in 1891, which operated for a few years under private auspices.

22. U.S. Congress, House, *Fine Arts Programs in Colleges. Hearings before the Subcommittee of the Committee on Education and Labor on H.R. 7494*, 82d Cong., 2d Sess. (1952). All of the testimony, including letters from the Bureau of the Budget and the Commission of Fine Arts, was favorable. For the full committee's amendments, see House Report No. 2428, 82d Cong., 2d Sess. (1952).

23. Senate Report No. 2072, 82d Cong., 2d Sess. (1952). S. 2300, sponsored by Sen. Murray, was passed over on 3 July 1952, after Sen. Kenneth McKellar (D-TN) objected to the bill's passage so close to the end of the session. Even though it was clear that the bill's cost would be incidental, McKellar cited the "enormous organizations" that often spring up, appearing before the Appropriations Committee to ask for funds. *Congressional Record*, 82d Cong., 2d Sess. (1952), pp. 9112–13.

24. House Report No. 2428, p. 2.

25. Alfred M. Frankfurter, "First Entry in a New Diary," *Art News* 51 (Jan. 1953), 17.

26. See, for example, Russell Lynes's 1952 speech at Barnard College, as reported in the *New York Times*, 9 Mar. 1952, p. 81; and Russell Lynes, "Government as Patron of the Arts," *Yale Review* 42 (Autumn 1952), 21–30, which favors the citizens' free and independent choice over the compromises that would arise from federally supported art.

27. In Feb. 1950, the State Dept. appointed Thomas C. Colt, Jr., of the Portland (OR) Museum to select works by American artists for exhibit in the Western Zone of occupied Germany. The plan was canceled less than a month later. See Dorothy Grafly, "How Shall We Support Our Artists?" *American Artist* 15 (Jan. 1951), p. 38.

28. Barrett spoke on 14 Nov. 1951 at a Town Hall conference arranged by the Institute of International Education. *New York Times*, 15 Nov. 1951, p. 12.

29. *New York Times*, 6 Apr. 1953, p. 21. A *New York Times* editorial applauded this effort, 7 Apr. 1953, p. 28. MOMA had always been associated with Rockefeller money, and Eva Cockcroft has traced the museum's involvement with American foreign policy from WW II ("fulfilling 38 contracts for cultural materials totaling $1,590,234") to the cold war, as chief disseminator of abstract expressionism. MOMA, for example, purchased the U.S. pavilion in Venice and represented the U.S. at the Biennales from 1958 to 1962. Eva Cockcroft, "Abstract Expressionism, Weapon of the Cold War," *Artforum* 12 (June 1974), 39–41.

30. Thomas W. Braden, "I'm Glad the CIA is 'Immoral'," *Saturday Evening Post*, 29 May 1967, p. 12. Braden, who had been MOMA's executive secretary from Apr. 1948 to Nov. 1949 before joining the CIA in 1950, explained the need for such a program: "Does anyone really think that congressmen would foster a foreign tour by an artist who has or has had left-wing connections?"

31. Cockcroft, "Abstract Expressionism," p. 40.

32. *Congressional Record*, 82d Cong., 2d Sess. (1952), pp. 2423–27; *New York Times*, 18 Mar. 1952, p. 24. For the NSS protest, which included an open letter to the *New York Times* signed by more than 600 artists, see the *New York Times*, 10 Feb. 1952, p. 1.

33. "The aims of the Artists League of America follow the Soviet pattern and are especially directed to Federal, State, and municipal patronage," Dondero claimed. He also railed against the biased economic studies of such radical groups: "Realizing that municipal, State, and Federal legislation is predicated upon a social need, the left wingers are conscious of the value of slanted surveys that attempt to prove need and justification for their socialistic bills." *Congressional Record*, 82d Cong., 2d Sess. (1952), pp. 2425, 2426.

34. The six other artists culled by Busbey from the HUAC files were

Antonio Frasconi, Milton Goldstein, Leona Price, William Rose, Alfred Russell, and Louis Schanker. Ibid., pp. 3520–23.

35. Quoted in William Hauptman, "Supression of Art in the Mc-Carthy Decade," *Artforum* 11 (Oct. 1973), 49–50.

36. Quoted in *New York Times Magazine*, 26 Oct. 1952, p. 32.

37. Ben Shahn, "The Artist and the Politicians," *Art News* 52 (Sept. 1953), 35.

38. Jane De Hart Mathews, "Art and Politics in Cold War America," *American Historical Review* 81 (Oct. 1976), 765–68.

39. Quoted in George V. Sherman [pseud.], "Dick Nixon: Art Commissar," *Nation*, 10 Jan. 1953, p. 21. See also Hauptman, "Suppression," pp. 51–52.

40. Scudder's resolution read:

> Whereas it has been brought to the attention of the House Committee on Public Works, that the mural paintings decorating the lobby of the Rincon Annex Post Office in San Francisco, Calif., have been criticized by civic groups, veterans' organizations, and patriotic and fraternal societies, as well as by local newspapers and numerous individuals, as being artistically offensive and historically inaccurate; and
> Whereas the murals cast a derogatory and improper reflection on the character of the pioneers and the history of the great State of California: Therefore be it
> Resolved by the Senate and the House of Representatives of the United States of America in Congress assembled, That the Administrator of General Services shall take such action as may be necessary for the prompt removal of the mural paintings on the lobby walls of the Rincon Annex Post Office Building in San Francisco, Calif.

U.S. Congress, House, *Rincon Annex Murals, San Francisco. Hearing before the Subcommittee on Public Grounds of the Committee on Public Works on H.J.R. 211*, 83d Cong., 1st Sess. (1953), p. 1. (Cited hereafter as *Rincon Annex Hearing.*)

41. *Congressional Record*, 83d Cong., 1st Sess. (1953), p. 1643.

42. *Rincon Annex Hearing*, p. 10.

43. For a list of the names of organizations and individuals for and against the murals, see ibid., pp. 78–86.

44. For Eisenhower's and Stevenson's views on arts subsidy, see "Money for Music—The Political Overtones," *Musical America* 72 (1 Nov. 1952), 14–15.

45. "There are many patriotic composers available without the long record of questionable affiliations of Copland," Busbey declared. *New York Times*, 17 Jan. 1953, p. 12.

Chapter Three

1. Alfred M. Frankfurter, "First Entry in a New Diary," *Art News* 51 (Jan. 1953), 17.

2. Following the announcement of Truman's decision, the CGA held what Goodrich recalled was an "acrimonious" meeting with Biddle and Finley. *Lloyd Goodrich Reminiscences*, interview with Dr. Harlan B. Phillips, Archives of American Art, Smithsonian Institution, 1963, pp. 358–70; interview with Lloyd Goodrich, 21 Feb. 1980.

3. For a brief history of the commission, see Commission of Fine Arts, *Art and Government: Report to the President by the Commission of Fine Arts on Activities of the Federal Government in the Field of Art* (Washington, D.C., 1953), pp. 7–12. The enabling legislation of 1910 makes the commission's limitations clear: "It shall be the duty of such Commission to advise upon the location of statues, fountains, and monuments. . . . The Commission shall also advise generally upon questions of art when required to do so by the President, or by any committee of either House of Congress." Nor did the 1953 version of the commission show any signs of wanting to expand its role:

> The Commission has always adhered strictly to its terms of reference: to serve in an advisory capacity concerning the special matters within its competence. . . . The Commission has opposed efforts to transform it into an administrative body, along the lines of government-supported arts councils and ministries of fine arts in other countries, with responsibility for the expenditure of large sums of money as government subsidies for public and private art projects. (*Art and Government*, pp. 10–11.)

The commission included at that time David E. Finley (chairman), Joseph Hudnut, Edward F. Neild, Sr., Felix W. de Welden, Pietro Belluschi, Elbert Peet, and George Biddle.

4. Ibid., p. 29. Biddle recommended the addition of three experts in painting and sculpture to the commission staff, appointed by the chairman from names suggested by a new permanent advisory committee.

5. For typical critiques of *Art and Government*, see Dorothy Grafly, "Art Mountain Conceives a Mouse," *American Artist* 17 (Dec. 1953), 62–66; Patrick Hayes, "A Review of the Commission of Fine Arts Report," *National Music Council Bulletin* 14 (Sept. 1953), 8–9; and Leslie Judd Portner, "What Does the Future Hold?" *Washington Post*, 16 Aug. 1953, sec. 6, p. 3L.

6. Quoted in U.S. Congress, House, *Federal Grants to Fine Arts Programs and Projects. Hearings before a Special Subcommittee of the Committee on Education and Labor on H.R. 452, 5136, 5330, 5397, 7106, 7185, 7192, 7383, 7433, 7533, 7953, 8047, and 9111*, 83d Cong., 2d Sess. (1954), pp. 88–89. (Cited hereafter as *Arts Hearings-1954*.)

7. H.R. 452 (1953) called for an appropriation of up to $1 million for the first year and up to $20 million annually thereafter, including funds

for the Smithsonian Gallery of Art and the Carter Barron Amphitheater as well. For a discussion of the bill, see Howard Taubman, "A Bill for Fine Arts," *New York Times*, 18 Jan. 1953, sec. 2, p. 7.

8. Aside from Javits's prophetic H.R. 5330, the "U.S. Arts Foundation Act," the several bills, introduced by Reps. Celler, Bolling, Metcalf, Miller, Blatnik, Rhodes, Multer, and Shelley, were all based on Howell's original H.R. 452. Bolling's H.R. 7106 listed the various arts disciplines to be served and added a program of grants to the states, while the final version, the focus of the hearings, was Howell's H.R. 9111. For a digest of proposed arts legislation through 1954, see *Arts Hearings-1954*, pp. 1–7.

9. Howell's H.R. 9111 included a broad range of proposed objectives: (1) assisting the states in fine arts projects; (2) increasing the accessibility and raising the standards of performance; (3) establishment of a federal arts agency and advisory council; (4) facilitating the formation of plans for federal arts programs during periods of depression or national emergency; (5) coordinating and raising standards of existing federal arts programs; (6) establishment of a theater and music center in Washington, along with a Smithsonian Gallery of Art; (7) encouraging American art through English-language productions in theater and opera, and stimulating the development of American art in general; (8) promoting the useful arts; (9) encouraging and securing local participation and autonomy; (10) encouraging fine arts programs for children and the elderly; (11) encouraging urban design and planning; (12) encouraging increased cooperation between the various arts and artists; (13) advancing general art education; (14) stimulating private-sector support of the arts; (15) encouraging historic preservation; and (16) counteracting Soviet propaganda regarding American materialism. The bill also included language pointing to eventual cabinet status for the arts: "The Congress . . . expresses the hope that, with more complete recognition of the importance of the fine arts in our society, action will be taken to establish in the Government, on an equal footing with other departments of the Government, a new Department of Education and Arts."

10. The European-born Leutze (1816–1868) is best known for his *Washington Crossing the Delaware*. During the Civil War, he painted *Westward the Course of Empire Makes Its Way* in the capitol. Healy (1813–1894) painted portraits of several presidents and other public figures both in the U.S. and abroad.

11. *Congressional Globe* 21, pt. 2 (1852), 105.

12. *Arts Hearings-1954*, pp. 29–30.

13. Ibid., pp. 9, 11. The leisure-time argument was a popular one.

14. *Congressional Record*, 82d Cong., 1st Sess. (1951), p. A6578; *Arts Hearings-1954*, p. 127. Henry Marx had earlier pointed out America's support of foreign culture. Henry Marx, "U.S. Money for Greek Music, but Not for U.S." *Music News* 41 (Oct. 1949), 6; and Marx, "Financial Insecurity of Orchestras Grows," *Music News* 42 (Oct. 1950), 3.

15. *Congressional Record*, 83d Cong., 2d Sess. (1954), pp. 5374–75; *Arts Hearings*-1954, p. 139.

16. *Congressional Record*, 82d Cong., 1st Sess. (1951), p. A6578; *Arts Hearings*-1954, p. 126.

17. *Arts Hearings*-1954, p. 30.

18. Ibid., p. 29.

19. Ibid., p. 42.

20. Ibid., pp. 59, 53.

21. Ibid., p. 29.

22. *Congressional Record*, 82d Cong., 1st Sess. (1951), p. A6578; *Arts Hearings*-1954, p. 126.

23. *Arts Hearings*-1954, pp. 50, 184–85.

24. Ibid., pp. 33, 12.

25. Ibid., pp. 12–13.

26. Ibid., p. 65.

27. Ibid., p. 78.

28. Ibid., p. 44.

29. Ibid., pp. 222–32.

30. Howell himself baited this trap with a stipulation in his bill that "all opera and drama productions presented by or under any arrangement with the Commission, with the exception of performances by visiting foreign companies, shall be presented in the English language to the maximum extent practicable. Suitable translations in English shall be provided when foreign opera and drama productions are presented."

31. In the fifties, the ASOL fashioned an alliance with the local- and state-oriented "arts council" movement (led by George Irwin and Philip Hanes) and reports from that group appeared regularly in the *ASOL Newsletter*. It was probably for this reason that the *Newsletter* was comparatively silent on the question of federal arts support throughout the fifties.

32. *Arts Hearings*-1954, pp. 148, 160–61.

33. Ibid., pp. 149, 159.

34. Ibid., pp. 32, 238.

35. Ibid., pp. 143, 151.

36. U.S. Congress, House, *Federal Grants for Fine Arts Programs and Projects. Report of a Special Subcommittee to the Committee on Education and Labor*, 83d Cong., 2d Sess. (Committee Print, 1954), p. 5. (Cited hereafter as *Arts Report*-1954.)

37. *National Music Council Bulletin* 14 (Jan. 1954), 8–15; "Music Leaders Give Views on Federal Aid," *Musical America* 73 (15 Nov. 1953), 4; "Petrillo Stresses Need for Government Subsidy," *Musical America* 74 (15 Feb. 1954), 29.

38. *Journal of the American Institute of Architects* 21 (Mar. 1954), 141–42. At its annual meeting in 1953, the institute passed a resolution opposing the creation of a national arts commission, calling instead for the "free and natural development" of the fine arts in America. *New York Times*, 20

June 1953, p. 25. Christopher Tunnard, "Government Bureau of Art," *Journal of the American Institute of Architects* 21 (May 1954), 234.

39. "Democratic Dilemma," *Art Digest* 27 (Aug. 1953), 7.

40. Emily Genauer, "New Federal Art Bill Introduced," *New York Herald Tribune*, 7 June 1953, sec. 4, p. 3.

41. *Arts Report*-1954, pp. 2, 3.

42. Ibid., p. 2.

43. Ibid., pp. 15–16.

44. Ibid., p. 20.

45. "The way to avoid the deplorable standards of the WPA arts projects," the joint statement read, "is to develop sound legislation and get it enacted into law before a national emergency is before us." The eight representatives, all Democrats who had sponsored arts bills identical to Howell's H.R. 452 (the National War Memorial Arts Commission), were John Blatnik (MN), Richard Bolling (MO), Charles Howell (NJ), Lee Metcalf (MT), George Miller (CA), Abraham Multer (NY), George Rhodes (PA), and John Shelley (CA). For an earlier, slightly different version of the joint statement (lacking the WPA reference), see *Musical America* 74 (1 Feb. 1954), 12.

46. Howell also introduced H.R. 10189, a condensed version of H.R. 9881, without the National Arts Commission.

Chapter Four

1. "Statement on Artistic Freedom," *College Art Journal* 14 (Winter 1955), inside back cover. The statement was drafted by Lloyd Goodrich, Alfred Barr, and a lawyer named Ralph Colin. *Lloyd Goodrich Reminiscences*, interview with Harlan P. Phillips, Archives of American Art, Smithsonian Institution, 1963, p. 386.

2. Professor Mary Colum of Columbia University, the actress Lillian Gish, television critic Harriet Van Horne, and choreographer Doris Humphrey all called for a cabinet post for the arts. Rep. Frank Thompson, Howell's successor, also spoke at the Columbia conference. *New York Times*, 27 Mar. 1955, p. 65; Lloyd Goodrich, "Government and Art: Committee Report," *College Art Journal* 14 (Fall 1954), 52–54. The CGA report itself was never published but a copy of the twenty-five-page document can be found in the Whitney Museum of American Art Papers (Lloyd Goodrich material), Archives of American Art, Smithsonian Institution.

3. Margaret French Cresson, "A Minority Opinion on the Goodrich Report," *American Artist* 18 (Nov. 1954), 16. See also the negative review in the National Sculpture Society's *National Sculpture Review* 4 (Fall 1954), 7.

4. The five proposed advisory commissions (two of which already existed) were an architectural panel, a panel concerned with the decoration of federal buildings, and a commission of museum workers, scholars,

and artists to advise the State Dept. and the USIA, plus the Smithsonian Art Commission and the Commission of Fine Arts (enlarged to include more professions). *New York Times*, 30 June 1954, p. 25.

5. Cresson, "Minority Opinion," p. 58; Goodrich, "Committee Report," p. 53.

6. *College Art Journal* 14 (Winter 1955), 95.

7. "Ike Likes the Arts, So—U.S. May Export Culture," *U.S. News and World Report*, 28 Jan. 1955, p. 68.

8. "Annual Message to Congress on the State of the Union," 6 Jan. 1955, *Public Papers of the President of the United States, Dwight D. Eisenhower, 1955* (Washington, D.C., 1959), pp. 28–29. Eisenhower reiterated his call for a federal advisory commission on the arts in his budget messages of 1955 and 1956. *New York Times*, 18 Jan. 1955, p. 17; 17 Jan. 1956, p. 20.

9. A copy of Secretary Hobby's letter to Rayburn is included in the *Congressional Record*, 84th Cong., 1st Sess. (1955), p. 6844.

10. Howell lost to Clifford Case by only 0.2 percentage points. The link between Howell's and Thompson's efforts for the arts was George Frain, a legislative assistant to both representatives who was responsible for drafting much of the arts legislation. Interview with Frank Thompson, 12 Feb. 1980; interview with George Frain, 25 Feb. 1980.

11. For the House debate on the proposed cultural center, see the *Congressional Record*, 84th Cong., 1st Sess. (1955), pp. 584–87.

12. "'Cultural Ambassadors' Get Results," *Musical America* 76 (15 Jan. 1956), 4.

13. U.S. Department of State, Advisory Commission on Educational Exchange, *Seventh Semiannual Report to the Congress*, 82d Cong., 2d Sess. (1952), p. 5.

14. U.S. Department of State, Advisory Commission on Educational Exchange, *Ninth Semiannual Report to the Congress* (July 1–Dec. 31, 1952), House Document No. 154, 83d Cong., 1st Sess. (1953), p. 11.

15. Quoted in the testimony of Abbott Washburn, deputy director of the USIA, in U.S. Congress, House, *Distinguished Civilian Awards and Cultural Interchange and Development. Hearings before a Subcommittee of the Committee on Education and Labor on Various Bills Relating to Awards of Medal for Distinguished Civilian Achievement, and Cultural Interchange and Development*, 84th Cong., (1955–56), p. 284. (Cited hereafter as *Arts Hearings-1955/56*.)

16. Robert Breen, "Cultural Envoys: Some Thoughts on Our Arts-Exchange Plan," *New York Times*, 5 Aug. 1956, sec. 2, p. 1.

17. Frank Thompson, "Are the Communists Right in Calling Us Cultural Barbarians?" *Music Journal* 13 (July-Aug. 1955), 5.

18. Lloyd Goodrich, "Spectrum," *Arts* 30 (Feb. 1956), 11.

19. *Arts Hearings-1955/56*, pp. 3–12.

20. The state grants, up to $100,000 per state, were to be awarded to those states with approved state plans for cultural programs and projects. The advisory commission in HEW was to consist of twenty-one members

appointed by the president for the purpose of undertaking studies of methods for encouraging the arts in America. The medal for distinguished civilian achievement (passed by the House in 1956 and 1958 but not acted upon by the Senate) was to involve a fifteen-member panel to select the design of the medal and recommend recipients to the president. Title V of Thompson's bill was somewhat misleading, since nonprofit symphony orchestras and opera associations had been granted exemptions from the admissions tax by special legislation in 1951.

21. Congress had issued a special award to Irving Berlin in 1954. The plan for a medal for Distinguished Civilian Achievements, contained in title IV of H.R. 6874, would make such awards a regular process. See *Arts Hearings*-1955/56, pp. 12–25, 31–48.

22. Ibid., p. 59.

23. Ibid., p. 131.

24. Ibid., pp. 276–77.

25. Ibid., p. 78.

26. Ibid., p. 82.

27. Ibid., p. 78. Even Thompson admitted, however, that two elements of his bill, the state grants and the tax reduction, "deserve long-time study."

28. *Congressional Record*, 83d Cong., 2d Sess. (1954), p. 5375. For similar comments by Sen. Wiley, see *CR*, 84th Cong., 1st Sess. (1955), pp. 8388–90.

29. *Arts Hearings*-1955/56, p. 4.

30. Ibid., p. 91. The source of Swire's figure for Soviet cultural exchange is not clear, and a more reliable figure involves the number of cultural and sports delegations that the USSR sent to other countries: 88 in 1954 and 148 in 1955 (plus representatives at 149 trade fairs in the latter year). In the two years of the Emergency Fund, by comparison, the U.S. had sent out 37 cultural delegations. As another example of Russia's commitment to culture, the Soviet cultural minister announced late in 1956 that $8,750,000 a year would be spent to encourage the production of works of art for museums and traveling exhibitions. *New York Times*, 7 Oct. 1956, p. 3.

31. U.S. Congress, Senate, *International Cultural Exchange and Trade Fair Participation Act of 1956. Hearing before the Committee on Foreign Relations on S. 3116 and S. 3172, Bills to Provide for the Promotion and Strengthening of International Relations through Cultural and Athletic Exchanges and Participation in International Fairs and Festivals*, 84th Cong., 2d Sess. (1956), p. 28.

32. Senate Report No. 1664, 84th Cong., 2d Sess. (1956).

33. "We are going to be judged, in the final analysis," Thompson told the committee, "not so much on how much steel we produce or how many nuclear bombs we can stockpile, but on our spiritual record." U.S. Congress, House, *Hearings before the Committee on Foreign Affairs on Draft Bills Proposed in Executive Communications No. 863, No. 953, and No. 1601, Amend-*

*ing the United States Information and Educational Exchange Act of 1948, and
No. 1409, Providing for Cultural and Athletic Exchanges and Participation in
International Fairs and Festivals,* 84th Cong., 2d Sess. (1956), p. 71. (Cited
hereafter as *Cultural Exchange Hearings, House*-1956.) The major departure
from H.R. 6874 in the various 1956 bills was the shift from HEW to the
executive office as the seat of authority for the cultural exchange program.

34. Eisenhower did, in fact, appoint a nine-member Advisory Committee on the Arts, as announced by Secretary of State Dulles in Oct. 1957.
New York Times, 17 Oct. 1957, p. 43. But with such obvious political appointments as actors Robert Montgomery and George Murphy on the committee, it accomplished little, if anything. See Frank Getlein, "Gesture Toward
the Arts," *Commonweal,* 6 Dec. 1957, pp. 251–53.

35. Rep. James Richards (D-SC), for example, inquired about the
rumors of Communists participating in American cultural-exchange tours
abroad, while Rep. Karl LeCompt (R-IA) suggested a "non-Communist
oath" for artists financed in part by taxpayers. *Cultural Exchange Hearings,
House*-1956, pp. 93–94, 150–51.

36. For Thompson's comments, see *Arts Hearings*-1955/56, pp. 275–
77.

37. See Dulles's comments on East-West contacts in *U.S. Department of
State Bulletin* 33 (28 Nov. 1955), 876–80.

38. *New York Times,* 4 Aug. 1955, p. 16; 24 Sept. 1955, p. 3; 4 Oct.
1955, p. 70. The following year, New York impresario Billy Rose made
plans for cultural exchanges with Russia, Poland, and Rumania. *New York
Times,* 30 July 1956, p. 6; 3 Aug. 1956, p. 11; 26 Aug. 1956, p. 71.

39. *New York Times,* 1 Aug. 1955, p. 1; 30 Aug. 1955, p. 17. See also
Haldore Hansen, "Two-Way Traffic to Moscow," *New Republic,* 7 Nov. 1955,
pp. 6–8.

40. *New York Times,* 6 Mar. 1956, p. 26; 25 May 1956, p. 2.

41. *New York Times,* 14 Feb. 1956, p. 4; 1 June 1956, p. 1; 4 Dec. 1956,
p. 1; 8 Dec. 1956, p. 11. See also Ross Parmenter, "The World of Music:
No Russians in U.S.", *New York Times,* 7 Apr. 1956, sec. 2, p. 9.

42. "United States and USSR Sign Agreement on East-West Exchanges," *U.S. Department of State Bulletin* 38 (17 Feb. 1958), 243–48; W. S. B.
Lacey, "Exchange Agreement with USSR," *U.S. Department of State Bulletin*
38 (3 Mar. 1958), 323–28.

43. Brooks Atkinson, "Affairs of State," *New York Times,* 17 June 1956,
sec. 2, p. 1.

44. The Dallas County Patriotic Council, a federation of sixteen organizations ranging from the Federation of Dallas Artists to the VFW and
the DAR, had originally been stirred to action by the anti-Communist crusades of H. L. Hunt and Karl Baarslag (who left Dallas in 1955 to become
HUAC's chief of research). The first attack on the Dallas Museum was
launched in Mar. 1955 by a patriotic women's club which accused the mu-

seum of overemphasizing "all phases of futuristic, modernistic, non-objective painting and statuary," and of promoting "the work of artists who have known Communist affiliations." See Charlotte Devree, "The U.S. Government Vetoes Living Art," *Art News* 55 (Sept. 1956), 34–35. See also Jane De Hart Mathews, "Art and Politics in Cold War America," *American Historical Review* 81 (Oct. 1976), 768–71; and William Hauptman, "The Supression of Art in the McCarthy Decade," *Artforum* 11 (Oct. 1973), 50–51. For Rep. Dondero's version of the story, see his comments in the *Congressional Record*, 84th Cong., 2d Sess. (1956), pp. 10422–23.

45. Quoted in Aline B. Saarinen, "Art Storm Breaks in Dallas," *New York Times*, 12 Feb. 1956, sec. 2, p. 15. See also Col. Owsley's letter to the *Times*, expressing his belief in the dangerous content of Communist art: "It is one of the basic premises of Communist doctrine that art should be used in the constant process of attempting to brainwash and create public attitudes that are soft toward Communism." *New York Times*, 4 Mar. 1956, sec. 2, p. 14.

46. According to Devree, none of the artists (including Kuniyoshi, who died in 1953) had maintained ties with Communist-front organizations.

47. *New York Times*, 19 Feb. 1956, sec. 2, p. 8; "Dallas Museum Trustees Take Stand in Policy," *The Museum News* 33 (15 Mar. 1956), 1.

48. Hauptman, "Suppression of Art," p. 51. In an interview with the *Milwaukee Journal*, USIA's Theodore Streibert denied the "post-1917" ban on art for USIA exhibitions, but he refused to comment on whether Rep. Dondero was a factor in shaping USIA policy. *Milwaukee Journal*, 7 Oct. 1956, sec. 5, p. 4.

49. *Congressional Record*, 84th Cong., 2d Sess. (1956), pp. 10918–20.

50. Eva Cockcroft, "Abstract Expressionism, Weapon of the Cold War," *Artforum* 12 (June 1974), 41.

51. *New York Times*, 2 Sept. 1956, sec. 4, p. 8.

Chapter Five

1. Frank Thompson to Brooks Atkinson, 11 Apr. 1955, Brooks Atkinson File, Library and Museum of the Performing Arts, Lincoln Center, New York.

2. Gish had been involved in the Federal Arts Committee that supported the Bureau of Fine Arts legislation of the late thirties, and spoke out publicly on the Secretary of Art issue on an Edward R. Murrow "Person-to-Person" broadcast in the early fifties; she later had an interview with President Eisenhower on the subject.

3. Along with Derwent and Weston, other active NCAG members included Howard Lindsay, Hy Faine of the American Guild of Musical

Artists, Robert Schnitzer of ANTA, and Howard Hanson of the National Music Council. The group was also involved in working for the establishment of the New York State Council on the Arts.

4. Interview with Lloyd Goodrich, 21 Feb. 1980; *Lloyd Goodrich Reminiscences*, interview with Harlan B. Phillips, Archives of American Art, Smithsonian Institution, 1963, pp. 371–73. Although they were not well organized, the Harold Weston Papers at the Archives of American Art contain a wealth of material on Weston's work with the NCAG.

5. "Such studies shall be conducted by special committees of persons, expert in the field of art involved, appointed by the Secretary [of HEW] after consultation with the Commission." S. 3419 (1956).

6. *Congressional Record*, 84th Cong., 2d Sess. (1956), pp. 4446–48.

7. U.S. Congress, Senate, *Federal Advisory Council on the Arts. Hearing before a Subcommittee of the Committee on Labor and Public Welfare on S. 3054, a Bill to Provide for the Establishment of a Federal Advisory Commission on the Arts, and for Other Purposes, and S. 3419, a Bill to Provide for the Establishment of a Federal Advisory Committee on the Arts, and for Other Purposes*, 84th Cong., 2d Sess. (1956). (Cited hereafter as *Arts Hearing, Senate*-1956.)

8. Senate Report No. 2409, 84th Cong., 2d Sess. (1956), p. 4.

9. *Congressional Record*, 84th Cong., 2d Sess. (1956), pp. 11818–20.

10. U.S. Congress, House, *Federal Advisory Commission on the Arts. Hearings before a Subcommittee of the Committee on Education and Labor on H.R. 3541, 1089, 1945, 4514, 6374, 6642, and 7606*, 85th Cong., 1st Sess. (1957), pp. 148–49. (Cited hereafter as *Arts Hearings*-1957.)

11. *Public Papers of the President of the United States, Dwight D. Eisenhower, 1957*, (Washington, D.C., 1958), p. 58. Eisenhower also called for a sizable increase in the budget for international information and exchange activities. *New York Times*, 17 Jan. 1957, p. 17.

12. The record of this hearing was never printed separately, although it is included in *Arts Hearings*-1957, pp. 37–74. This subcommittee considered S. 930 (Humphrey, Douglas, and Javits) and S. 1716 (Smith, Ives, Cooper, Hennings, and Javits), to establish an advisory commission/council, and S. 2081 (Javits and Clark), to create a federal arts foundation.

13. For a copy of the bill and Javits's comments regarding it, see the *Congressional Record*, 85th Cong., 1st Sess. (1957), pp. 6926–28. The bill would create a U.S. Arts Foundation in the executive branch, administered by twelve trustees appointed by the president, and designed to provide assistance to nonprofit professional civic and educational performing arts groups, "for the purpose of enabling such groups to provide productions of such types or in such regions as would not otherwise be available to the prospective audiences."

14. *Arts Hearings*-1957, p. 51.

15. Ibid., pp. 62–63.

16. Ibid., pp. 170–74, 85–99. The cabaret tax dated to 1919, when

it was instituted to help pay for WW I. Originally set at 20%, it was raised briefly to 30% during WW II and remained at 20% even after the admissions tax was reduced to 10% in 1954 (and subsequently removed for nonprofit arts organizations).

17. For a copy of the NCAG letter and a list of signatories, see ibid., pp. 151–56.

18. "It would seem to me," Thompson wrote Goodrich in regard to Williams, "that this whole matter must be met head-on and that it calls for immediate action and draconian methods. I would think you and Mr. Weston would want to confer immediately with Nelson Rockefeller, Rep. Wainwright, the Secretary of Health, Education, and Welfare and his top officials, and perhaps others." Frank Thompson to Lloyd Goodrich, n.d. [1956], copy in Harold Weston Papers, Archives of American Art, Smithsonian Institution. Thompson was responding to a letter critical of the advisory council legislation that Williams had written to Graham Barden, chairman of the House Committee on Education and Labor, and sent to other members of the committee.

19. Born in Chicago in 1897, Williams was educated at Yale, Harvard Graduate School of Architecture, and the Beaux Arts in Paris. A veteran of both World Wars, he was the recipient of several government sculptural commissions. For examples of his work, see *Wheeler Williams* (New York, 1957); for examples of his politics, see the American Artists Professional League's "War Cry" in *Arts Hearings*-1957, pp. 189–90.

20. *Arts Hearings*-1957, p. 200.

21. U.S. Congress, House, *Federal Advisory Council on the Arts. Hearing before a Subcommittee of the Committee on Education and Labor on H.R. 2569 and Related Bills to Provide for the Establishment of a Federal Advisory Commission on the Arts and to Assist in the Growth and Development of the Fine Arts in the United States*, 86th Cong., 1st Sess. (1959).

22. Milton Bracker, "Federal Role on the Arts Has Increased in Decade," *New York Times*, 8 Dec. 1958, p. 28.

23. *Museum News* 17 (1 Sept. 1939), 1. For a copy of the 1938 resolution, see Frank Thompson's comments in the *Congressional Record*, 84th Cong., 2d Sess. (1956), p. 4529. See also his earlier comments and his original NCFA bill in *CR*, 84th Cong., 2d Sess. (1956), pp. 1615–17.

24. For a concise summary of the capital cultural center movement, see Frank Thompson's testimony in U.S. Congress, Senate, *Public Buildings. Hearings before a Subcommittee of the Committee on Public Works on S. 1985, a Bill to Authorize the Preparation of Plans and Specifications for the Construction of a National Air Museum, S. 3335, a Bill to Provide for a National Capital Center of the Performing Arts, and S. 3560, a Bill to Authorize the Construction of a Courthouse and Federal Office Building in Memphis, Tenn.*, 85th Cong., 2d Sess. (1958), pp. 27–33. (Cited hereafter as *Public Buildings Hearings*-1958.)

25. *Congressional Record*, 85th Cong., 1st Sess. (1957), pp. 14090, 14094–

14101. In addition to the expense, several members of the House seemed offended by the action of the Senate, which had amended a simple bill to extend the life of the auditorium commission to include an appropriation for the purchase of the Foggy Bottom site. The vote in the House was 115 in favor and 284 opposed, thus killing the cultural center plans for 1957.

26. See Thompson's comments and a draft of his bill in the *Congressional Record*, 85th Cong., 1st Sess. (1957), pp. 16987–99; and his comments on introducing the bill in 1958, *CR*, 85th Cong., 2d Sess. (1958), pp. 121–23.

27. *Congressional Record*, 85th Cong., 2d Sess. (1958), pp. 3705–6.

28. For a copy of the bill, see *Public Buildings Hearings*-1958, pp. 2–4.

29. Ibid., pp. 22–23.

30. Senate Report No. 1700, 85th Cong., 2d Sess. (1958); House Report No. 2623, 85th Cong., 2d Sess. (1958). For the Senate's discussion of the bill, see the *Congressional Record*, 85th Cong., 2d Sess. (1958), pp. 11832–36; Richard Coe, "Capital Idea," *New York Times*, 31 Aug. 1958, sec. 2, p. 1; *CR*, 85th Cong., 2d Sess. (1958), pp. 19180–93.

31. Jacob K. Javits, "Plan to Aid Our Lagging Culture," *New York Times Magazine*, 5 Apr. 1959, p. 28.

32. *New York Times*, 13 Jan. 1958, p. 23; 12 Feb. 1958, p. 32. Both Frank Thompson and Hubert Humphrey introduced legislation for a supplemental appropriation of $2,054,000 for Brussels. For Humphrey's comments on the need to insure that the best of American art was sent to Brussels, see the *Congressional Record*, 85th Cong., 2d Sess. (1958), pp. 192–97. Conservatives in the House, led by Rep. Rooney, resisted full funding, agreeing to only $1.1 million.

33. Best known among the "Seventeen Contemporary Artists" (i.e., artists under forty-five) included in the American exhibit were Robert Motherwell, Grace Hartigan, and Ad Reinhardt. In defense of its exclusion of older, more important figures, the committee in charge of the American exhibit pointed out that artists like Marin, DeKooning, Pollock, and Hopper were included in the fair's own "Fifty Years of Modern Art" exhibit.

The Senator Bridges episode began with an angry letter to the senator from one of his constituents, a businessman who was appalled by the American exhibit, particularly the art on display. Bridges read the letter to Eisenhower, who promptly dispatched USIA chief George V. Allen to Brussels for a report. "U.S. Art at Brussels; Why Ike Is Irritated," *U.S. News and World Report* 27 June 1958, p. 8. For Allen's report to the president, which was generally favorable but which did recommend some improvements (including a broadening of the art exhibit with a few more representational works), see the *Congressional Record*, 85th Cong., 2d Sess. (1958), p. 12897. The leading congressional art critic of 1958 was Rep. Albert Morano (R-CT), who repeatedly blasted the American exhibit, but whose charges seemed much better informed and more reasonable than Dondero's earlier tirades. For the remarks of Morano, who finally persuaded U.S. Commissioner General Howard S. Cullman to add several works from the Whitney collection, see *CR*, 85th Cong., 2d Sess. (1958), pp. 4687, 5263, 6443, 12108–9, 14631.

34. The government's two standing art advisory committees (those of the State Dept. and the USIA) had appointed a joint subcommittee to select the jury for the Moscow show. *New York Times*, 4 July 1959, p. 17.

35. Aline B. Saarinen, "Thoughts on U.S. Art for Moscow," *New York Times*, 22 Feb. 1959, sec. 2, p. 20.

36. *Congressional Record*, 86th Cong., 1st Sess. (1959), p. 9756. "It appears to me," Walter declared in the House, "that we are sending the so-called art of men who have prostituted whatever talents they possess to the foulest conspiracy in the history of man. . . . It is repulsive to me that a U.S. government agency should glorify so-called artists who stand for nothing this country represents and for everything it is opposed to, men who stand for, promote, and defend Communist slavery, mass murder, and destruction of freedom." Ibid., pp. 9746–48.

37. Genauer's commentary was placed in the *Congressional Record* by Sen. Philip Hart (D-MI) on the day following Rep. Walter's initial outcry. Ibid., pp. 9813–14.

38. The twenty-three sculptures were equally diverse, ranging from classical pieces by Sol Baizerman and William Zorach to the freer forms of Calder and Noguchi. For a list of the forty-nine paintings and twenty-three sculptures, see the *New York Times*, 31 May 1959, p. 60.

39. U.S. Congress, House, *The American National Exhibition, Moscow, July 1959. Hearings before the Committee on Un-American Activities*, 86th Cong., 1st Sess. (1959), p. 900. (Cited hereafter as *HUAC Hearings-1959*.) See also HUAC's *Control of the Arts in the Communist Empire: Consultation with Ivan P. Bahrianz*, 86th Cong., 1st Sess. (1959), in which the exiled Ukrainian writer testified on 3 June 1959 regarding the absence of artistic freedom in the Soviet Union, the folly of cultural exchange with Russia, and the danger of the U.S. sending the works of Communist artists to the Moscow exhibition.

40. Walter Goodman, *The Committee* (New York, 1968), pp. 399–404.

41. "I know him to be dishonest, self-seeking and dangerous," Dorothy Drew wrote George Dondero in 1960, in reference to Williams. "While he is exploiting the work done by others to uncover the red art monopoly—he is doing it in a very reckless manner. I consider him anti-semitic and he is so considered by many of our best artists." Dorothy Drew to George Dondero, 17 Jan. 1960, George A. Dondero Papers, Archives of American Art, Smithsonian Institution.

42. *HUAC Hearings-1959*, pp. 910, 914–15.

43. Ibid., pp. 941–63. The committee also heard friendly testimony from another AAPL member, Frank C. Wright, whose experience with

psychological warfare in WW II apparently enabled him to "decipher" abstract expressionism—"the distortion and subversion of the images in the way they use art for this business of confusing people." And Rep. Thomas M. Pelly (R-WA) submitted a statement supporting HUAC's effort. Ibid., pp. 933–39.

44. *New York Times*, 2 July 1959, p. 10. As Lloyd Goodrich reminded the president in an open letter two days later, a White House press release of 24 Feb. 1959 announced the appointment of the four-man jury with the "approval" of the president. *New York Times*, 4 July 1959, p. 17; interview with Lloyd Goodrich, 21 Feb. 1980.

45. Eisenhower refused to comment further on the paintings, explaining that "I have nothing to say about them because I am not an artist . . . ," but he repeated his earlier promise: "I am not now going to be any censor. . . ." He seemed, in fact, to be rather confused by the whole matter: "It seems strange all of this editorial opinion I have seen on this defending the committee very strenuously, and so I don't know what's right."

46. Among those congratulating the president were the Museum of Modern Art; the American Federation of Arts, the Brooklyn Museum, and the American Association of Museum Directors. *New York Times*, 3 July 1959, p. 7.

47. *New York Times*, 8 July 1959, p. 31; 23 July 1959, p. 5. The works were being added, according to a spokesman for the USIA, because the president "felt more attention should be given to artists of the pre–World War I period." Works by Bellows, Eakins, and Homer had previously been added to the exhibit.

48. This is not to suggest that government cultural exchange programs were suddenly free of problems or that they were universally accepted as a proper expenditure of government funds. For typical USIA problems late in 1959 (including the cancellation of a sculpture show organized by the Yale University Gallery and the curtailment of a "25 Years of American Art" show touring in Italy), see John Canaday, "Art Disinherited," *New York Times*, 27 Dec. 1959, sec. 2, p. 17.

49. *New York Times Book Review*, 12 Nov. 1958, p. 2. See also the *New York Times* editorial on *Horizon* and the culture boom, 21 Sept. 1958, sec. 4, p. 8.

50. *New York Times*, 7 Oct. 1959, p. 45.

51. Frank Thompson, "Our Cultural Crisis," *Progressive* 22 (June 1958), 24.

52. *Congressional Record*, 85th Cong., 2d Sess. (1958), p. 10466.

53. For a useful survey of the cultural legislation of the late fifties (including the two important measures that passed—the National Cultural Center and the Old Patent Office bills), see Frank Thompson, "Federal Legislation to Foster the Fine Arts," *American Institute of Architects Journal* 32 (July 1959), 36–41.

54. *Congressional Record*, 86th Cong. 1st Sess. (1959), p. 5437.

55. U.S. President's Commission on National Goals, *Goals for Americans* (Englewood Cliffs, NJ, 1960), pp. 126–46.

56. For Nixon's and Kennedy's statements on the arts, see "Nixon, Kennedy View Music and the Arts," *Musical America* 80 (Oct. 1960), 8; and "The Candidates and the Arts," *Saturday Review*, 29 Oct. 1960, pp. 42–44. See also their responses to questions posed by Artists Equity (*Equity Magazine*, Nov. 1960), reprinted in U.S. Congress, House, *Aid to Fine Arts. Hearing before the Select Subcommittee on Education of the Committee on Education and Labor on H.R. 4172, H.R. 4174 and Related Bills to Aid the Fine Arts of the United States*, 87th Cong., 1st Sess. (1961), pp. 167–69; and Harold Schonberg, "Candidates on Culture," *New York Times*, 30 Oct. 1960, sec. 2, p. 9.

57. For all of his apparent reluctance in 1960 to subsidize the arts, upon reaching the White House eight years later Nixon proved to be the most munificent presidential patron in the nation's history, raising the budget of the National Endowment for the Arts from $8.25 million to $74.75 million during his term of office.

58. For the Democratic arts plank (actually several scattered references to culture), see the *Congressional Record*, 86th Cong., 2d Sess. (1960), p. A7102.

59. "The Candidates and the Arts," p. 44.

60. "Nixon, Kennedy View Music and the Arts," p. 11. For a response to Kennedy's promises, see "A New Frontier in the Arts—the Why and the How," *Musical America* 80 (Dec. 1960), 8.

61. *New York Times*, 23 Nov. 1960, p. 14. Clearly unprepared for the White House's new tenants, the Commission of Fine Arts objected to Letitia Baldridge's announcement of Jackie's plans. "The White House isn't a place to show off American paintings," protested Linton R. Wilson, the commission's secretary. "Who would see them? We have museums and art galleries for exhibitions." *New York Times*, 6 Dec. 1960, p. 30. In response, Baldridge assured Wilson that discretion would be used by the new first lady; early American paintings rather than abstract expressionist works would be displayed. *New York Times*, 11 Dec. 1960, p. 134.

Chapter Six

1. *New York Times*, 13 Apr. 1962, p. 38. For the full text of Schlesinger's speech to the AFA's annual meeting, see the *Congressional Record*, 88th Cong., 1st Sess. (1963), pp. 15135–37.

2. *New York Times*, 15 Jan. 1961, p. 39.

3. August Heckscher, recorded interview by Wolf Von Eckardt, 10 Dec. 1963, p. 3, John F. Kennedy Library Oral History Program. (Cited hereafter as Heckscher Interview—JFK Lib.) Kay Halle, a White House aide, came up with the idea to invite artists to the inauguration. Kay Halle, recorded interview by William M. McHugh, 7 Feb. 1967, John F. Kennedy

Library Oral History Program. Of the 155 artists and scholars invited, 58 attended the inauguration.

4. The contributions of Heckscher, the president's special consultant on the arts, and of Secretary of Labor Goldberg, will be discussed below. Walton, a close friend of the president, unofficially advised Kennedy on culture until being named chairman of the Commission of Fine Arts in 1963. Schlesinger was probably the key cultural influence in the White House, although Salinger, a classically trained pianist and the president's press secretary, also contributed to the administration's cultural tone. It was Salinger, for example, who suggested a program of White House prizes in art and music. *Congressional Record*, 87th Cong., 1st Sess. (1961), pp. A1969–70. Kennedy's cabinet sponsored a performance series, including Secretary Udall's "Evening with Robert Frost" and Secretary Ribicoff's "Evening with Thornton Wilder." *New York Times*, 2 May 1961, p. 25; 1 May 1962, p. 31.

5. Heckscher Interview—JFK Lib., p. 14. There is also evidence that Kennedy's interest in (or tolerance for) the arts increased during his term in the White House. *New York Times*, 19 Dec. 1962, p. 5.

6. Arthur and Barbara Gelb, "Culture Makes a Hit at the White House," *New York Times Magazine*, 28 Jan. 1962, p. 9.

7. A copy of Isenbergh's essay, dated 11 Sept. 1961 and sent to Arthur Goldberg by Arthur Schlesinger on 15 Sept. 1961, is included in the Records of the Secretary of Labor, Arthur J. Goldberg, R.G. 134 ("Metropolitan Opera File"), National Archives. (Cited hereafter as the Goldberg Papers.)

8. Additionally, three of the nation's most prestigious orchestras (the New York Philharmonic and the Cleveland and Philadelphia orchestras) experienced labor problems at the start of the 1961 season. *New York Times*, 15 Oct. 1961, sec. 2, p. 11.

9. For Kennedy's message on the opening of the Met in Oct., delivered by Goldberg, see the *New York Times*, 24 Oct. 1961, p. 1.

10. *New York Times*, 30 Aug. 1961, p. 32.

11. For the text of Goldberg's decision, see the *New York Times*, 15 Dec. 1961, pp. 1, 40.

12. Ross Parmenter, "The Goldberg Award Will Cost the 'Met' an extra $300,000 over Three Years," *New York Times*, 24 Dec. 1961, p. 13.

13. The files on the Metropolitan Opera decision, including an early, edited draft of section three, are found in the Goldberg Papers, Boxes 60–62, and in the Records of the Executive Assistant to the Secretary of Labor, Stephen H. Shulman, R.G. 174, Box N, National Archives.

14. A copy of the memo, along with another on increasing the allowable tax deduction for contributions to arts organizations—also included in the Met decision—can be found in the Goldberg Papers, Box 62. Goldberg sent a copy of his decision to Rockefeller and thanked him for his contribution to section three.

15. Goldberg Papers, Box 62. Goldberg also received letters encouraging federal action from Howard S. Cullman, former U.S. commissioner general at the 1958 Brussels exhibition; Rep. Frank Thompson; and Rep. Victor Anfuso (D-NY). He received letters as well from private citizens, only a small percentage of whom opposed federal subsidy.

16. Corporate support of the arts was not a major factor at this time. According to surveys conducted by the Conference Board, business giving to cultural and civic causes amounted to only 2.9% of all corporate philanthropy in 1959 and 5.3% in 1962. Not until 1965 was corporate support of cultural activities listed separately in the Conference Board survey, with 2.8% of corporate giving going to the arts and humanities. John H. Watson, *Biennial Survey of Company Contributions* (New York, 1973), pp. 12–13. Foundation support of the arts was just beginning to become a major factor in arts support in the early sixties, especially with the Rockefeller Brothers and Twentieth Century Fund studies of the arts, and the expanded support of the Ford Foundation.

17. See Goldberg's testimony in U.S. Congress, House, *Economic Conditions of the Performing Arts. Hearings before the Select Subcommittee on Education of the Committee on Education and Labor*, 87th Cong., 1st and 2d Sess. (1961–62), p. 426. (Cited hereafter as *Arts Hearings-1961/62*.) The Goldberg Papers include 95 letters responding to the Metropolitan decision, with 70 of those letters in support of the secretary. Supporters included orchestras (Austin, Oakland, Cedar Rapids), the Museum of Modern Art, Assistant Secretary of State Phillip Coombs, the National Association of Schools of Music, the United Steelworkers of America, and U.S. Commissioner of Education Sterling M. McMurrin.

18. Ibid., p. 1.

19. Quoted in ibid., p. 435.

20. Ibid., p. 2.

21. A former editorial writer for the *New York Herald Tribune*, Heckscher experienced his first professional arts involvement in the fifties with the Museum of Modern Art's International Council. He later served on the New York City Art Commission, and on Eisenhower's National Goals Commission as the writer of the arts essay.

22. John F. Kennedy to August Heckscher, 5 Dec. 1961, August Heckscher Papers, Box 6, John F. Kennedy Library. (Cited hereafter as the Heckscher Papers.)

23. August Heckscher to Arthur Schlesinger, Jr., 18 Jan. 1962, Heckscher Papers, Box 6.

24. For a brief overview of Heckscher's activities as special consultant, see *The Arts and the National Government, Report to the President Submitted by August Heckscher, Special Consultant on the Arts, May 28, 1963*, pp. 2–3. For a list of Heckscher's major speeches, articles, and official participation at cultural events during his tenure as special consultant, see ibid., Appendix 1, pp. 29–30.

25. August Heckscher Interview, Archives of American Art, p. 31.

26. Although the president himself was not intimately concerned with the National Culture Center, he was, according to Heckscher, anxious to see the project completed during his administration. Thus in the ongoing debate over the proper location for the center, the president favored maintaining the Foggy Bottom site, if only to hasten the center's completion. Heckscher Interview—JFK Lib., p. 46. The president also contributed an essay (written by Heckscher) to the collection of photographs and essays produced for the center as a fund-raising device. *Creative America* (New York, 1962), pp. 4–8.

27. The *New York Times* writer was Tom Wicker, 16 June 1963, p. 1. It was *Commonweal's* Washington correspondent who labeled the report "historic"; William Shannon, "Government and Art," *Commonweal*, 23 Aug. 1963, p. 494.

28. *Congressional Record*, 87th Cong., 1st Sess. (1961), p. 20499.

29. Ibid., pp. 20499–500.

30. Earlier, the advisory council bill had faced a similar roadblock in the person of Graham Barden (D-NC), who, as chairman of the House Committee on Education and Labor, regularly pigeonholed arts legislation.

31. *Congressional Record*, 87th Cong., 1st Sess. (1961), pp. 20535–36.

32. Excerpts from the debate are included in John Kenneth Galbraith and Russell Lynes, "Should the Government Subsidize the Arts?" *Print* 15 (May 1961), 47–49. Lynes continued his campaign the following year with an article entitled "Case Against Government Aid to the Arts," *New York Times Magazine*, 25 Mar. 1962, p. 26. René d'Harnoncourt, director of the Museum of Modern Art, rebutted Lynes the following month. *New York Times Magazine*, 15 Apr. 1962, p. 14.

33. *Arts Hearings*-1961/62, p. 362.

34. Charles C. Mark to Russell Lynes, 17 Mar. 1961, Russell Lynes Papers, Archives of American Art, Smithsonian Institute. For background information on the arts council movement, see Charles C. Mark, "Genesis and Import of the Arts Council Concept," *Arts in Society* 1 (Fall 1960), 15–19. Mark stated his opposition to federal arts support, calling it "premature," in "Common Sense about Citizen Support for Arts and Culture," *Arts in Society*, vol. 2, no. 4 (1963), pp. 4–11.

35. *New York Times*, 6 July 1961, p. 19. Fulbright's bill (S. 1154) called for a $149 million exchange program, $106 million more than the previous year. It passed the Senate by an overwhelming 79–5 vote on 14 July 1961, but was subsequently scaled down to a $40 million by the House. *New York Times*, 15 July 1961, p. 21; 17 Sept. 1961, p. 32. The president signed the bill on 21 Sept. 1961. *New York Times*, 22 Sept. 1961, p. 8.

36. *New York Times*, 18 May 1962, pp. 33. 63. Interview with Jack Golodner, 21 Feb. 1980; *Washington International Arts Letter* 1 (Dec. 1962–Jan. 1963), 39; Memoranda, Barbara Donald to August Heckscher, 19

Apr. 1962, 20 Aug. 1962, Heckscher Papers, Box 20. The Rodgers committee emerged in late 1962 as the National Committee for the Arts in America.

37. *New York Times*, 22 June 1962, p. 12.

38. U.S. Congress, Senate, *Government and the Arts. Hearings before a Special Subcommittee of the Committee on Labor and Public Welfare on S. 741, S. 785, and S. 1250*, 87th Cong., 2d Sess. (1962), pp. 329–40. (Cited hereafter as *Arts Hearings*-1962.)

39. *Congressional Record*, 87th Cong., 2d Sess. (1962), pp. 13823–26. Based loosely on the National Science Foundation, Fogarty's bill also provided authority for investigations of national needs in the arts and humanities; the creation of a Cultural Service Center to serve as a national clearinghouse of information; "a major research and demonstration program within the federal government to stimulate new approaches and new techniques for the creative application of the arts and humanities throughout our society"; a fellowship and training program for teachers and talented students in the arts and humanities; matching grants for arts and humanities projects conducted by public and nonprofit agencies; and "cooperation with state and local agencies in the development of leadership programs for schools, colleges, and cultural institutions." The Office of Education drew up the NIAH bill at Fogarty's request. Memorandum, Barbara Donald to August Heckscher, 28 Aug. 1962, Heckscher Papers, Box 35.

40. *Congressional Record*, 88th Cong., 1st Sess. (1963), pp. 106–07.

41. *New York Times*, 24 May 1963, p. 19.

42. *Arts Hearings*-1962, p. 43.

43. The National Cultural Development Act had the following purposes: (1) to assist the states to inventory their existing arts programs and develop new programs; (2) to assist existing state arts programs; (3) to assist in the construction of arts centers; (4) to assist states in historic preservation; (5) to assist states in developing arts administration and training projects; and (6) to authorize the secretary of HEW to make grants for research and demonstration projects in the arts.

The act also required each state to designate a state arts agency and to submit a plan for the use of federal funds, to be approved by the secretary of HEW before the matching grant would be made. In 1963 thirteen states had either established state arts agencies or were working on plans for their establishment: New York, New Jersey, California, Connecticut, North Carolina, Michigan, Minnesota, Missouri, Ohio, Nebraska, Nevada, Washington, and Virginia. Milton Esterow, "Cultural Councils in 13 States Reflect an Upsurge of Interest," *New York Times*, 17 June 1963, p. 22; Ralph Burgard, "Variations on the Lincoln Center Theme," *New York Times*, 28 Apr. 1963, sec. 2, p. 11. The New York State Arts Council, established in 1960 and with a $560,000 budget in 1962, was the shining example of the arts advocates. See Ross Parmenter, "Colored Pins Mark the Tour," *New York Times*, 18 June 1961, sec. 2, p. 1. For the Library of Congress studies of state and selected municipal arts support, see the *Congressional Record*, 87th Cong., 1st Sess. (1961), pp. 1625–32, 9489–90. See also "Cities, States, and the Arts," *Musical Courier* 163 (Sept. 1961), 11–13.

Javits's arts foundation bill, meanwhile, was designed to provide, along with direct financial assistance to nonprofit professional and educational arts groups, stimulation and encouragement of the study and presentation of the arts. But to remind all concerned that the days of the Federal Theater Project were indeed over, Javits's bill included the following caveat: "The Foundation shall not produce or present any production."

44. The full committee overruled the subcommittee (9–4), which had recommended only the advisory council. *New York Times*, 26 Sept. 1962, p. 33; Senate Report No. 2260, 87th Cong., 2d Sess. (1962); *Washington International Arts Letter* 1 (Nov. 1962), 29.

45. Claiborne Pell to Mrs. Kennedy, 24 Oct. 1962, included in the appendix to Claiborne Pell, recorded interview by John F. Stewart, 6 Feb. 1967, p. 50, John F. Kennedy Library Oral History Program.

46. U.S. Congress, Senate, *National Arts Legislation. Hearings before the Special Subcommittee on the Arts of the Committee on Labor and Public Welfare on S. 165 and S. 1316*, 88th Cong., 1st Sess. (1963). (Cited hereafter as *Arts Hearings*-1963.) S. 165, sponsored by Javits, Clark, and Humphrey, would create a U.S. National Arts Foundation, while S. 1316, sponsored by Humphrey, Javits, Clark, Cooper, Pell, Long of Missouri, Metcalf, Randolph, Ribicoff, and Scott (all Democrats except Javits, Cooper, and Scott) would establish both the advisory council (renamed the National Council on the Arts and placed in the executive office rather than HEW) and the foundation (now covering all of the arts). *1963 NCAG Annual Report*. For the text of S. 1316, see *Arts Hearings*-1963, pp. 18–41.

47. Memorandum, August Heckscher to Arthur Schlesinger, Jr., 2 May 1962, Goldberg Papers, Box 61.

48. "Notes on Meeting to Discuss White House Policy on Advisory Committee on the Arts, May 12, 1962"; Heckscher Interview—JFK Lib., pp. 26–27; August Heckscher to Frank Thompson, 14 Dec. 1962, 13 Feb. 1963; Hubert Humphrey to August Heckscher, 16 Jan. 1963, 5 Feb. 1963, 18 Apr. 1963; Memorandum, Arthur Schlesinger, Jr., to John F. Kennedy, n.d. [ca. 30 Jan. 1963], Heckscher Papers, Boxes 6 and 35; *New York Times*, 13 Mar. 1963, p. 5; 1 Apr. 1963, p. 1; 13 June 1963, p. 28. For the text of the executive order and Kennedy's accompanying statement, see *The Arts and the National Government*, pp. 33–36. In addition to the thirty private citizens, the advisory council was to include several federal officials, whose agencies were to contribute $10–15,000 annually in cash or services.

49. The list approved by Kennedy included representatives in ten categories: (public) K. Lemoyne Billings, Anthony Bliss, Dorothy B. Chandler,* John Fischer,* R. Philip Hanes,* Huntington Hartford, August Heckscher, and Frederic R. Mann*; (architecture) Pietro Belluschi and Catherine B. Wurster*; (dance) Katherine Dunham; (drama) Ralph Bel-

lamy,* Eva Le Gallienne,* Alan J. Lerner, and Dore Schary*; (education) Albert Bush-Brown; (literature) Marchette Chute,* Ralph Ellison, and John Hersey; (motion pictures) Katherine Hepburn,* Stanley Kramer, and George Stevens; (music) Aaron Copland,* Herman Kenin, and Isaac Stern; (television) Fred Coe*; (visual arts) René d'Harnoncourt,* Lloyd Goodrich,* Charles Nagel, and Ben Shahn. (Those names marked with an asterisk were subsequently removed from the list by Richard Goodwin. Bliss, Hanes, Hartford, Bush-Brown, Ellison, Stevens, Kenin, Stern, and d'Harnoncourt eventually served on the National Council on the Arts.) Heckscher Papers, Box 7.

50. August Heckscher to Richard Goodwin, 24 July 1963. It was thought that Goodwin, deputy assistant secretary of state for Inter-American Affairs, would add a needed Latin American emphasis to America's cultural exchange efforts. *New York Times*, 3 Aug. 1963, p. 9. For the text of the second executive order, see *Arts Hearings*-1963, p. 45. An entirely new list compiled by Goodwin in consultation with the president included representatives in nine categories: (public) J. Ford Bell, William Benton, Eugene Block, Joyce Hall, Roy Larsen, McNeil Lowrey, John D. Rockefeller III, and Angus Wymar; (architecture) Lewis Mumford, I. M. Pei, William Pereira, and Paul Rudolph; (dance) George Balanchine; (drama) Julie Harris, Elia Kazan, Oliver Rea, and Richard Rodgers; (literature) Cass Canfield; (motion pictures) Paul Newman, James Stewart, Lew Wasserman, and Fred Zinneman; (music) Leopold Mannes and George Szell; (television) Mort Werner; (visual arts) Richard Diebenkorn, Philip Guston, Harold Rosenberg, and Theodore Roszak. Of the twenty-nine new names, only Pei, Pereira, Rodgers, and Diebenkorn have served on the National Council on the Arts. For other lists of candidates, including their congressional endorsements, see the file FG 716, "President's Advisory Council on the Arts," White House Central File (WHCF), Box 395, Lyndon Baines Johnson Memorial Library.

Among the candidates considered for Heckscher's job before Goodwin was selected were John Gardner, Lloyd Goodrich, McNeil Lowrey, Michael Straight, George Stevens, Jr., and Harold Taylor. Heckscher Papers, Boxes 6 and 7.

51. Memorandum, Arthur Schlesinger, Jr., to Lyndon B. Johnson, 29 Nov. 1963, Heckscher Papers, Box 6; *New York Times*, 22 Nov. 1963, p. 34.

52. Even after the passage of the resolution renaming the cultural center and providing matching funds for the center's completion, however, the project received a fair amount of criticism, especially from Rep. William Widnall (R-NJ).

Chapter Seven

1. Memorandum, Arthur Schlesinger, Jr., to Lyndon B. Johnson, 29 Nov. 1963, August Heckscher Papers, Box 6, John F. Kennedy Library. (Cited hereafter as the Heckscher Papers.)

2. Cosponsors of Humphrey's S. 2379 were Joseph Clark (D-PA), John Cooper (D-KY), Jacob Javits (R-NY), Edward Kennedy (D-MA), Edward Long (D-MO), Lee Metcalf (D-MT), Claiborne Pell (D-RI), Jennings Randolph (D-WV), Abraham Ribicoff (D-CT), and Hugh Scott (R-PA). Calling for both the National Council on the Arts and the National Arts Foundation, the bill had been introduced on 12 Dec. 1963, was reported four days later by the Committee on Labor and Public Welfare (Senate Report No. 780), and was debated in the Senate on 23 Dec. 1963. For that debate, including Pell's and Javits's remarks, see the *Congressional Record*, 88th Cong., 1st Sess. (1963), pp. 25263–73.

3. *New York Times*, 21 Dec. 1963, p. 17.

4. Memorandum for the President, August Heckscher to Lyndon B. Johnson, 7 Jan. 1964, Heckscher Papers, Box. 6.

5. *New York Times*, 17 Feb. 1964, p. 28.

6. Abe Fortas's memorandum to Johnson offered the following description of Roger Stevens: "Stevens is Chairman of the Board of Trustees of the Kennedy Center. He is a businessman and the outstanding theatrical producer in the country; a Democrat; experienced fund raiser (both for the Democratic party and cultural events); a real estate developer (Empire State Building, New Haven redevelopment, etc.); fine, attractive, energetic man who has dealt with Congress successfully. He will command the respect of the artistic world." Memorandum for the President, "Re: Cultural Policy," Abe Fortas to Lyndon B. Johnson, 29 Jan. 1964, Ex FG 716, "President's Advisory Council on the Arts," White House Central File (WHCF), Box 395, Lyndon Baines Johnson Library.

Born in Detroit on 12 Mar. 1910, Stevens dropped out of the University of Michigan during the Depression, eventually drifting into the real estate business; by 1951 he had made a fortune, that year heading up the syndicate that bought and sold the Empire State Building. Since that time he has been equally successful as a Broadway producer, whose 200-plus shows have included *West Side Story*, *Cat on a Hot Tin Roof*, and *A Man for All Seasons*. That experience and his work as a Democratic fund raiser led to his appointment as chairman of the National Cultural Center (now the Kennedy Center) in 1961, a position he still holds.

7. Suggested names for the Presidential Board included Isaac Stern, René d'Harnoncourt, William Walton, Edward R. Murrow, Fred Coe, Fred Friendly, George Stevens, Sr., Agnes deMille, Richard Rodgers, Pietro Belluschi, Lewis Mumford, I. M. Pei, Elizabeth Janeway, and Lucius Battle.

8. *New York Times*, 17 Feb. 1964, p. 28; 18 Feb. 1964, p. 1; 20 Feb. 1964, p. 28.

9. *Washington Post*, 25 Feb. 1964, p. 1.

10. Heckscher's remarks came in an address to the Federation of Protestant Welfare Agencies on 4 Mar. 1964. *New York Times*, 5 Mar. 1964, p. 36. Heckscher sounded a more positive note the following month in a Washington speech, noting that "although the organizational continuity has been broken sharply," Johnson was "going forward in his own way" in the matter of a federal arts policy. *New York Times*, 30 Apr. 1964, p. 29.

11. *New York Times*, 17 Apr. 1964, pp. 14–15. Stevens was sworn in 13 May. *New York Times*, 14 May 1964, p. 39. The executive order for the "Presidential Committee for Cultural Activites," as it was to have been called, was held in abeyance until the fate of the arts council and foundation bill, passed in the Senate in Dec. 1963, was decided in the House. Ex FG 716, "President's Advisory Council on the Arts," WHCF, Box 395, LBJ Library.

12. U.S. Congress, House, *National Arts and Cultural Development Act of 1963. Hearings before the Special Subcommittee on Labor of the Committee on Education and Labor, on H.R. 9587*, 88th Cong., 2d Sess. (1964). (Cited hereafter as *Arts Hearings*-1964.)

13. Ibid., p. 57.

14. Ibid., p. 11, 127. It is unlikely that any studies existed at the time showing the 8:1 ratio that Thompson cited. Those figures probably came from the testimony regarding the New York State Arts Council experience, often cited by Jacob Javits, that the council's 1960 budget of $50,000 yielded $400,000 in private arts spending.

15. Ibid., pp. 115, 71.

16. House Report No. 1476, 88th Cong., 2d Sess. (1964), p. 1.

17. Ibid., p. 7. The five representatives were Donald Bruce (R-IN), John Ashbrook (R-OH), David Martin (R-NB), Paul Findley (R-IL), and M. G. Snyder (R-KY). "Let us be prudent," the minority report concluded. "Let us forestall the deluge. Let us, in tuneful harmony, and clarion chorus, reject this bill."

18. Quoted in Dael Wolfe, "National Humanities Foundation," *Science* 145 (31 July 1964), 449.

19. *New York Times*, 24 June 1964, p. 27. *Report of the Commission on the Humanities* (New York, 1964). The commission's report itself ("Statements and Recommendations") was only fifteen pages, but it was supplemented by appendixes on "The Humanities and the Schools" and "Libraries and the Humanities," along with reports from twenty-four learned societies, ranging from the American Historical Association and the Modern Language Association of America to the American Studies Association and the Metaphysical Society of America. The Humanities Commission was replete with academic heavyweights, a roster of names certain to impress Congress.

20. Harold Weston, interview by Alvin Reiss, 20 Oct. 1965, Harold Weston Papers, Archives of American Art, Smithsonian Institution.

21. *Report . . . Humanities*, p. 1. "This Commission conceives of the humanities, not merely as academic disciplines confined to schools and colleges, but as functioning components of society which affect the lives and well-being of all the population. It regards the arts, both visual and performing, as part of the humanities and indeed essential to their existence" (p. 2).

22. Ibid., p. 5.

23. Fred Hechinger, "Balancing Act: Scholars Seek National Agency to Aid Humanities Teaching," *New York Times*, 28 June 1964, sec. 4, p. 7.

24. *New York Times*, 16 Aug. 1964, sec. 4, p. 7. Moorhead recognized that his bill had no chance of passage in 1964, but planned to reintroduce the bill the following January. William S. Moorhead, "A National Humanities Foundation," *America* 111 (14 Nov. 1964), 597.

25. "There just simply must be no neglect of the humanities," Johnson declared, after citing figures that showed that nearly half of the graduate students in the life sciences received federal support, while only 10% of humanities students received such aid. "The values of our free and compassionate society are as vital to our national success as the skills of our technical and scientific age." *Public Papers of the President, Lyndon B. Johnson, 1963–64*, vol. 2 (Washington, D.C., 1965), p. 1141.

26. *Congressional Record*, 88th Cong., 2d Sess. (1964), p. 20649.

27. For the debate, see ibid., pp. 20645–64. For background information on the NCA bill and Stevens's role in its passage, see "The National Council on the Arts and the National Endowment for the Arts during the Administration of Lyndon B. Johnson," vol. 1, "The History" (mimeographed, 1968), pp. 5–8, NEA Library.

28. *Congressional Record*, 88th Cong., 2d Sess. (1964), p. 20647.

29. Sec 2(1) of the NCA bill stated "that the encouragement and support of the arts, while primarily a matter for private and local initiative, is also an appropriate matter of concern to the Federal Government." Further, sec. 3 stated: "In the administration of this Act no department, agency, officer, or employee of the United States shall exercise any direction, supervision or control over the policy or program determination of any group, State or State agency involved in the arts."

Sec 7(b) described the duties of the NCA:

The Council shall (1) recommend ways to maintain and increase the cultural resources of the United States, (2) propose methods to encourage private initiative in the arts, (3) advise and consult with local, State, and Federal departments and agencies, on methods by which to coordinate existing resources and facilities, and to foster artistic and cultural endeavors and the use of the arts, both nationally and internationally, in the best interests of our country, and (4) conduct studies and make recommendations with a view to formulating methods or ways by which creative activity and high standards and increased opportunities in the arts may be encouraged and promoted in the best interests of the Nation's artistic and cultural progress, and a greater appreciation and enjoyment of the arts by our citizens can be encouraged and developed.

The chairman of the NCA was authorized to appoint advisory committees or panels to assist the council in its deliberations; and the council was required to submit an annual report to the Congress and the president outlining its activities.

30. *Congressional Record,* 88th Cong., 2d Sess. (1964), p. 20658.

31. Rep. John Ashbrook's proposed amendment stated "that the Council shall not consider, study, or recommend activities or programs which involve, directly or indirectly, the use of Federal funds for grants or loans." It was defeated 42–65. Rep. Paul Findley introduced the balanced-budget amendment; it, too, failed, 36–60. The only amendment to pass was introduced by Peter Frelinghuysen (R-NJ), placing a ceiling of $150,000 on the NCA budget; this figure was subsequently reduced to a $50,000 appropriation. Ibid., p. 23640. The failure to include the words "per annum" following the $150,000 figure in the bill resulted in a potential crisis the following year, until legislation to amend the original bill was passed.

32. Ibid., pp. 20664, 20923–25; *New York Times,* 21 Aug. 1964, p. 14; 4 Sept. 1964, p. 18. Including paired votes, the NCA tally was 226 in favor (176 Democrats and 50 Republicans) and 149 opposed (44 Democrats and 105 Republicans; 33 of the Democrats were from southern states). *Washington International Arts Letter* 3 (Sept. 1964) 164. For a copy of Public Law 88–579, see U.S., *Statutes at Large,* vol. 78 (1964), pp. 905–7.

33. Howard Taubman, "A Sign of Grace: U.S. Takes Modest First Step in the Arts," *New York Times,* 20 Sept. 1964, sec. 2, p. 1. Congress, in fact, persuaded itself—with the help of fifteen years of outside pressure—of the need for arts subsidy before the NCA had much opportunity to act.

34. *Public Papers of the President, Lyndon B. Johnson, 1963–64,* vol 2 (Washington, D.C., 1965), p. 1141.

35. Mark Harris, "Government as Patron of the Arts," *New York Times Magazine,* 13 Sept. 1964, p. 35.

36. *Congressional Record,* 89th Cong., 1st Sess. (1965), p. 2397.

37. *Public Papers of the President, Lyndon B. Johnson, 1965,* vol. 1 (Washington, D.C., 1966), p. 8; *New York Times,* 5 Jan. 1965, p. 16.

38. The National Humanities Foundation Act would establish in the executive branch an independent agency "to develop and promote a broad policy of support" for the humanities and the arts, with a twenty-member board appointed by the president and authorized to award scholarships and graduate fellowships and to support various educational and cultural projects.

39. *Congressional Record,* 89th Cong., 1st Sess. (1965), pp. 1688–90. Sen. Ernest Gruening (D-AK) was the chief sponsor of the humanities legislation in the Senate.

40. Ibid., pp. 36–37. See also the similar comments by Rep. Moorhead, including a summary of his bill and a list of sponsors of humanities legislation in the House. Ibid., pp. 39–40.

41. Ibid., p. 17041.

42. Frank Thompson provided a brief history of the arts and humanities foundation legislation in the *Congressional Record*, 89th Cong., 1st Sess. (1965), pp. 4717–18. For Sen. Javits's comments on his arts foundation bill, see ibid., pp. 377–79. The printed records of both subcommittees include the following joint session transcript: U.S. Congress, House and Senate, *National Arts and Humanities Foundation. Joint Hearings before the Special Subcommittee on Arts and Humanities of the Committee on Labor and Public Welfare, U.S. Senate, and the Special Subcommittee on Labor of the Committee on Education and Labor, House, on Bills to Establish National Foundations on the Arts and Humanities*, pt. 1, 89th Cong., 1st Sess. (1965). (Cited hereafter as *Arts Hearings—House and Senate-1965*, with page numbers referring to the Senate version.)

See also, U.S. Congress, Senate, *National Arts and Humanities Foundations. Hearings before the Special Subcommittee on Arts and Humanities of the Committee on Labor and Public Welfare*, pt. 2, 89th Cong., 1st Sess. (1965). (Cited hereafter as *Arts Hearings—Senate-1965*); and U.S. Congress, House, *National Arts and Humanities Foundations. Hearings before the Special Subcommittee on Labor of the Committee on Education and Labor, on H.R. 334, H.R. 2043, and H.R. 3617 and Similar Bills to Establish National Foundations on the Arts and Humanities*, pt. 2, 89th Cong., 1st Sess. (1965). (Cited hereafter as *Arts Hearings—House-1965*.)

The major legislation considered by these House and Senate subcommittees were Moorhead's H.R. 334 (National Humanities Foundation), Thompson's H.R. 3617 (National Arts Foundation), Gruening's S. 111 (National Humanities Foundation), and Pell's S. 315 (National Arts Foundation) and S. 316 (National Humanities Foundation), along with the administration's National Foundation on the Arts and Humanities bill—Pell's S. 1483 and Thompson's H.R. 6050. See also "The National Council on the Arts . . . During the Administration of President Lyndon B. Johnson", vol. 1, pp. 9–12.

43. *Arts Hearings—House and Senate-1965*, pp. 2–3.

44. The standard arguments of the arts advocates were repeated ad infinitum at the hearings; only R. Philip Hanes, president of the Arts Councils of America and the North Carolina Arts Council (in a written statement, ibid., pp. 572–73) and his colleague George Irwin of the Illinois Arts Council (*Arts Hearings—House-1965*, pp. 289–98) opposed federal arts subsidy. Much of the testimony came from representatives of the academic community, who wholeheartedly supported the humanities legislation. The infrequent opposing comments came from Reps. Robert Griffin and Paul Findley, who feared federal control and the drying up of private support. The most useful and important testimony at the hearings was

offered by Roger Stevens (*Arts Hearings—House and Senate*-1965, pp. 10–18); Barnaby Keeney (*Arts Hearings—Senate*-1965, pp. 200–35); Harold Weston (*Arts Hearings—Senate*-1965, pp. 263–300); Frederick Dorian, author of *Commitment to Culture* (Pittsburgh, 1964), a study of foreign practices of state arts subsidy (*Arts Hearings—Senate*-1965, pp. 379–82); Glenn T. Seaborg, chairman of the U.S. Atomic Energy Commission (*Arts Hearings—Senate*-1965, pp. 404–8); Helen S. Thompson, ASOL executive vice president (*Arts Hearings—Senate*-1965, pp. 419–29); John Hightower, New York State Arts Council executive director (*Arts Hearings—Senate*-1965, pp. 551–55); and Rep. William S. Moorhead (*Arts Hearings—House*-1965, pp. 250–57).

45. *Arts Hearings—House and Senate*-1965, p. 7.

46. Ibid., p. 6. For Frank Thompson's comments, see ibid., p. 107; for Jacob Javits's comments, see *Arts Hearings—Senate*-1965, p. 228.

47. *New York Times*, 11 Mar. 1965, p. 1. (The bill also included a provision for $1 million funding for the Office of Education to strengthen education in the arts and humanities and for teacher training in those fields.) Memorandum to the President, Richard Goodwin to Lyndon B. Johnson, 8 Mar. 1965, Ex FG 266, WHCF, "National Foundation on the Arts and Humanities," Box 298, LBJ Library. Livingston L. Biddle, Pell's assistant, was instrumental in the process of writing the bill and the president's statement. Interview with Livingston Biddle, 11 Feb. 1980. Also working on the measure were Jack Golodner, arts lobbyist for Actors Equity, and Barbara Donald, representing the National Council on the Arts and Government. Interview with Barbara Donald, 25 Feb. 1980. Pell introduced the bill in the Senate (S. 1483), along with forty-three cosponsors (thirty-six Democrats and seven Republicans), while Thompson sponsored the administration bill in the House (H.R. 6050), bringing the total number of arts and humanities bills introduced in the House in 1965 to 148. *Congressional Record*, 89th Cong., 1st Sess. (1965), pp. 4594–98, 4717–18.

48. *Congressional Record*, 89th Cong., 1st Sess. (1965), p. 4594.

49. In addition to the chairmen of the NEA and NEH, the proposed FCAH was to include the U.S. commissioner of education, the secretary of the Smithsonian Institution, the director of the National Science Foundation, the Librarian of Congress, and a member designated by the Secretary of State. Other federal officials were added in later years.

50. The Humanities Endowment was authorized to develop a national policy for "progress and scholarship in the humanities," to support research through fellowships to individuals and grants to institutions, to foster the interchange of information in the humanities, to foster public understanding of the humanities, and to support the publication of scholarly works in the humanities.

51. The total amount of any grant could not exceed 50% of the total cost of any project or production. Up to 20% of the funds were not subject

to this stipulation, if the applicant could demonstrate that matching funds were not available.

52. Rockefeller Brothers Fund, *The Performing Arts: Problems and Prospects* (New York, 1965). The appearance of the report was announced on the front page of the *New York Times*, 8 Mar. 1965. The panel included sixteen arts patrons, eight educators, one journalist, one economist, one architect, and three arts administrators.

53. *The Performing Arts*, p. 50.

54. In summary, the panel concluded that while private support should remain dominant, the federal government—together with state and local governments—should give strong support to the arts, including the performing arts, by appropriate recognition of their importance, by direct and indirect encouragement, and by financial cooperation." Ibid., p. 148. The panel favored federal matching grants to meet the capital construction needs of arts organizations.

55. The Baumol and Bowen report, *The Performing Arts: The Economic Dilemma* (New York, 1966), was not published until the following year, but a preview was offered shortly after the release of the Rockefeller report. William Baumol and William Bowen, "On the Performing Arts: The Anatomy of Their Economic Problems," *American Economic Review, Papers and Proceedings* 55 (May 1965), 495–502. Their research focused on the "income gap" in the arts, whose institutions are unable to offset rising costs with increased productivity. Although primarily concerned with the development of a mass audience for culture in America, Alvin Toffler's *The Culture Consumers* (New York, 1964) also examined the arts' "economic dilemma." And in a chapter entitled "Art and Politics," Toffler discussed the arts-support debate, recommending a modest program of indirect federal subsidy based on tax incentives for artists and patrons.

56. *Arts Hearings—House and Senate*-1965, p. 4.

57. John Steinbeck replaced David Brinkley, who resigned in 1966.

58. Herman Kenin, president of the American Federation of Musicians, replaced David Smith, who died 22 May 1965.

59. The Council, *The Nation* wrote, "is an experiment handicapped from the start by the fact that President Johnson has seen fit to place at its head a man whose professional life has been shaped by the very situation the Council is designed to relieve. . . . It is inconceivable that he is the best man available to free art from the shackles of commerce." "The Real Conflict," *The Nation*, 18 Nov. 1964, p. 234.

60. See note 29, above, for the full legislative reference to the NCA's duties and responsibilities.

61. Quoted in *Library Journal* 90 (15 Jan. 1965), 210. Six days after his "Magna Carta" speech in New York, Stevens spoke even more boldly in a memorandum to the president, outlining a plan for a $10 million national arts foundation, with half of the money to be devoted to matching grants for the states (allocated according to population) and the rest de-

voted mainly to various "outreach" projects. Memorandum for the President, Roger Stevens to Lyndon B. Johnson, 16 Dec. 1964, Bill Moyers File, "Arts and Humanities, National Foundation," WHCF, Box 5, LBJ Library.

62. Frank Thompson's H.R. 4714, to add the words "per annum" to the NCA bill, failed by only a few votes on 15 Mar. 1965 to get the two-thirds majority it needed. Proceedings of the National Council on the Arts, First Meeting—Apr. 9 and 10, 1965, Washington, D.C., p. 1; *Congressional Record*, 89th Cong., 1st Sess. (1965), pp. 8871–74, 19645.

63. Proceedings . . . First meeting, pp. 1–4. Hanes was also concerned by the "prevailing minimum wage" requirement of the bill.

64. *New York Times*, 10 Apr. 1965, p. 18.

65. Proceedings . . . First Meeting, pp. 2–9. Resolutions were also offered by various task forces of the council, to be taken up at the second meeting in June, and the formation of panels and regional committees was discussed. Additionally, council member Isaac Stern suggested two goals for the council—"enlarging audience participation and (providing) opportunities for wider professional activities and training"—which were subsequently cited as basic NCA principles in the *First Annual Report of the National Council on the Arts*, 1964–65, p. 16.

66. *New York Times*, 11 Apr. 1965, p. 80. The council did issue a "Statement by the National Council on the Arts at the Termination of its First Meeting in Washington, D.C. Apr. 9–10, 1965," stressing the need for an arts and humanities foundation to make "manifest . . . the quality that is implicit in the American promise."

67. Of particular interest at the second NCA meeting was a policy paper proposing the "central concept of the National Council," stressing the coordinating role of that body, the importance of the availability of the arts, arts education, and the need for improved arts administration, all of which foreshadowed eventual Arts Endowment policies. "Whatever practical programs are developed . . . ," the report noted, "cultural progress can only be measured in terms of greater enjoyment and participation in the arts by its citizens. . . . It might be said that the goal of the National Council on the Arts is to increase *artistic appreciation* in the nation." These themes were woven at the meeting into a public policy statement, one which deftly combined the grandiloquence of Congress ("our national inner life," "the promise of our democracy") with some of the more immediate and pragmatic concerns of the council itself. For the statement, see the *First Annual Report*, p. 36.

68. Ibid., p. 35. See also "The National Council on the Arts . . . During the Administration of Lyndon B. Johnson," vol. 1, pp. 12–17.

69. The Senate Labor and Public Welfare Committee had unanimously approved the NFAH bill in May, amending the bill slightly (including restoring Javits's original state-aid plan by earmarking $2.75 million, from the $5 million available in federal matching funds, for state grants—$50,000 matching grants for states with official arts agencies and $25,000

nonmatching grants for surveys leading to the establishment of such agencies). The committee report also included a statement on the importance of freedom of expression suggested by Sen. Ralph Yarborough (D-TX). Other changes in the bill included a clarification of the prevailing minimum wage stipulation to apply only to professional artists, and an increase in the membership of the NCA by two, to twenty-six. For these and other, technical amendments, see Senate Report No. 300, 89th Cong., 1st Sess. (1965), pp. 13–18. For a discussion of the bill, a list of cosponsors, and the Senate's voice-vote passage on 10 June 1965, see the *Congressional Record*, 89th Cong., 1st Sess. (1965), pp. 12793–94, 13103–11.

70. "Art and Politics at the White House Festival of the Arts," *U.S. News and World Report*, 28 June 1965, pp. 10–11.

71. Memorandum for the President, Eric F. Goldman to Lyndon B. Johnson, 25 Feb. 1965, Gen AR/MC, "11/23/63–6/4/65," WHCF, Box 2, LBJ Library. Details on the festival were released in May. *New York Times*, 27 May 1965, p. 30; 11 June 1965, p. 19.

72. "Cavalcade of Culture," *The Economist* 215 (19 June 1965), 1401.

73. Eric Goldman, "The White House and the Intellectuals," *Harper's*, Jan. 1969, p. 32. There were actually two guest lists for the festival, and most of those artists who were invited were included on the second list, for the evening program only. Dwight Macdonald, "A Day at the White House," *New York Review of Books*, 15 July 1965, pp. 10–15.

74. *New York Times*, 3 June 1965, pp. 1–2; *Washington Post*, 4 June 1965, p. 1. Goldman prepared a response to Lowell for the president, but Johnson refused to send it out over his signature. Goldman, "The White House," p. 35.

75. The artists and writers included Jules Feiffer, Philip Guston, Mark Rothko, Larry Rivers, Lillian Hellman, Alfred Kazin, Dwight Macdonald, Mary McCarthy, Hannah Arendt, Bernard Malamud, Philip Roth, William Styron, Peter Taylor, Edgard Varèse, and six Pulitzer Prize–winning poets: John Berryman, Alan Dugan, Stanley Kunitz, Louis Simpson, W. D. Snodgrass, and Robert Penn Warren. *New York Times*, 4 June 1965, p. 2. Others who refused invitations, according to Goldman, were Paul Strand, Alexander Calder, Jack Levine, and Robert Brustein.

76. The behind-the-scenes details are provided by Goldman in "The White House." That *Harper's* article, it should be noted, appearing nearly four years after the event, was not without its critics. Both Richard Goodwin and Saul Maloff responded unfavorably in a later issue of *Harper's*, with the latter dismissing Goldman's essay as a "self-serving concoction of distorted hearsay, plain error, inept fiction, and damn lie." *Harper's*, Mar. 1969, p. 4. For an expanded version of Goldman's account, see Eric Goldman, *The Tragedy of Lyndon Johnson* (New York, 1969), pp. 418–75.

77. The display of painting and sculpture (selected by David Scott and Adelyn Breeskin of the National Collection of Fine Arts and Carter Brown of the National Gallery, from collections throughout the U.S.) fea-

tured an impressive array of artists, including Andrew Wyeth, Jack Levine, Ben Shahn, Georgia O'Keeffe, Edward Hopper, Thomas Hart Benton, Jackson Pollock, Jasper Johns, Peter Hurd, Charles Burchfield, Alexander Calder, Louise Nevelson, Theodore Roszak, Stuart Davis, Willem de-Kooning, David Smith, Robert Motherwell, Mark Rothko, Adolph Gottleib, and Robert Rauschenberg.

78. Hersey introduced his reading from *Hiroshima* with the following statement: "I read these passages on behalf of the great number of citizens who have become alarmed in recent weeks by the sight of fire begetting fire. Let these words be a reminder. The step from one degree of violence to the next is imperceptibly taken, and cannot be taken back. The end point of these little steps is horror and oblivion. . . . Wars have a way of getting out of hand." Quoted in "Festival of the Arts," *Time*, 25 June 1965, p. 31.

79. "We wish to make it clear, that, in accepting the President's kind invitation," Macdonald's statement to the press read, "we do not mean to repudiate the courageous stand taken by Robert Lowell nor to endorse the Administration's foreign policy. We quite share Mr. Lowell's dismay at our country's recent action in Vietnam and the Dominican Republic." According to Macdonald, he collected nine signatures. Macdonald, "A Day at the White House," p. 15; *New York Times*, 24 June 1965, p. 43; "Polit Art," *The Nation*, 21 June 1965, pp. 687–88.

80. Memorandum, Jack Valenti to Lyndon B. Johnson, 8 June 1965, Gen AR/MC, "6/565–6/12/65," WHCF, Box 2, LBJ Library.

81. For the full text of Johnson's speech, see the *Congressional Record*, 89th Cong., 1st Sess. (1965), p. 13599.

82. Goldman, "The White House," p. 45; Saul Maloff, "Art and Vietnam: White House Festival," *Commonweal*, 9 July 1965, pp. 485–87.

83. *Harper's*, Mar. 1965, p. 8; Thomas B. Hess, "Artists in the Great Society," *Art News* 64 (Sept. 1964), 21.

84. House Report No. 618, 89th Cong., 1st Sess. (1965), p. 19. The seven representatives were William H. Ayres (R-OH), Robert Griffin (R-MI), Albert Quie (R-MN), Charles Goodell (R-MI), Dave Martin (R-NB), Glenn Andrews (R-AL), and Edward J. Gurney (R-FL). Besides the alleged haste with which the full committee acted, these representatives criticized the bureaucratic maze of the NFAH bill, its potential for a "more lavish expenditure of federal funds" in the future, and the absence of any NCA study of the matter.

85. Details of the final passage of the NFAH bill in the House are found in, "The National Council on the Arts . . . During the Administration of Lyndon B. Johnson," vol. 1, pp. 19–22. The session on 13 Sept. lasted from noon until 12:31 A.M., with resolutions on the release of seven bills from the Rules Committee being considered. At one point, reportedly, it appeared that only three of the seven bills, not including the arts and humanities bill, would succeed, until President Johnson, through Law-

rence O'Brien, sent word to Speaker McCormack that the cultural legislation was a "must." *Congressional Record*, 89th Cong., 1st Sess. (1965), pp.
23618–21; *New York Times*, 14 Sept. 1965, p. 18.

86. *Congressional Record*, 89th Cong., 1st Sess. (1965), pp. 23937–84.
As chairman of the House Committee on Education and Labor, Rep. Adam
Clayton Powell (D-NY) led the debate.

87. Ibid., p. 23957.

88. Ibid., p. 23973.

89. *Washington Post*, 16 Sept. 1965, p. 1; *New York Times*, 16 Sept.,
1965, 49; *Congressional Record*, 89th Cong., 1st Sess. (1965), pp. 24617–18;
Washington Post, 30 Sept. 1965, p. 1; "An Historic Occasion," *Dance Magazine* 39 (Nov. 1965), 34.

90. "This government," Rep. Gross wrote, "with a $325 billion debt,
facing a yawning deficit in this fiscal year and spending billions on a war
in Southeast Asia, has no business initiating the spending of $20 million
annually on so-called art and culture. Let's win this war and balance the
budget before subsidizing the longhairs and little twinkletoes. I ask you to
veto H.R. 9460." Telegram, Rep. H. R. Gross to Lyndon B. Johnson, 18
Sept. 1965, Gen LE/AR, "Arts," WHCF, Box 28, LBJ Library.

91. For the full text of Johnson's speech at the bill-signing ceremony,
see *Public Papers of the President, Lyndon B. Johnson, 1965*, vol. 2 (Washington, D.C., 1966), pp. 1022–23. For a copy of Public Law 89–209, see U.S.,
Statutes at Large, vol. 79 (1965), pp. 845–55.

92. "The National Council on the Arts . . . During the Administration
of Lyndon B. Johnson," vol., 1, p. 24.

Epilogue

1. August Heckscher, *The Public Happiness* (New York, 1962), pp.
291–92.

2. *New York Times*, 22 Oct. 1965, pp. 1, 50. Between 1956 and 1964,
the Ford Foundation expended $55,400,000 on the arts and humanities.
William Murray, "Culture Boom," *Holiday*, Mar. 1966, pp. 70–75.

3. Richard B. Stolley, "The Problem of How to Spend $3 Million,"
Life, 26 Nov. 1965, pp. 75–76.

4. "The National Council on the Arts and the National Endowment
for the Arts During the Administration of President Lyndon B. Johnson,"
vol. 1 (mimeographed, 1968), pp. 28–33, NEA Library; *New York Times*, 16
Nov. 1965, pp. 49, 53; 21 Nov. 1965, p. 86. See also Frank Getlein, "Disbursement of Funds," *New Republic*, 15 Jan. 1966, p. 36; Roger L. Stevens,
"State of the Arts: A 1966 Balance Sheet," *Saturday Review*, 12 Mar. 1966,
pp. 24–25; "Government and the Arts: How Much to Whom?" *Newsweek*,
18 July 1966, pp. 56–60; and the annual reports of the NEA.

Selected Bibliography

Except for the expanding collection of works on the New Deal arts projects, there has been very little study in the area of government and art in America. Both Grace Overmyer, *Government and the Arts* (New York, 1939), and Ralph Purcell, *Government and Art: A Study of the American Experience* (Washington, D.C., 1956), are out of date, although a forthcoming book by Milton Cummings promises to fill the gap in the broad overview accounts of the subject. Recent treatments of current federal programs, Dick Netzer's *The Subsidized Muse: Public Support for the Arts in the United States* (New York, 1978), and Michael Mooney's *Ministry of Culture: Connections among Art, Money and Politics* (New York, 1980), have suffered from the authors' distance from their subject; Netzer focuses, if rather narrowly, on economic concerns, while Mooney ranges wildly over federal culture, "humanism," and conspiratorial politics. The forthcoming work on the subject by Edward C. Banfield should be equally wide of the mark, if one judges from his work in the past (*The Unheavenly City*).

Among the doctoral dissertations on government and the arts, two are pertinent: Meitzl Miller's "Factors Affecting Government Sanction of the Performing Arts" (Ball State University, 1966), and Lawrence Mankin's "The National Government and the Arts: From the Great Depression to 1973" (University of Illinois, Urbana-Champaign, 1976). Neither, however, is useful. Miller's is an early, ill-written, and poorly researched account of the origins of the Arts Endowment, while Mankin's, poorly organized and bogged down in political science jargon, attempts to do too much in its 221 pages.

If useful scholarly studies on government and the arts between the WPA and the Arts Endowment are lacking, there is no scarcity of other material. Journal and newspaper literature (selectively listed below and variously indexed in the *Art Index, Music Index,* the *Social Science and Humanities Index, Readers Guide to Periodical Literature,* and the *New York Times Index*) has proved to be immensely valuable. So, too, is the *Congressional Record,* not only for the entertaining floor debates, but for the considerable amount of editorial material inserted into the record by both friends and foes of the arts legislation. And of course the records of the several congressional hearings on the arts (also listed below), and the resulting committee reports, are indispensable to a study of art and government. Like the *Congressional Record,* these hearings include a great deal of reprinted material, and thus constitute veritable anthologies of arts advocacy. The opposition camp, with less of a need than the advocates to rally its forces, is less accessible, although good examples of that position are available in the periodical literature, the *Congressional Record,* and the records of the early arts hearings.

Personal interviews (listed below) and archival sources, finally, have provided a wealth of information, illuminating in particular the work of some of the key figures in the federal arts movement. The notebooks of Lloyd Goodrich (covering the years 1953–57 in great detail) at the Whitney Museum of American Art, and Harold Weston's papers (Archives of American Art, Smithsonian Institution), provide insight into the work of the Committee on Government and Art and the National Council on the Arts and Government, respectively. Also of interest at the Archives of American Art are the papers of Leon Kroll, Russell Lynes, and George Dondero, and interviews with Goodrich and August Heckcher. Heckscher's voluminous files are housed at the John F. Kennedy Library, while the Lyndon B. Johnson Library has well-catalogued holdings on government and art. Material pertaining to Arthur Goldberg's landmark Metropolitan Opera decision is included with his papers at the National Archives, while the New York Public Library and Museum of the Performing Arts (Lincoln Center) and the libraries of the American Council for the Arts in New York and the National

Endowment for the Arts in Washington all have scattered materials of interest to the scholar working in the field of government and art.

Books

Baumol, William, and Bowen, William. *Performing Arts—The Economic Dilemma; a Study of Problems Common to Theater, Opera, Music, and Dance*. New York: Twentieth Century Fund, 1966.

Carpenter, Paul. *Music: An Art and a Business*. Norman, OK: University of Oklahoma Press, 1950.

Commission on the Humanities. *Report*. New York: American Council of Learned Societies, 1964.

Creative America. New York: Ridge Press, 1962.

Dorian, Frederick. *Commitment to Culture: Art Patronage in Europe, Its Significance for America*. Pittsburgh: University of Pittsburgh Press, 1961.

Goldman, Eric. *The Tragedy of Lyndon Johnson*. New York: Alfred A. Knopf, 1969.

Goodman, Walter. *The Committee: The Extraordinary Career of the House Committee on Un-American Activities*. New York, 1968.

Leiter, Robert D. *The Musicians and Petrillo*. New York: Bookman Associates, 1960.

President's Commission on National Goals. *Goals for Americans*. Englewood Cliffs: Prentice-Hall, 1960.

Purcell, Ralph. *Government and Art: A Study of the American Experience*. Washington, D.C.: Public Affairs Press, 1956.

Rockefeller Brothers Fund. *The Performing Arts: Problems and Prospects; Rockefeller Panel Report on the Future of Theatre, Dance, Music in America*. New York: McGraw-Hill, 1965.

Toffler, Alvin. *The Culture Consumers: A Study of Art and Affluence in America*. New York: St. Martin's Press, 1964.

Periodical and Newspaper Articles

1943

Biddle, George. "The Victory and Defeat of Modernism." *Harper's*, June 1943, pp. 32–37.

Boswell, Peyton. "A Federal Art Bureau." *Art Digest* 18 (15 Nov. 1943), 3.

———. "The Government and Art." *Art Digest* 18 (1 Dec. 1943), 3.

Davis, Stuart. "What About Modern Art and Democracy?" *Harper's*, Dec. 1943, pp. 16–23.

"The Government and the Arts: A Proposal by George Biddle, with Comment and Criticism by Others." *Harper's*, Oct. 1943, pp. 427–34.

Mangrivite, Pepino. "Congress Vetoes Culture." *Magazine of Art* 36 (Nov. 1943), 264–65.

1944

"Cut-Rate Culture; Relics of the WPA Art Project." *Time*, 6 Mar. 1944, p. 56.

"End of WPA." *Life*, 17 Apr. 1944, pp. 85–86.

Gibbs, Josephine. "End of the Project." *Art Digest* 18 (15 Feb. 1944), 7.

Reid, Albert T. "WPA—RIP!" *Art Digest* 18 (15 Mar. 1944), 28.

"WPA and the Junkie." *Newsweek*, 6 Mar. 1944, p. 96.

1945

American Artists Professional League. "Another Bureau of Fine Arts." *Art Digest* 20 (1 Dec. 1945), 32–33.

"Leaders Discuss Arts after War." *New York Times*, 23 June 1945, p. 10.

Porterfield, Robert, and Breen, Robert. "Toward a National Theatre." *Theatre Arts* 29 (Oct. 1945), 599–602.

1946

"American Art Abroad: The State Department Collection." *Art News* 45 (Oct. 1946), 20–31.

Davis, Hallie Flanagan. "Postman Sometimes Rings Twice: Need for a National Theater." *Theatre Arts* 30 (Sept. 1946), 514–16.

Frankfurter, Alfred M. "60 Americans Since 1800." *Art News* 45 (Dec. 1946), 30–39.

Gibbs, Josephine. "State Dept. Sends Business-Sponsored Art as U.S. Envoys." *Art Digest* 21 (15 Nov. 1946), 8.

Pearson, Ralph M. "Hearst, the A.A.P.L., and Life." *Art Digest* 21 (15 Dec. 1946), 25.

"Showing the World." *Newsweek*, 14 Oct. 1946, p. 116.

1947

Boswell, Peyton. "Killed by Politics." *Art Digest* 21 (1 May 1947), 7.

"It's Striking, But Is It Art or Extravagance?" *Newsweek*, 25 Aug. 1947, p. 17.

Lansford, Alonzo. "Artists Protest." *Art Digest* 21 (15 May 1947), 16.

Louchheim, Aline. "Disputable Art Placed on Display." *New York Times*, 21 May 1947, p. 21.

———. "The Government and Our Art Abroad." *New York Times*, 23 May 1947, sec. 2, p. 8.

Morse, John D. "Americans Abroad." *Magazine of Art* 40 (Jan. 1947), 21–25.

Pearson, Ralph M. "State Department Requests." *Art Digest* 22 (1 Oct. 1947), 29.

———. "They Asked for It." *Art Digest* 21 (15 Sept. 1947), 32.

Read, Herbert. "The State as Patron." *The University Observer* 1 (Winter 1947), 3–9.

1948

Gibbs, Josephine. "State Department Art Classed as War Surplus." *Art Digest* 22 (June 1948), 9.

Goodrich, Lloyd. "Art and Government." *College Art Journal* 8 (Fall 1948), 41–42.

———. "Federal Government and Art." *Magazine of Art* 41 (Oct. 1948), 236–38.

Lansford, Alonzo. "Sic Transit: State Department's Collection of Modern American Paintings; Final Awards to Bidders." *Art Digest* 22 (July 1948), 13.

Mr. Harper [pseud.]. "After Hours." *Harper's*, Aug. 1948, pp. 115–16.

"Plan to Interpret American Culture." *New York Times*, 9 Dec. 1948, p. 35.

"Retired American Art." *Newsweek*, 5 July 1948, p. 68.

Robb, Marilyn. "Art News from: Chicago." *Art News* 46 (Jan. 1948), 39.

Shanley, J. P. "Toward Subsidy: Drive to Gain Governmental Support for National Theatre Planned." *New York Times*, 14 Nov. 1948, sec. 2, p. 3.

Taubman, Howard. "Art and Money." *New York Times*, 12 Sept. 1948, sec. 2, p. 6.

———. "Major Music Units Cannot Pay Way." *New York Times*, 1 Sept. 1948, p. 26.

———. "Music Groups Due to Ask Aid of U.S." *New York Times*, 2 Sept. 1948, p. 25.

———. "Philharmonic Bid for Aid Revealed." *New York Times*, 3 Sept. 1948, p. 16.

1949

Beyer, William. "State of the Theatre: Renaissance in Embryo." *School and Society* 69 (26 Mar. 1949), 228–31.

Boswell, Peyton. "Assassination by Implication." *Art Digest* 23 (15 Mar. 1949), 7.

———. "True and the False: Dondero's Assaults on Freedom of Expression and the Press." *Art Digest* 23 (Sept. 1949), 7.

"Death for the Javits Bill." *Music News* 41 (May 1949), 13.

DeVree, Howard. "Modernism under Fire." *New York Times*, 11 Sept. 1949, sec. 2, p. 6.

Frankfurter, Alfred M. "Abstract Red Herring." *Art News* 48 (Summer 1949), 15.
————. "Is There a Gentleman in the House?" *Art News* 48 (Sept. 1949), 13.
Genauer, Emily. "Still Life with Red Herring." *Harper's*, Sept. 1949, pp. 88–91.
"Government and Art; Digest of a Symposium at the Meeting of the College Art Association." *College Art Journal* 8 (Spring 1949), 171–77.
"Government Subsidy: A Dangerous Expedient." *Musical America* 69 (Sept. 1949), 14.
Ives, Irving, and Javits, Jacob K. "Toward a National Theatre." *Theatre Arts* 33 (Apr. 1949), 10–13.
Javits, Jacob. "A National Theatre and a National Opera and Ballet." *National Music Council Bulletin* 10 (Sept. 1949), 3–4.
"The Javits Resolution." *Music News* 41 (Mar. 1949), 4.
Kees, Weldon. "Essays and Asides: Dondero and Dada." *Nation*, 1 Oct. 1949, p. 327.
Marx, Henry. "Radio Discussion on Government Subsidy Skirts Fundamental Issues." *Music News* 41 (Feb. 1949), 3.
————. "Theatrical People Are More Alert than Are Musicians." *Music News* 41 (Jan. 1949), 27.
Pearson, Ralph M. "Representative Dondero's Blast." *Art Digest* 23 (July 1949), 20.
"Plea for Tolerance; Dondero's Attack." *Art Digest* 23 (June 1949), 7.
Soby, James Thrall. "A Going into the Mulberry Trees." *Saturday Review*, 2 July 1949, pp. 30–31.

1950

Biddle, George. "United States Bureau of Fine Arts." *Art Digest* 24 (Aug. 1950), 5.
Grafly, Dorothy. "How Can We Support an American Art?" *American Artist* 14 (May 1950), 48.
Javits, Jacob. "Address on a Bill to Establish a National Theatre, Opera, and Ballet." *National Music Council Bulletin* 10 (Jan. 1950), 6–7.
Marx, Henry. "Financial Insecurity of Orchestras Grows." *Music News* 42 (Oct. 1950), 3.
————. "Government Shows Interest in Support of Music." *Music News* 42 (Jan. 1950), 3.
————. "Subsidies for Musical Organizations Are Part of a Cultural Mobilization." *Music News* 42 (Nov. 1950), 3.
Sherek, Henry. "Why Not a Subsidy for the Theatre?" *New York Times Magazine*, 16 Apr. 1950, p. 27.
'A Symposium: Government and Art." *Magazine of Art* 43 (Nov. 1950), 242–59.

Taubman, Howard. "Trouble Ahead: Musical Institutions of Nation Face Peril Unless New Support Is Found." *New York Times*, 1 Oct. 1950, sec. 2, p. 7.

1951

Downes, Olin. "Financial Woes: Musical Organizations of America Face Critical Times and Need Help." *New York Times*, 1 Apr. 1951, sec. 2, p. 7.

Goodrich, Lloyd. "Politics and Policies in American Art." *Art Digest* 26 (1 Nov. 1951), 20.

Grafly, Dorothy. "How Shall We Support Our Artists?" *American Artist* 15 (Jan. 1951), 38.

———. "How Shall We Support Our Artists—Continuing the Discussion of 'The American Way'." *American Artist* 15 (Mar. 1951), 45.

Mitropoulos, Dimitri, and Malkin, J., et al. "Is Subsidy in Music Necessary?" *National Music Council Bulletin* 11 (Jan. 1951), 7–14.

Morrison, J. L. "That Inevitable Symphony Deficit." *Etude* 69 (Feb. 1951), 17.

"President Petrillo as Guest Columnist." *International Musician* 50 (Aug. 1951), 9.

Spaeth, Eloise A. "America's Cultural Responsibilities Abroad." *College Art Journal* 11 (Winter 1951), 115–20.

Specht, P. L. "Is a Federal Fine Arts Office Needed?" *Music News* 43 (May 1951), 3–4.

1952

"American Art Abroad." *Magazine of Art* 45 (Jan. 1952), 2.

Barr, Alfred H. "Is Modern Art Communistic?" *New York Times Magazine*, 14 Dec. 1952, p. 22.

Downes, Olin. "Subsidy for Arts: British System Could Be Considered by the U.S." *New York Times*, 21 Dec. 1952, sec. 2, p. 9.

Javits, Jacob K. "For an Academy of Music, Drama, and Ballet." *Music News* 44 (Sept. 1952), 13.

Lynes, Russell. "Government as a Patron of the Arts." *Yale Review* 42 (Autumn 1952), 21–30.

Marx, Henry. "Butter, Guns—and Culture." *Music News* 44 (Jan. 1952), 3–4.

———. "Music in Cultural Relations." *Music News* 44 (Sept. 1952), 3.

———. "Opera Economics." *Music News* 44 (Dec. 1952), 8.

"Money for Music—the Political Overtones." *Musical America* 72 (1 Nov. 1952), 14–15.

Peters, H. F. "American Culture and the State Department." *American Scholar* 21 (July 1952), 265–74.

Stevens, S. H. "Canada Shows the Way; Report on Needs of Music by Royal

Commission Should Not Go Unnoticed in This Country." *Music News* 44 (Jan. 1952), 5–6.

1953

"Democratic Dilemma." *Art Digest* 27 (Aug. 1953), 7.

"The Economic Situation of the Orchestra Player." *National Music Council Bulletin* 13 (Jan. 1953), 5–8.

Faison, S. L. "Refregier Murals in the Rincon Annex Post Office." *College Art Journal* 12 (Spring 1953), 287–88.

Fradier, George. "Freedom of the Artist." *Arts and Architecture* 70 (Feb. 1953), 15.

"Government Sifting Music Biz for Red Activities." *Billboard* 65 (2 May 1953), 14.

Grafly, Dorothy. "Art Mountain Conceives a Mouse: Comments on the Report of the Commission of Fine Arts." *American Artist* 17 (Dec. 1953), 62–66.

Hayes, Pat. "A Review of the Commission of Fine Arts Report." *National Music Council Bulletin* 14 (Sept. 1953), 8–9.

"H.R. 452: Federal Sponsorship." *Art Digest* 27 (July 1953), 21–22.

Josephson, Matthew. "Vandals Are Here." *Nation*, 26 Sept. 1953, pp. 244–48.

"Language of Reaction: Subversive." *Art Digest* 27 (July 1953), 7.

Louchheim, Aline B. "America and Art." *New York Times*, 6 Sept. 1953, sec. 2, p. 8.

———. "The Case of the Criticized Mural." *New York Times*, 10 May 1953, sec. 2, p. 13.

———. "Commission on Art." *New York Times*, 30 Aug. 1953, sec. 2, p. 8.

"Music Leaders Give Views on Federal Aid." *Musical America* 73 (15 Nov. 1953), 4.

Portner, Leslie Judd. "What Does the Future Hold?" *Washington Post*, 16 Aug. 1953, sec. G, p. 3.

Preston, Stuart. "Support for Art." *New York Times*, 8 Nov. 1953, sec. 2, p. 11.

Shahn, Ben. "The Artist and the Politicians." *Art News* 52 (Sept. 1953), 34–35.

Taubman, Howard. "A Bill for Fine Arts." *New York Times*, 18 Jan. 1953, sec. 2, p. 7.

———. "Cultural Policy: National Leaders Urged to Unite in Shaping It." *New York Times*, 5 Apr. 1953, sec. 2, p. 7.

Thompson, Helen M. "Report on Proposed Federal Government Participation in the Fine Arts." *National Music Council Bulletin* 14 (Sept. 1953), 3–7.

1954

Blatnik, John A., et al. "Joint Statement on Pending Arts Subsidy Legislation." *Musical America* 74 (1 Feb. 1954), 12.

Cresson, Margaret F. "Minority Opinion on the Goodrich Report." *American Artist* 18 (Nov. 1954), 16.

Eyer, Ronald. "Federal Aid to Art—Boon or Bane? Orchestral Heads Give Their Ideas on Subsidies." *Musical America* 74 (May 1954), 6.

Goodrich, Lloyd. "Government and Art: Committee Report." *College Art Journal* 14 (Fall 1954), 52–54.

———. "Government and the Arts." *Art in America* 42 (Dec. 1954), 272–73.

Grafly, Dorothy. "Art Bills in Congress." *American Artist* 18 (Jan. 1954), 51–53.

———. "Toward a Federal Art Program." *American Artist* 18 (Oct. 1954), 32.

"Letter from Congressman Charles R. Howell on Government Grants-in-Aid for the Arts." *Musical Courier* 149 (1 Apr. 1954), 5.

Louchheim, Aline B. "Cultural Diplomacy: An Art We Neglect." *New York Times Magazine*, 3 Jan. 1954, pp. 16–17.

Petrillo, James C. "Petrillo Stresses Need for Government Subsidy." *Musical America* 74 (15 Feb. 1954), 29.

"Symposium: Freedom and Art." *Art Digest* 29 [28] (1 Mar. 1954), 10–11.

"Symposium: Government and Art." *Art Digest* 28 (June 1954), 10–11.

Tunnard, Christopher. "Government Bureau of Art." *American Institute of Architects Journal* 21 (May 1954), 234.

1955

"Art and Entertainment: Latest 'Cold War' Weapon for U.S." *U.S. News and World Report*, 1 July 1955, pp. 57–59.

"Cultural Ambassador?" *Senior Scholastic* 66 (20 Apr. 1955), 7–9.

"Cultural Exports to Win Friends." *America*, 12 Feb. 1955, p. 494.

"Culture on the Road." *Newsweek*, 7 Feb. 1955, p. 72.

Devree, Charlotte. "Is This Statuary Worth More than a Million of Your Money?" *Art News* 54 (Apr. 1955), 34–37.

DeVree, Howard. "Our Art Travels: Many Shows Circulate at Home and Abroad." *New York Times*, 13 Feb. 1955, sec. 2, p. 15.

Frankfurter, Alfred. "Souls of Clay." *Art News* 54 (Apr. 1955), 17.

Goodrich, Lloyd, and Barr, Alfred. "Mrs. Cresson Draws Fire." *American Artist* 19 (Jan. 1955), 12–13.

Hanson, Haldore. "Two-Way Traffic to Moscow." *New Republic*, 7 Nov. 1955, pp. 6–8.

Ike Likes the Arts, So—U.S. May Export Culture." *U.S. News and World Report*, 28 Jan. 1955, p. 68.

Kearns, Carroll D. "Music vs. Guns." *Etude* 73 (Sept. 1955), 13–14.

Portner, Leslie. "Can Art and Politics Mix?" *Washington Post*, 27 Feb. 1955, sec. E, p. 7.

———. "Government Gets Behind Art." *Washington Post*, 6 Mar. 1955, sec. E, p. 7.

"Post in Cabinet Asked for Arts." *New York Times*, 27 Mar. 1955, p. 65.

Saarinen, Aline B. "Art and the Official Mind." *New York Times*, 27 Mar. 1955, sec. 2, p. 13.

Smith, Harrison. "American Culture for Export: Salute to France." *Saturday Review*, 30 July 1955, p. 22.

"Statement by Secretary Dulles on East-West Contacts." *U.S. Department of State Bulletin* 33 (28 Nov. 1955), 376–80.

"Statement on Artistic Freedom." *College Art Journal* 14 (Winter 1955), inside back cover.

Thompson, Frank. "Are the Communists Right in Calling Us Cultural Barbarians?" *Music Journal* 13 (July–Aug. 1955), 5.

———. "Congressman's Report." *Musical America* 75 (May 1955), 14.

"U.S. Lifts Curtain on Cultural Drive." *New York Times*, 28 Feb. 1955, p. 19.

1956

"Art and Prudence." *Commonweal*, 6 July 1956, pp. 336–37.

Atkinson, Brooks. "Affairs of State." *New York Times*, 17 June 1956, sec. 2, p. 1.

Austin, Holcombe M. "American Artist and the Cold War." *College Art Journal* 15 (Spring 1956), 205–11.

Breen, Robert. "Cultural Envoys; Some Thoughts on Our Arts-Exchange Plan." *New York Times*, 5 Aug. 1956, sec. 2, p. 1.

"Capitol Cats Bare Claws as Senators Go Longhair; No Funds for Jazz Mission." *Billboard* 68 (28 July 1956), 16.

Castle, E. W. "Ambassadors of Anti-Americanism." *American Mercury*, Feb. 1956, pp. 85–89.

Cooper, David S. "American Music Abroad." *Musical Courier* 153 (June 1956), 8–10.

"'Cultural Ambassadors' Get Results." *Musical America* 76 (15 Jan. 1956), 4.

"Cultural Exchange . . . or International Short-Change?" *Senior Scholastic* 69 (13 Dec. 1956), 7–8.

"Dallas Museum Trustees Take Stand on Policy." *The Museum News* 33 (15 Mar. 1956), 1.

Devree, Charlotte. "U.S. Government Vetoes Living Art." *Art News* 55 (Sept. 1956), 34–35.

Goodrich, Lloyd. "Spectrum." *Arts* 30 (Feb. 1956), 11.

Guthrie, Tyrone. "Case for an 'Arts Council' Here." *New York Times Magazine*, 25 Nov. 1956, p. 26.

Hall, Mildred. "Uncle Sam's a Cool Cat, Digs Jazz Beat." *Billboard* 68 (24 Nov. 1956), 1.

Holland, Kenneth. "Art and Exchange of Persons." *College Art Journal* 15 (Spring 1956), 228–33.

Kent, Norman. "It's About Time." *American Artist* 20 (Oct. 1956), 3.

Marshall, Jonathan. "Dondero, Dallas, and Defeatism." *Arts* 30 (July 1956), 9.

Marshall, Jonathan, and Rosenberg, James N. "Open Letter to the President of the United States, the Honorable D. D. Eisenhower." *Arts* 30 (Sept. 1956), 11.

Martin, John. "Austerity: Export Subsidies Make for Local Scarcity." *New York Times*, 16 Sept. 1956, sec. 2, p. 11.

Parmenter, Ross. "U.S. Helps Out; Bill Passed to Make Cultural Tours a Branch of Our Foreign Policy." *New York Times*, 5 Aug. 1956, sec. 2, p. 7.

"Political Critics of Art." *Commonweal*, 8 June 1956, p. 241.

Saarinen, Aline B. "Art Storm Breaks on Dallas." *New York Times*, 12 Feb. 1956, sec. 2, p. 15.

Schnitzer, Robert C. "America's Ambassadors of the Arts." *Musical Courier* 153 (June 1956), 12–13.

Schnitzer, Robert, and Martin, John. "In Dissent: Manager of ANTA's Exchange Program Rises to Object." *New York Times*, 30 Sept. 1956, sec. 2, p. 19.

Taubman, Howard. "Strange Thanks: Symphony's Asian Tour Repaid with a Slap." *New York Times*, 8 Apr. 1956, sec. 2, p. 9.

1957

Coe, Richard L. "Behind the Culture Curtain." *Nation*, 19 Jan. 1957, pp. 54–56.

Conly, John M. "Who'll Pay the Fiddler?" *High Fidelity*, Nov. 1957, p. 43.

Getlein, Frank. "Gesture toward the Arts." *Commonweal*, 6 Dec. 1957, pp. 251–53.

"Government Subsidy of Music?" *Instrumentalist* 11 (June 1957), 63.

"Marshall Plan for American Artists." *Musical America* 77 (July 1957), 4.

"Panel: Government and the Arts." *American Institute of Architects Journal* 28 (June 1957), 106–13.

Parmenter, Ross. "Congress and Art." *New York Times*, 8 Sept. 1957, sec. 2, p. 11.

———. "The World of Music: No Russians in U.S." *New York Times*, 7 Apr. 1957, sec. 2, p. 9.

Thompson, Frank. "Federal Government's Role in Art." *Educational Theater Journal* 9 (Dec. 1957), 300–305.

1958

"Americans at Brussels: Soft Sell, Range, and Controversy." *Time*, 11 June 1957, pp. 70–75.

Bracker, Milton. "Federal Role in the Arts Is Found to Have Increased in Decade Since WW II." *New York Times*, 8 Dec. 1958, p. 1.

Brinkley, David. "Downright Shameful That Brussels Exhibit." *New Republic*, 7 July 1958, p. 8.

Hess, Thomas B. "Innocents to Brussels." *Art News* 57 (Mar. 1958), 23.

Hope, Henry R. "Art at the Worlds Fair." *College Art Journal* 18 (Fall 1958), 68–71.

Hynes, Sam. "Cultural Exchange with Russia." *Commonweal*, 11 July 1958, pp. 369–71.

Javits, Jacob K. "Proposed U.S. Arts Foundation." *National Music Council Bulletin* 18 (Winter 1958), 3.

Lacy, W. S. B. "Exchange Agreement with U.S.S.R." *U.S. Department of State Bulletin* 38 (3 Mar. 1958), 323–28.

Lynes, Russell. "Proof that We Are Not Barbarians." *New York Times Magazine*, 6 July 1958, p. 5.

Marshall, Jonathan. "A Call for Action." *Arts* 32 (Apr. 1958), 15.

"New Approach to Old Problem." *Musical America* 78 (15 Dec. 1958), 4.

Strickland, William. "Some Thoughts on Subsidy and the Arts." *Musical Courier* 157 (1 Jan. 1958), 10–12.

Taubman, Howard. "Brussels: American Mistakes and Lessons." *New York Times Magazine*, 1 June 1958, p. 11.

———. "Cold War on the Cultural Front." *New York Times Magazine*, 13 Mar. 1958, pp. 12–13.

———. "Who Should Pay the Bill for the Arts?" *New York Times Magazine*, 7 Dec. 1958, pp. 61–62.

———. "Windows to the Souls of Nations." *New York Times Magazine*, 7 Sept. 1958, pp. 20–21.

Thompson, Frank. "A New Look at the Proposed Performance Center in Washington." *National Music Council Bulletin* 18 (Winter 1958), 5–7.

———. "Our Cultural Crisis." *Progressive* 22 (June 1958), 22–24.

"United States and U.S.S.R. Sign Agreement on East-West Exchange." *U.S. Department of State Bulletin* 38 (17 Feb. 1958), 243–48.

"U.S. Art at Brussels; Why Ike Is Irritated." *U.S. News and World Report*, 27 June 1958, p. 8.

1959

Canady, John. "Art Disinherited." *New York Times*, 27 Dec. 1959, sec. 2, p. 17.

Getlein, Frank. "Politicians as Art Critics; Thoughts on the U.S. Exhibition in Moscow." *New Republic*, 27 July 1959, pp. 11–14.

Goodrich, Lloyd. "American Painting and Sculpture, 1930–1959." *College Art Journal* 18 (Summer 1959), 288–301.

Halpert, Edith G. "Moscow Greeting." *New York Times*, 2 Aug. 1959, sec. 2, p. 15.

Javits, Jacob K. "Plan to Aid Our Lagging Culture." *New York Times Magazine*, 5 Apr. 1959, p. 21.

Kenin, Herbert D. "Governmental Support of Music." *Instrumentalist* 13 (7 Aug. 1959), 46–47.

Pelletier, Wilfred. "Music Is Everybody's Business." *Music Journal* 17 (Oct. 1959), 14.

Saarinen, Aline B. "Thoughts on U.S. Art for Moscow." *New York Times*, 22 Feb. 1959, sec. 2, p. 20.

———. "U.S. Art for Moscow." *New York Times*, 14 June 1959, sec. 2, p. 9.

Taubman, Howard. "Arts Council: A Dream for Investing a Foundation's Money." *New York Times*, 2 Aug. 1959, sec. 2, p. 7.

Thompson, Frank. "Federal Legislation to Foster the Fine Arts." *American Institute of Architects Journal* 32 (July 1959), 36–41.

———. "Politicians Are Interested in Music." *Music Journal* 17 (Apr.–May 1959), 11.

"U.S.I.A.: the Entertainers." *Wall Street Journal*, 15 June 1959, p. 10.

"U.S.I.A.: the Singing Commercials." *Wall Street Journal*, 5 June 1959, p. 8.

Watkins, Franklin. "U.S. Art to Moscow." *Art in America* 47 (Summer 1959), 90–93.

1960

Alessandro, Victor. "Give the Orchestra a Break." *Music Journal* 18 (Oct. 1960), 16.

"Art in U.S. International Programs: A Statement on Policy." *Art Journal* 20 (Winter 1960), 69.

Atkinson, Brooks. "Not Very Cheerful: Some Dark Facts that Plague the Theatre." *New York Times*, 19 June 1960, sec. 2, p. 1.

Boswell, Peyton. "Modern Manifesto." *Art Digest* 24 (Apr. 1950), 5.

"The Candidates and the Arts." *Saturday Review*, 29 Oct. 1960, pp. 42–44.

Getlein, Frank. "Federal Aid to Art: Distribution." *New Republic*, 8 Aug. 1960, pp. 21–22.

Grafton, Samuel. "Trouble in Our Symphony Orchestras." *McCalls*, Nov. 1960, pp. 84–85.

"How Art-Government Alliance Works in Europe—The Problem as Viewed by Our Editorial Board." *Musical America* 88 (Nov. 1960), 8–9.

Humphrey, Hubert. "The Cultural Arts and the Nation." *Arts in Society* 1 (Fall 1960), 4–12.

Janta, Alexander. "Art as Its Own Patron." *Saturday Review*, 18 June 1960, p. 14.

Lindsay, Howard. "Governmental Recognition of Music." *Music Journal* 18 (Mar. 1960), 28.

Mark, Charles C. "Genesis and Import of the Arts Council Concept." *Arts in Society* 1 (Fall 1960), 15–19.

"A New Frontier in the Arts—the Why and the How." *Musical America* 80 (Dec. 1960), 8.

"Nixon, Kennedy View Music and the Arts." *Musical America* 80 (Oct. 1960), 8.

Papp, Joseph. "Government Aid." *New York Times*, 24 July 1960, sec. 2, p. 1.

Parmenter, Ross. "Cultural Center." *New York Times*, 31 July 1960, sec. 2, p. 7.

Riegger, Wallingford. "For a Department of Fine Arts." *American Composers Alliance*, vol. 9, no. 3 (1960), p. 12.

Rockefeller, John D. "Financing the Arts—a Community Responsibility." *ASOL Newsletter*, vol. 11, nos. 5–6 (1960), pp. 4–5.

Schonberg, Harold C. "Candidates on Culture." *New York Times*, 30 Oct. 1960, sec. 2, p. 9.

Thompson, Frank. "Government Aid for the Arts." *International Musician* 58 (June 1960), 9.

———. "The Thompson-Wainwright Bill." *Musical America* 80 (June 1960), 19–20.

1961

Atkinson, Brooks. "Critic at Large." *New York Times*, 26 Dec. 1961, p. 22.

Bliss, Anthony. "Subsidy and the Met." *International Musician* 60 (Nov. 1961), 8.

Booth, John E. "Theatre Lobbying: Public Support Needed to Back Legislation." *New York Times*, 3 Dec. 1961, sec. 2, p. 1.

Cater, Douglas. "The Kennedy Look in the Arts." *Horizon* 4 (Sept. 1961), 4–17.

"Cities, States—and the Arts." *Musical Courier* 163 (Sept. 1961), 11–13.

"Federal Support of the Arts Debated on TV." *Musical America* 81 (Mar. 1961), 7.

Galbraith, John, and Lynes, Russell. "Should the Government Subsidize the Arts?" *Print* 15 (May 1961), 47–49.

"Government and the Arts." *Musical Courier* 163 (Sept. 1961), 5.

Haley, Hope. "Government and the Arts; the Washington Climate." *Musical Courier* 163 (Sept. 1961), 6.

Humphrey, Hubert H. "Government Aid for the Arts." *International Musician* 59 (June 1961), 8.

Javits, Jacob K. "America's Cultural Heritage." *Music Journal* 19 (May 1961), 12.

————. "Culture and the Struggle for Freedom." *American Music Teacher* 10 (Mar.–Apr. 1961), 4.

————. "National Arts Program." *Art in America*, vol. 49, no. 4 (1961), pp. 86–87.

————. "New Cultural Climate." *New York Times*, 7 May 1961, sec. 2, p. 1.

————. "A Senator's Plea." *Musical Courier* 163 (Sept. 1961), 7–8.

Kearns, Carroll. "Government Aid for the Arts." *International Musician* 59 (June 1961), 10.

Kuh, Katherine. "New Frontier in Art?" *Saturday Review*, 23 Dec. 1961, p. 32.

Lipman, Joseph. "Artist Manager Says Yes and No." *Musical Courier* 163 (Sept. 1961), 10.

McCreery, Mrs. Hugh E. "A Dissenting Voice." *Musical America* 81 (May 1961), 3–4.

McDowell, Harris B. "Our Government and Music." *Music Journal* 19 (Feb. 1961), 38–39.

McNaspy, C. J. "How Can We Pay for Music?" *International Musician* 60 (Dec. 1961), 8.

Mannes, Marya. "They're Cultural, but Are They Cultured?" *New York Times Magazine*, 9 July 1961, p. 14.

Robertson, Nan. "Artists Forced to Take Side Jobs." *New York Times*, 31 July 1961, p. 21.

Schonberg, Harold C. "Arts Hero, 1961." *New York Times*, 31 Dec. 1961, sec. 2, p. 9.

————. "Seen from Afar: Some Answers the Metropolitan Seeks Have Already Been Found in Europe." *New York Times*, 27 Aug. 1961, sec. 2, p. 9.

"Subsidy a European Tradition." *Musical Courier* 163 (Sept. 1961), 16–19.

Taubman, Howard. "Hunger for Arts: Trend Running Strong for Federal Action." *New York Times*, 16 July 1961, sec. 2, p. 1.

————. "A Subsidy for the Arts." *New York Times*, 24 Dec. 1961, Sec. 2, p. 3.

————. "Winds of Change: New Administration Has Chance to Help Arts." *New York Times*, 5 Feb. 1961, sec. 2, p. 1.

"Thank You, Mr. President." *Music Educators Journal* 48 (Nov.–Dec. 1961), 33–36.

"This Has Been Said." *Musical Courier* 163 (Sept. 1961), 14–15.

Thompson, Frank. "A Congressman's Plea." *Musical Courier* 163 (Sept. 1961), 9.

————. "Does Government Assistance Mean Government Control?" *Dance Magazine* 35 (June 1961), 36–37.

————. "Government Aid for the Arts." *International Musician* 59 (June 1961), 11.

————. "Subsidy as Sound Policy." *International Musician* 60 (July 1961), 16.

1962

Benton, Thomas Hart. "Random Thoughts on Art." *New York Times Magazine,* 25 Oct. 1962, p. 42.

Berdahl, R. O. "Laissez Faire or Aid?" *New York Times,* 18 Feb. 1962, sec. 2, p. 1.

Booth, John E. "How to Get Shakespeare to Pay the Bill." *New York Times,* 1 Apr. 1962, sec. 2, p. 1.

Burgard, Ralph. "Arts Councils—A New Approach to Cultural Leadership." *Arts in Society* 2 (Fall–Winter 1962–63), 120–31.

Calta, Louis. "Community Plan for Arts Urged." *New York Times,* 16 Mar. 1962, p. 22.

"Culture Chief." *New Yorker,* 31 Mar. 1962, p. 25.

Feron, James. "British Arts Plan May Guide U.S." *New York Times,* 11 Feb. 1962, p. 24.

Frankenstein, Alfred. "State Support for the Arts." *Hi Fi,* May 1962, p. 35.

Gelb, Arthur, and Gelb, Barbara. "Culture Makes a Hit at the White House." *New York Times Magazine,* 28 Jan. 1962, p. 9.

Goldberg, Arthur J. "The State of the Performing Arts." *Music Educators Journal* 48 (Feb.–Mar. 1962), 51–54.

———. "What Place the Arts?" *International Musician* 60 (June 1962), 8–9.

"Government and the Arts: Reprise Three." *Music Magazine/Musical Courier* 164 (Feb. 1962), 4–5.

"Government and the Arts: Subsidy? Yes, No, Maybe." *Music Magazine/Musical Courier* 164 (May 1962), 6–9.

Grutzner, Charles. "Schlesinger Sees Gains in the Arts." *New York Times,* 13 Apr. 1962, p. 38.

Hale, William Harlan. "When Government Went All Out for the Arts: A Memorandum to the President from the Secretary of Arts and Leisure." *Horizon* 5 (Nov. 1962), 18–19.

Heckscher, August. "The Nation's Culture: New Age for the Arts." *New York Times Magazine,* 23 Sept. 1962, pt. 2, p. 15.

———. "Role of Government." *Art in America* 50 (Winter 1962), 30.

Kerr, Russell. "Heckscher, U.S. Culture Consultant, Tells Plans." *Music Magazine/Musical Courier* 164 (May 1962), 9.

Kolodin, Irving. "Secretary Goldberg and the Opera Dilemma." *Saturday Review,* 27 Jan. 1962, p. 39.

Levine, Joseph. "The Vanishing Musician." *Music Journal* 20 (Mar. 1962), 38–40.

"New Era for Arts? National Policy Supports Them." *Architectural Record* 131 (Apr. 1962), 23.

"Parkinsonian Culture." *National Review* 12 (13 Mar. 1962), 157.

Sabin, Robert. "Government and the Arts: A Survey." *Musical America* 82 (Jan. 1962), 16–19.

Schlesinger, Arthur. "Government and the Arts: A New Era." *Show* 2 (Oct. 1962), 74.

Shapiro, Karl. "No Patronage." *Arts in Society* 2 (Fall–Winter 1962–63), 16–19.

Thompson, Frank. "A Congressman Suggests an Approach to Arts Legislation." *Instrumentalist* 16 (June 1962), 32–33.

———. "The Musical State of the Union." *Musical Journal* 26 (Apr. 1962), 28.

Thompson, Helen M. "Report on Federal Arts Legislation and Attitudes of Orchestra Governing Boards." *ASOL Newsletter*, vol. 13, nos. 5–6 (1962), p. 1.

1963

"Art and Politics." *Newsweek*, 17 June 1963, p. 85.

Blau, Herbert. "A Comment on the Heckscher Report." *Arts in Society* 2 (Spring–Summer 1963), 114–15.

Burgard, Ralph. "Variations on the Lincoln Center Theme." *New York Times*, 28 Apr. 1963, sec. 2, p. 11.

Esterow, Milton. "Arts Encouraged by the Kennedys." *New York Times*, 23 Nov. 1963, p. 10.

———. "Cultural Councils in 13 States Reflect an Upsurge of Interest." *New York Times*, 17 June 1963, p. 22.

Fogarty, John E. "Education: The Key to Music's Future." *International Musician* 61 (Mar. 1963), 8.

Heckscher, August. "The Attention Now Being Given to Music in the Executive Branch of the Government." *National Music Council Bulletin*, vol. 23, no. 2 (1962–63), pp. 11–12.

———. "Government and the Arts." *Music Journal* 21 (Mar. 1963), 17.

———. "The President and the Arts: Remembering JFK." *Saturday Review*, 14 Dec. 1963, p. 6.

"The Heckscher Report." *New Republic*, 29 June 1963, p. 8.

Mark, Charles C. "Common Sense about Citizen Support for Arts and Culture." *Arts in Society* 2 (Spring–Summer 1963), 4–11.

Shannon, William V. "Government and Art." *Commonweal*, 23 Aug. 1963, pp. 493–94.

Thompson, Helen M. "Report on Recent Federal Arts Legislation." *ASOL Newsletter*, vol. 14, nos. 4–5 (1963), pp. 18–20.

Von Eckardt, Wolf. "Public Happiness." *American Institute of Architects Journal* 40 (Sept. 1963), 10.

1964

Brustein, Robert. "Art, Non-Art: The Curse of Official Culture." *New Republic*, 7 Nov. 1964, p. 85–88.

Childs, Marquis. "President Keeps Society in Mind." *Washington Post*, 5 Aug. 1964, p. A17.

"Federal Architecture Policy: Will It Be Worthy of Great Society?" *Architectural Record* 136 (Oct. 1964), 10.

Frankfurter, Alfred. "Kennedy Pro Arte, et Sequitur?" *Art News* 62 (Jan. 1962), 23.

Getlein, Frank. "Government in Art." *New Republic*, 15 Feb. 1964, pp. 36–37.

Harris, Mark. "Government as Patron of the Arts." *New York Times Magazine*, 13 Sept. 1964, p. 35.

Hechinger, Fred. "Balancing Act: Scholars Seek National Agency to Aid Humanities Teaching." *New York Times*, 28 June 1964, sec. 4, p. 7.

Javits, Jacob K. "The Arts and the Federal Government." *National Music Council Bulletin* 24 (Spring 1964), 13–14.

"Johnson Inherits Cultural Leadership." *Architectural Forum* 120 (Jan. 1964), 5.

Kent, Norman. "To Encourage the Arts." *American Artist* 28 (Nov. 1964), 3.

Lekachman, Robert. "Everybody Is in the Queue." *New York Times Book Review*, 13 Dec. 1964, p. 1.

Moorhead, William S. "A National Humanities Foundation." *America* 111 (14 Nov. 1964), 597.

Oakes, George W. "Federal Arts Bill Endangered in Election Year Tactics." *Washington Evening Star*, 31 May 1964, p. C-2.

Schonberg, Harold C. "Culture—By Numbers, or by Quality." *New York Times*, 27 Dec. 1964, sec. 2, p. 13.

Spaeth, Sigmund. "In and Out of Tune." *Music Journal* 22 (Apr. 1964), 66.

Taubman, Howard. "A Sign of Grace: U.S. Takes a Modest First Step in the Arts." *New York Times*, 20 Sept. 1964, sec. 2, p. 1.

Thompson, Frank. "The Arts in Congress." *Music Journal* 22 (Sept. 1964), 27.

Udall, Stewart L. "The Arts as a National Resource." *Saturday Review*, 28 Mar. 1964, pp. 14–16.

Von Eckardt, Wolf. "Stalling on the Arts: Plans for JFK Library." *New Republic*, 21 Mar. 1964, p. 8.

Wolfe, Dael. "National Humanities Foundation." *Science* 145 (31 July 1964), 449.

1965

"Art, and Politics, at the White House Festival." *U.S. News and World Report*, 28 June 1965, pp. 10–11.

"The Arts: Crash Program." *Nation*, 22 Mar. 1965, p. 294.

Baumol, William, and Bowen, William. "On the Performing Arts: The

Anatomy of Their Economic Problems." *American Economic Review, Papers and Proceedings* 55 (May 1965), 495–502.

"Biting the Hand." *New Republic*, 2 Oct. 1965, p. 8.

"Cavalcade of Culture." *The Economist* 215 (19 June 1965), 1401.

Conte, Luther J. "Congress: Birth of NSF Recalled as New Foundation Is Established to Strengthen Arts, Humanities." *Science* 150 (1 Oct. 1965), 40–42.

"Festival of the Arts." *Time*, 25 June 1965, pp. 30–31.

Getlein, Frank. "My Day at the White House—White House Festival of the Arts." *New Republic*, 26 June 1965, p. 33.

————. "Roger and the Rabbits." *New Republic*, 3 April 1965, p. 25.

Greenberg, D. S. "Humanities: Proposals to Set Up National Foundation Are Gathering Support in the House and Senate." *Science* 147 (15 Jan. 1965), 273–74.

Hess, Thomas. "Artists in the Great Society." *Art News* 64 (Sept. 1965), 21.

"An Historic Occasion." *Dance Magazine* 39 (Nov. 1965), 34.

Kauffmann, Stanley. "Can Culture Explode? Notes on Subsidizing the Arts." *Commentary*, Aug. 1965, pp. 19–28.

Keeney, Barnaby C. "Why We Need a National Humanities Foundation." *Saturday Review*, 20 Mar. 1965, pp. 68–70.

Kolodin, Irving. "The Future of the Performing Arts." *Saturday Review*, 13 Mar. 1965, p. 21.

Lynes, Russell. "Mrs. Johnson's Cultural Cookout." *Harper's*, Sept. 1965, p. 28.

Macdonald, Dwight. "A Day at the White House." *New York Review of Books*, 15 July 1965, p. 10–15.

Maloff, Saul. "Art and Vietnam: White House Festival." *Commonweal*, 9 July 1965, pp. 485–87.

Morley, Felix. "Now Being Human Is an Art." *Nation's Business*, Sept. 1965, pp. 27–38.

"The New Patron." *Nation*, 18 Jan. 1965, p. 42.

"Next on the Subsidy List: Plays, Operas, Orchestras." *U.S. News and World Report*, 15 Mar. 1965, pp. 64–65.

"Patrons of Mediocrity." *Wall Street Journal*, 8 Mar. 1965, p. 12.

"Polit Art." *Nation*, 28 June 1965, pp. 687–88.

Stolley, Richard B. "The Problem of How to Spend $3 Million." *Life*, 26 Nov. 1965, pp. 75–76.

Taubman, Howard. "Rx for the Arts, U.S. and British." *New York Times*, 14 Mar. 1965, sec. 2, p. 1.

Taylor, Harold. "The Arts in America." *Dance Magazine* 39 (Nov. 1965), 35–39.

"Thanks, Without Enthusiasm." *Time*, 8 Oct. 1965, p. 30.

Weston, Harold. "The Federal Government and the Arts." *National Music Council Bulletin*, vol. 25, no. 3 (1965), pp. 9–11.

1966–1977

Braden, Thomas W. "I'm Glad the CIA Is 'Immoral'." *Saturday Evening Post*, 20 May 1967, p. 10.

Cockcroft, Eva. "Abstract Expressionism, Weapon of the Cold War." *Artforum* 12 (June 1974), 39–41.

Getlein, Frank. "Disbursement of Funds." *New Republic*, 15 Jan. 1966, p. 36.

"Government and the Arts: How Much to Whom?" *Newsweek*, 18 July 1966, pp. 56–60.

Goldman, Eric. "The White House and the Intellectuals." *Harper's*, Jan. 1969, pp. 31–45.

Hauptman, William. "The Suppression of Art in the McCarthy Decade." *Artforum* 11 (Oct. 1973), 48–52.

Mathews, Jane De Hart. "Art and Politics in Cold War America." *American Historical Review* 81 (Oct. 1976), 762–87.

Shapiro, David, and Shapiro, Cecile. "Abstract Expressionism: the Politics of Apolitical Painting." *Prospects* 3 (1977), 175–214.

Stevens, Roger L. "State of the Arts: A 1966 Balance Sheet." *Saturday Review*, 12 Mar. 1966, pp. 24–25.

Government Publications

Hearings

U.S. Congress, House. *Fine Arts Programs in Colleges. Hearings before a Subcommittee of the Committee on Education and Labor, on H.R. 7494.* 82d Cong., 2d Sess. 1952.

———. *Rincon Annex Murals, San Francisco. Hearings before the House Subcommittee on Public Buildings and Grounds of the Committee on Public Works on H.J.R. 211.* 83d Cong., 1st Sess. 1953.

———. *Federal Grants to Fine Arts Programs and Projects. Hearings before a Special Subcommittee of the Committee on Education and Labor, on H.R. 452, 5136, 5330, 5397, 7106, 7185, 7192, 7383, 7433, 7533, 7953, 8047, and 9111.* 83d Cong., 2d Sess. 1954.

———. *Distinguished Civilian Achievement. Hearings before a Subcommittee of the Committee on Education and Labor on Various Bills Relating to Awards of Medal for Distinguished Civilian Achievement, and Cultural Interchange and Development.* 84th Cong., 1st and 2d Sess. 1955–56.

———. *Hearings before the Committee on Foreign Affairs on Draft Bills Proposed in Executive Communications No. 863, No. 953, and No. 1601, Amending the United States Information and Educational Exchange Act of 1948, and No. 1409, Providing for Cultural and Athletic Exchanges and Participation in International Fairs and Festivals.* 84th Cong., 2d Sess. 1956.

————. *Federal Advisory Commission on the Arts. Hearings before a Subcommittee of the Committee on Education and Labor on H.R. 3541, 1089, 1945, 6374, 6642, and 7606.* 85th Cong., 1st Sess. 1957.

————. *Federal Advisory Council on the Arts. Hearing before a Subcommittee of the Committee on Education and Labor, on H.R. 2569 and Related Bills to Provide for the Establishment of a Federal Advisory Commission on the Arts to Assist in the Growth and Development of the Fine Arts in the United States.* 86th Cong., 1st Sess. 1959.

————. *The American National Exhibition, Moscow, July 1959. (The Record of Certain Artists and an Appraisal of Their Works Selected for Display.) Hearings before the Committee on Un-American Activities.* 86th Cong., 1st Sess. 1959.

————. *Aid to Fine Arts. Hearing before the Select Subcommittee on Education of the Committee on Education and Labor on H.R. 4172, H.R. 4174 and Related Bills to Aid the Fine Arts in the U.S.* 87th Cong., 1st Sess. 1961.

————. *Economic Conditions in the Performing Arts. Hearings before the Select Subcommittee on Education of the Committee on Education and Labor.* 87th Cong., 1st and 2d Sess. 1961–62.

————. *National Arts and Cultural Development Act of 1963. Hearings before the Special Subcommittee on Labor of the Committee on Education and Labor, on H.R. 9587.* 88th Cong., 2d Sess. 1964.

————. *National Arts and Humanities Foundations. Hearings before the Special Subcommittee on Labor of the Committee on Education and Labor, on H.R. 334, H.R. 2043, H.R. 3617, and Similar Bills to Establish National Foundations on the Arts and Humanities.* 89th Cong., 1st Sess. 1965.

U.S. Congress, House and Senate. *National Arts and Humanities Foundations. Joint Hearings before the Special Subcommittee on Arts and Humanities of the Committee on Labor and Public Welfare, U.S. Senate, and the Special Subcommittee on Labor of the Committee on Education and Labor, House, on Bills to Establish National Foundations on the Arts and Humanities.* 89th cong., 1st Sess. 1965.

U.S. Congress, Senate. *International Cultural Exchange and Trade Fair Participation Act of 1956. Hearing before the Committee on Foreign Relations on S. 3116 and S. 3172, Bills to Provide for the Promotion and Strengthening of International Relations through Cultural and Athletic Exchanges and Participation in International Fairs and Festivals.* 84th Cong., 2d Sess. 1956.

————. *Federal Advisory Council on the Arts. Hearing before a Subcommittee of the Committee on Labor and Public Welfare on S. 3054, a Bill to Provide for the Establishment of a Federal Advisory Commission on the Arts, and for other Purposes, and S. 3419, a Bill to Provide for the Establishment of a Federal Advisory Committee on the Arts, and for other Purposes.* 84th Cong., 2d Sess. 1956.

————. *Public Buildings. Hearings before a Subcommittee of the Committee on Public Works on S. 1985, a Bill to Authorize the Preparation of Plans and Specifications for the Construction of a National Air Museum, S. 3335, a Bill to Provide for a National Capital Center for the Performing Arts, and S. 3560, a Bill to Authorize the Construction of a Courthouse and Federal Office Building in Memphis, Tenn.* 85th Cong., 2d Sess. 1958.

U.S. Congress, Senate. *Providing for a National Academy of Culture. Hearing before the Subcommittee on Labor and Public Welfare on S. 2207, a Bill to Provide for a National Academy of Culture.* 86th Cong., 2d Sess. 1960.

————. *Government and the Arts. Hearings before a Special Subcommittee of the Committee on Labor and Public Welfare on S. 741, S. 785, and S. 1250.* 87th Cong., 2d Sess. 1962.

————. *National Arts Legislation. Hearings before the Special Subcommittee on the Arts of the Committee on Labor and Public Welfare on S. 165 and S. 1316.* 88th Cong., 1st Sess. 1963.

————. *National Arts and Humanities Foundations. Hearings before the Special Subcommittee on Arts and Humanities of the Committee on Labor and Public Welfare.* 89th Cong., 1st Sess. 1965.

Reports

Commission of Fine Arts. *Art and Government. A Report to the President by the Commission of Fine Arts, on Activities of the Federal Government in the Field of Art.* Washington, D.C., 1953.

U.S. Congress, Senate. *The Arts and the National Government. Report to the President Submitted by August Heckscher, Special Consultant on the Arts, May 28, 1963.* Senate Document No. 28, 88th Cong., 1st Sess. 1963.

Interviews

Livingston Biddle, 11 February 1980, Washington, D.C.
Barbara Donald, 25 February 1980, Washington, D.C.
George Frain, 25 February 1980, Washington, D.C.
Lloyd Goodrich, 21 February 1980, New York, NY
August Heckscher, 20 February 1980, New York, NY
Daniel Millsaps, 13 February 1980, Washington, D.C.
Dick Moore, 22 February 1980, New York, NY
Frank Thompson, 12 February 1980, Washington, D.C.
Elihu Winer, 21 February 1980, New York, NY

Index

Arts: model for federal program, 184, 226, 261; proposed, 40, 239
Nixon, Richard (R-CA), 61, 148, 231, 257
Noguchi, Isamu, 255
Northwest Grand Opera, 128
Nureyev, Rudolf, 196

O'Brien, Lawrence, 273–74
O'Hara, Barratt (D-IL), 240
Oistrakh, David, 114
O'Keeffe, Georgia, 25, 139, 272–73
"100 American Artists of the Twentieth Century," 117
Osver, Arthur, 237
Owsley, Alvin, 116, 251
Oxford Players, 151

Papp, Joseph, 140
Patterson, James (R-CT), 238
Peck, Gregory, 206
Peet, Elbert, 244
Pei, I. M., 263, 264
Pell, Claiborne (D-RI): on importance of arts legislation, 177, 182, 184, 198–200, 220; sponsors National Foundation on the Arts and Humanities bill, 201; urges National Council on the Arts to endorse foundation bill, 207
Pelly, Thomas (R-WA), 255–56
Pepper, Claude (D-FL), 42–44, 215
percent-for-art proposals, 207
Pereira, Irene Rice, 237
Pereira, William, 205, 263
Performing Arts: Problems and Prospects, The (Rockefeller Brothers Fund), 203–4, 218
Performing Arts: The Economic Dilemma, The (Baumol and Bowen), 270

Petrillo, James C., 51, 88, 128–29, 258
Philadelphia Orchestra, 102
Philbin, Philip (D-MA), 195–96
Piatigorski, Gregor, 51
Picasso, Pablo, 31, 60, 237
Pierpoint, Robert, 101
Pollock, Jackson, 139, 140, 254, 272–73
Poor, Henry Varnum, 234
Porgy and Bess (Gershwin), 97, 101, 102, 114
Pound, Ezra, 36–37, 107
Powell, Adam Clayton (D-NY), 274
Presidential Board on the Arts, proposed, 183–84
Presidential Citation for Excellence in the Arts, proposed, 207
Presidential Task Force on the Arts and the Humanities, 233
President's Advisory Council on the Arts, 154, 177–80, 262
President's Commission on National Goals, 10, 145–48, 181, 218, 228
President's Committee for Cultural Activities, proposed, 264
President's Science Advisory Committee, 188
Price, Leona, 242–43
Pucinski, Roman (D-IL), 162

Quie, Albert (R-MN), 273

Randolph, Jennings (D-WV), 262, 264
Rankin, John (D-MI), 237
Rattner, Abraham, 237
Rauschenberg, 272–73
Rayburn, Sam (D-TX), 99
Rea, Oliver, 263
Reagan, Ronald, 3, 11, 222, 223
Reeves, Ruth, 93
Refregier, Anton, 9, 25, 61–62, 243